Rick Steves®

SNAPSHOT

Norway

T0018168

CONTENTS

Post-Pandemic Travels: Expect a Warm Welcome...and a Few Changes
Research for this guidebook was limited by the COVID-19 outbreak, and the long-term impact of the crisis on our recommended destinations is unclear. Some details in this book will change for post-pandemic travelers. Now more than ever, it's smart to reconfirm specifics as you plan and travel. As always, you can find major updates at RickSteves.com/update.

SIGHTS

1. Akershus Fortress
2. City Hall
3. Fram Museum
4. Historical Museum
5. Karl Johans Gate
6. Kon-Tiki Museum
7. Munch Museum
8. National Gallery
9. National Museum
10. Nobel Peace Center
11. Norwegian Folk Museum
12. To Norwegian Holocaust Center & Huk Beach
13. Norwegian Maritime Museum
14. Opera House
15. Oslo Cathedral
16. Parliament
17. Royal Palace
18. Vigeland Museum
19. Viking Ship Museum

Let's Keep on Travelin'

Your trip doesn't need to end.

Follow Rick on social media!

Avalon Travel
Hachette Book Group
1700 Fourth Street
Berkeley, CA 94710

Printed in Canada by Friesens.
Fifth Edition. Third printing May 2023.

ISBN 978-1-64171-426-6

For the latest on Rick's talks, guidebooks, tours, public television series, and public radio show, contact Rick Steves' Europe, 130 Fourth Avenue North, Edmonds, WA 98020, 425/771-8303, www.ricksteves.com, rick@ricksteves.com.

Rick Steves' Europe
Managing Editor: Jennifer Madison Davis
Assistant Managing Editor: Cathy Lu
Editors: Glenn Eriksen, Suzanne Kotz, Rosie Leutzinger, Jessica Shaw, Carrie Shepherd
Editorial & Production Assistant: Megan Simms
Researchers: Glenn Eriksen, Cameron Hewitt, Pål Bjarne Johansen, Suzanne Kotz
Research Assistance: Rich Earl, Lisa Friend, Robyn Stencil, Laura Terrenzio
Contributor: Gene Openshaw
Graphic Content Director: Sandra Hundacker
Maps & Graphics: David C. Hoerlein, Lauren Mills, Mary Rostad
Digital Asset Coordinator: Orin Dubrow

Avalon Travel
Senior Editor and Series Manager: Madhu Prasher
Associate Managing Editors: Jamie Andrade, Sierra Machado
Indexer: Stephen Callahan
Production & Typesetting: Lisi Baldwin, Jane Musser
Cover Design: Kimberly Glyder Design
Maps & Graphics: Kat Bennett, Mike Morgenfeld

Photo Credits

POCKET GUIDES
Compact color guides for shorter trips

Amsterdam	Paris
Athens	Prague
Barcelona	Rome
Florence	Venice
Italy's Cinque Terre	Vienna
London	
Munich & Salzburg	

SNAPSHOT GUIDES
Focused single-destination coverage

Basque Country: Spain & France
Copenhagen & the Best of Denmark
Dublin
Dubrovnik
Edinburgh
Hill Towns of Central Italy
Krakow, Warsaw & Gdansk
Lisbon
Loire Valley
Madrid & Toledo
Milan & the Italian Lakes District
Naples & the Amalfi Coast
Nice & the French Riviera
Normandy
Northern Ireland
Norway
Reykjavík
Rothenburg & the Rhine
Sevilla, Granada & Southern Spain
St. Petersburg, Helsinki & Tallinn
Stockholm

CRUISE PORTS GUIDES
Reference for cruise ports of call

Mediterranean Cruise Ports
Scandinavian & Northern European
  Cruise Ports

Complete your library with...

TRAVEL SKILLS & CULTURE
Study up on travel skills and gain insight on history and culture

Europe 101
Europe Through the Back Door
Europe's Top 100 Masterpieces
European Christmas
European Easter
European Festivals
For the Love of Europe
Italy for Food Lovers
Travel as a Political Act

PHRASE BOOKS & DICTIONARIES
French
French, Italian & German
German
Italian
Portuguese
Spanish

PLANNING MAPS
Britain, Ireland & London
Europe
France & Paris
Germany, Austria & Switzerland
Iceland
Ireland
Italy
Scotland
Spain & Portugal

BEST OF GUIDES

Full-color guides in an easy-to-scan format. Focused on top sights and experiences in the most popular European destinations

Best of England
Best of Europe
Best of France
Best of Germany
Best of Ireland
Best of Italy
Best of Scotland
Best of Spain

COMPREHENSIVE GUIDES

City, country, and regional guides printed on Bible-thin paper. Packed with detailed coverage for a multi-week trip exploring iconic sights and venturing off the beaten path

Amsterdam & the Netherlands
Barcelona
Belgium: Bruges, Brussels,
  Antwerp & Ghent
Berlin
Budapest
Croatia & Slovenia
Eastern Europe
England
Florence & Tuscany
France
Germany
Great Britain
Greece: Athens & the Peloponnese
Iceland
Ireland
Istanbul
Italy
London
Paris
Portugal
Prague & the Czech Republic
Provence & the French Riviera
Rome
Scandinavia
Scotland
Sicily
Spain
Switzerland
Venice
Vienna, Salzburg & Tirol

Rick Steves books are available from your favorite bookseller.
Many guides are available as ebooks.

guides and small groups. We follow Rick's favorite itineraries, ride in comfy buses, stay in family-run hotels, and bring you intimately close to the Europe you've traveled so far to see. Most importantly, we take away the logistical headaches so you can focus on the fun.

Join the fun

This year we'll take thousands of free-spirited travelers—nearly half of them repeat customers—along with us on 50 different itineraries, from Athens to Istanbul. Is a Rick Steves tour the right fit for your travel dreams?

Find out at ricksteves.com, where you can also check seat availability and sign up. Europe is best experienced with happy travel partners. We hope you can join us.

See our itineraries at ricksteves.com

Experience maximum Europe

Save time and energy

This guidebook is your independent-travel toolkit. But for all it delivers, it's still up to you to devote the time and energy it takes to manage the preparation and logistics that are essential for a happy trip. If that's a hassle, there's a solution.

Rick Steves Tours

A Rick Steves tour takes you to Europe's most interesting places with great

Gear up for your next adventure at ricksteves.com

Light Luggage

Pack light and right with Rick Steves' affordable, custom-designed rolling carry-on bags, backpacks, day packs and shoulder bags.

Accessories

From packing cubes to moneybelts and beyond, Rick has personally selected the travel goodies that will help your trip go smoother.

Shop at ricksteves.com

Rick's Free Travel App

Get your FREE **Rick Steves Audio Europe**™ app to enjoy…

- Dozens of self-guided tours of Europe's top museums, sights and historic walks

- Hundreds of tracks filled with cultural insights and sightseeing tips from Rick's radio interviews

- All organized into handy geographic playlists

- For Apple and Android

With Rick whispering in your ear, Europe gets even better.

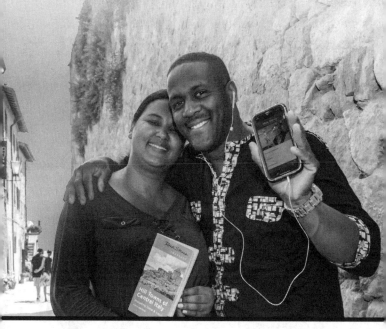

Find out more at ricksteves.com

your travel dreams into affordable reality

Radio Interviews

Enjoy ready access to Rick's vast library of radio interviews covering travel tips and cultural insights that relate specifically to your Europe travel plans.

Travel Forums

Learn, ask, share! Our online community of savvy travelers is a great resource for first-time travelers to Europe, as well as seasoned pros.

Travel News

Subscribe to our free Travel News e-newsletter, and get monthly updates from Rick on what's happening in Europe.

Classroom Europe®

Check out our free resource for educators with 500 short video clips from the *Rick Steves' Europe* TV show.

Explore Europe

At ricksteves.com you can browse through thousands of articles, videos, photos and radio interviews, plus find a wealth of money-saving travel tips for planning your dream trip. And with our mobile-friendly website, you can easily access all this great travel information anywhere you go.

TV Shows

Preview the places you'll visit by watching entire half-hour episodes of *Rick Steves' Europe* (choose from all 100 shows) on-demand, for free.

Oslo

BEYER BRIDGE
RINGNES BREWERY

ULLEVÅLSVEIEN
VALLEGATA
COLLETTS GATE
THERESES GATE
SOFIES GATE
SENBORGGATA
GT.
BES GATE
SANNERGATE
MARIDALSVEIEN
UELANDS GATE
SCHLEPPEGRELLS GATE
ST. HANS-HAUGEN
GEITMYRSVEIEN
WALDEMAR THRANES GATE
ÅMOT BRIDGE
THOR. MEYERS GATE
MARIDALSVEIEN
HELGESENS GATE
JOSEFINES GATE
PILESTREDET
BJERREGAARDS GATE
GAMLE AKER CHURCH
AKERSBAKKEN
AKERSVEIEN
Akerselva
FOSSVEIEN
MARKVEIEN
Olaf Ryes Plass
SOFIENBERGGATA
KOGNITOGATA
ARKVEIEN
STEENBERGGATA
ULLEVÅLSVEIEN
Vår Frelsers Cemetery
NORDRE GATE
GRÜNER-LØKKA
To E-6 & Airport
Slotts-parken
ST. OLAF'S CHURCH
TREFOLDIGHETS CHURCH
HAUSMANNS GATE
TRONDHEIMSVEIEN
HEIMDALSGATA
SARS GATE
Botanic Garden

17 **ROYAL PALACE**
4 **8**
KRISTIAN IV'S GATE
UNIV.-GATA
AKERSGATA
Youngs-torget
GRUBBEGATA
MØLLERGATA
TOGGATA
HAMMERS BORGATA
STORGATA
C. KROGHS GATE
BRUGATA
NORBYGATA
GRØNLAND
TØYENGATA

Nationaltheatret
NATIONAL THEATER
KARL JOHANS GATE
Stortorvet
16 Stor-tinget
5
15
Jernbane-torget
OSLO SPEKTRUM
Grønland

10 **2** **CITY HALL** **CENTER**
Rådhus-plassen
PRINSENS GATE
TRAIN STATION
BISKOP GUNNERUS GATAN
SCHWEIGAARDS
AKER BRYGGE MALL
TOLLBUGATA
KIRGATA
DRONN.
SKIPPERGATE
STRANDGATA
BARCODE PROJECT
162

Piperveka
RÅDHUSGATA
MYNTGATA
NORWEGIAN RESISTANCE MUSEUM
1
AKERSHUS FORTRESS
14 **OPERA HOUSE**
OPERAGATA
DRONNING EUFEMIAS GATE

AKERSHUSSTRANDA
REVIERKAIA CRUISE BERTH
7 **MUNCH MUSEUM**
Bjørvika
Bispe-vika

SØNDRE AKERSHUSKAIA CRUISE BERTH
RUINS OF MEDIEVAL OSLO
KONG HÅKON 5s GATE

VIPPETANGEN (AKERSHUS) CRUISE BERTH
DFDS TICKET OFFICE
162
KONGSVEIEN

fjord
To Ekeberg Sculpture Park

To Copenhagen, Denmark
GRESSHOLMEN

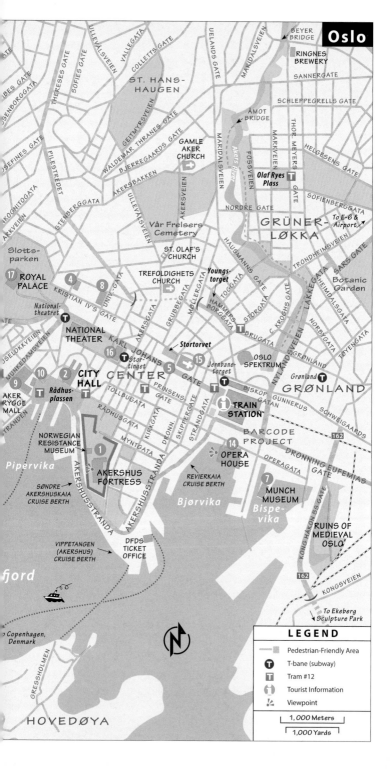

HOVEDØYA

LEGEND

- ▬ ■ Pedestrian-Friendly Area
- 🚇 T-bane (subway)
- Ⓣ Tram #12
- ℹ️ Tourist Information
- 📷 Viewpoint

| 1,000 Meters |
| 1,000 Yards |

Bergen

To Norwegian
Fisheries Museum

SKOLTEN
CRUISE
TERMINAL

SKOLTEGRUNNS-
KAIEN

INTERNATIONAL
FERRIES

Harbor

SKUTEVIKSTORGET

(B)

E85

**BERGENHUS
FORTRESS**

HÅKON'S
HALL

9

ROSEN-
KRANTZ
TOWER

FESTNINGS-
KAIEN

NORDNES

TOTEM
POLE

AQUARIUM

1

STRANDGATEN

C. SUNDTS GATE

HAUGEVEIEN

Nordnesparken

POOL

SWIMMING
BEACH

STRANDSIDEN

NORDNESVEIEN

HARBOR
FERRIES

NYKIRKEN

C. SUNDTS GATE

STRANDGATEN

HAUGEVEIEN

HOLBERGSALLM.

Puddefjorden

KLOSTERGATEN

SKOTTEGATEN

NØSTEGATEN

ENGEN

NØSTEGATEN

HURTIGRUTEN
TERMINAL
(COASTAL
CRUISES)

555

TORBORG NEDREAASGATE

JEKTEVIKEN/DOKKEN
CRUISE PORT

SIGHTS

1. Aquarium
2. Bergenhus Fortress
3. Bryggens Museum
4. Cathedral
5. Fish Market
6. Fløibanen Funicular
7. Fortress Museum
8. To Gamle Bergen
9. Håkon's Hall
10. Hanseatic Museum
11. KODE Art Museums
12. Leprosy Museum
13. Ole Bulls Plass
14. Rosenkrantz Tower
15. St. Mary's Church
16. Theta Museum
17. Torgallmenningen (Main Square)
18. Bus to Ulriken643 Cable Car
19. Bybanen Tram to Troldhaugen, Fantoft Stave Church & Airport

To 8

N

200 Meters

200 Yards

BERGEN-HUS

FORTRESS MUSEUM 1

NYE SANDVIKSVEIEN

HELGESENS GATE

LADEGÅRDSGATEN

STEINKJELLERGT.

HENRIK WERGELANDSGATE

DYRE HALSESGATE

DYRE BLEKKVEIEN

FJELLVEIEN

SKANSELIEN

FLØYVEIEN

FJELLVEIEN

SKANSEBAKKEN

SANDBROGATEN

ST. MARY'S CHURCH 15

SCHØTSTUENE

3 BRYGGENS MUSEUM

16

BRYGGEN VISITORS CENTER

B

BRYGGEN

RADISSON BLU ROYAL HOTEL

Vågen Harbor

BRYGGEN

ØVREGATEN

ROSENKRANTZ-GATEN

6 FLØIBANEN FUNICULAR STATION

Fløibanen

TUNNELS

To Mt. Fløyen

SKANSEMYREN

HANSEATIC MUSEUM 10

FISH MARKET

EXPRESS BOAT TO SOGNEFJORD

5

STRANDKAIEN

TORGET

HOLLENDER-GATEN

LILLE ØVREGATEN

KONG OSCARS GATE

BISPENGSGATE

CATHEDRAL 4

BRATTLIEN

STRANDGATEN

BØRSEN

SKOSTREDET

RÅDSTUPLASS

SKIVEBAKKEN

KONG OSCARS GATE

18 **B**

SENTRUM

SEAFARERS' MONUMENT

MARKEVEIEN

TORGALLMENNINGEN

SMÅSTRANDGT.

GALLERIET MALL

RÅDHUSGATEN

POLICE STN.

12

MARKEN

J MURALLM.

TEATERGATEN

NATIONAL THEATER

17

Byparken T

13 **Ole Bulls Plass**

KING OLAV V MONUMENT

VASKERELVEN

OLAV KYRRES GATE

Byparken

CHRISTIES GATE

19

Fest-plassen

RASMUS MEYERS ALLE

Lille Lungegårdsvannet (Lake)

KAIGATEN

TRAIN STATION

Nonne-seteren T

LIBRARY

BUS STATION

Bystasjonen T

HÅKONS GATEN

PERMANENTEN

STENERSEN

11

RASMUS MEYER

KODE ART MUSEUMS

LYSVERKET

ROSENBERGSGATEN

NYGÅRDSGATEN

FOSSWINCKELS GATE

GRIEG HALL

LARS HILLES GATE

STRØMGATEN

FLØSANGER VEIEN

LARS HILLES GATE

P

JOHANNES-KIRKEN

UNIVERSITY OF BERGEN

ALLEGATEN

NYGÅRDSGATEN

FOSSWINCKELSGATE

E-39

NATIONAL HISTORY MUSEUM

To Airport 555

ALLE GATEN

MØHLENPRIS

Nygård Park

To Fantoft Stave Church & Troldhaugen

INTRODUCTION

This Snapshot guide, excerpted from my guidebook *Rick Steves Scandinavia*, introduces you to a land with modern European values and a great outdoors like nowhere else—Norway.

Start in Oslo, Norway's sharp capital city, with its historic and walkable core and mural-slathered City Hall. Down on the pedestrian-friendly waterfront stroll along the promenade, clamber on the roof of the striking Opera House, marvel at the modernistic new Munch Museum, explore the Nazi Occupation at the stirring WWII Resistance Museum, and enjoy the outstanding National Museum (home to a version of Munch's *Scream*). A quick ferry ride takes you to the Bygdøy peninsula and museums dedicated to famous ships—Viking, *Fram*, and *Kon-Tiki*—plus the Norwegian Folk Museum. Just beyond the center, hundreds of bronze and granite nudes adorn the majestic Vigeland Sculpture Park. Or, ride a tram above the city to relive Olympic memories at the Holmenkollen Ski Jump and breathe in sweeping views.

Then head for Norway's countryside for a dose of natural wonder. The famous "Norway in a Nutshell" ride—by train, ferry, and bus—showcases the scenic splendor of the country, from snowcapped mountains to the striking Sognefjord. Choose a cozy fjordside hamlet (such as Balestrand, Solvorn, or Aurland) as your home base for touring mighty glaciers and evocative stave churches. Explore the Gudbrandsdal Valley, Lillehammer's excellent open-air folk museum, and the impressive Jotunheimen Mountains.

Dip into Bergen, Norway's salty port town, with its lively fish market, colorful Hanseatic quarter, and funicular to spectacular city views from the top of Mount Fløyen. You can round out your Norwegian experience in the lively city of Stavanger (with a side trip to soaring Pulpit Rock), the time-passed Setesdal Valley, or the port of Kristiansand (with ferries to Denmark).

To help you have the best trip possible, I've included the following topics in this book:

• **Planning Your Time,** with advice on how to make the most of your limited time

• **Orientation,** including tourist information (abbreviated as TI), tips on public transportation, local tour options, and helpful hints

• **Sights,** and strategies for meaningful and efficient visits

• **Sleeping** and **Eating,** with good-value recommendations in every price range

• **Connections,** with tips on trains, buses, boats, and driving

Practicalities, near the end of this book, has information on money, staying connected, hotel reservations, transportation, and other helpful hints.

To travel smartly, read this little book in its entirety before you go. It's my hope that this guide will make your trip more meaningful and rewarding. Traveling like a temporary local, you'll get the absolute most out of every mile, minute, and dollar.

God tur! Happy travels!

Rick Steves

NORWAY

NORWAY

Norge

Norway is stacked with superlatives—it's the most mountainous, most scenic, and most prosperous of all the Scandinavian countries. It is also a land of rich harvests—timber, oil, and fish. In fact, Norway's wealth of resources is a major reason why Norwegians have voted *"nei"* to membership in the European Union. They don't want to be forced to share fishing rights with EU countries.

The country's relatively recent independence (in 1905, from Sweden) makes Norwegians notably patriotic and proud of their traditions and history. They have a reputation for insularity, and controversially have tightened immigration laws over the past several years.

Norway's Viking past (c. AD 800-1050) can still be seen today in the country's 28 remaining stave churches—with their decorative nods to Viking ship prows—and the arti- facts housed in Oslo's Viking Ship Museum. The Vikings, who also lived in present-day Denmark and Sweden, were great traders, shipbuilders, and explorers. However, they are probably best known for their infamous invasions, which terrorized much of Europe. The sight of their dragon-prowed ships on the horizon struck fear into the hearts of people from Ireland to the Black Sea.

Named for the Norse word *vik,* which means "bay" or "inlet," the Vikings sailed their sleek, seaworthy ships on extensive voyages, laden with amber and furs for trad- ing—and weapons for fighting. They traveled up the Seine and deep into Russia, through the Mediterranean east to Constantinople, and across the Atlantic to Greenland and even "Vinland" (Canada). They touched the soil of the Americas centuries before Columbus, causing proud "ya sure ya betcha" Scandinavian immigrants in the US to display bumper stickers that boast, "Columbus used a Viking map!"

Southern Norway

History and Hollywood have painted a picture of the Vikings as fierce barbarians, an image reinforced by the colorful names of leaders like Sven Forkbeard, Erik Bloodaxe, and Harald Bluetooth. Unless you're handy with an ax, these don't sound like the kind of men you want to hoist a tankard of mead with. They kept slaves and were all-around cruel (though there is no evidence that they forced their subjects to eat lutefisk).

But the Vikings also had a gentle side. Many were farmers, fishermen, and craftsmen who created delicate works with wood and metal. Faced with a growing population constrained by a lack of arable land, they traveled south not just to pillage and plunder, but in search of greener pastures. Sometimes they stayed and colonized, as in northeast England, which was called the "Danelaw," or in northwest France, which became known as Normandy ("Land of the North-men").

Norway Almanac

Official Name: Kongeriket Norge—"The Kingdom of Norway"—or simply Norge (Norway).

Size: At 148,700 square miles, Norway is slightly larger than Montana, and has a population of 5.4 million people (about 35 per square mile)

Geography: Sharing the Scandinavian Peninsula with Sweden, Norway also has short northern borders with Finland and Russia. Its 51,575-mile coastline extends from the Barents Sea in the Arctic Ocean to the Norwegian Sea and North Sea in the North Atlantic. Shaped by glaciers, Norway has a rugged landscape of mountains, plateaus, and deep fjords. In the part of Norway that extends north of the Arctic Circle, the sun never sets at the height of summer, and never rises in the depth of winter.

Latitude and Longitude: 62°N and 10°E, similar latitude to Canada's Northwest Territories.

Biggest Cities: Norway's capital city, Oslo, has a population of 680,000; more than 1 million live in its metropolitan area. Bergen, Norway's second-largest city, has a population of about 284,000.

Economy: The Norwegian economy grows around 1.5-2 percent each year, contributing to a healthy $434 billion gross domestic product and a per capita GDP of $80,200. Its primary exports are oil and gas—Norway produces less than 5 percent of the world's oil but exports 95 percent of it; the country is second only to Russia in natural gas production. Oil and gas make Norway one of the world's richest countries. The two commodities account for more than 50 percent of the Norwegian economy. By law, the country must save a portion of its oil revenue; the fund is currently worth almost $1 trillion.

Currency: 9 Norwegian kroner (NOK) = about $1.

Government: As the leader of Norway's parliamentary constitutional monarchy, King Harald V has largely ceremonial powers. Norway's legislative body is the Stortinget (Parliament), with 169 members elected for four-year terms.

Flag: Red with a blue Scandinavian cross outlined in white.

The Average Norwegian is 39 years old, has 1.8 children, will live to be 82, and enjoys a good coffee buzz, drinking nearly four cups a day.

The Vikings worshipped many gods and had a rich tradition of mythology. Epic sagas were verbally passed down through generations or written in angular runic writing. The sagas told the heroic tales of the gods, who lived in Valhalla, the Viking heaven, presided over by Odin, the god of both wisdom and war. Like the Egyptians, the Vikings believed in life after death, and chieftains were often buried in their ships within burial mounds, along with prized possessions such as jewelry, cooking pots, food, and Hagar the Horrible cartoons.

Similar to the Greeks and Etruscans before them, the Vikings never organized on a large national scale and eventually faded away due to bigger, better-organized enemies and the powerful influence of Christianity. By 1150, the Vikings had become Christianized and assimilated into European society. But their memory lives on in Norway.

Beginning in the 14th century, Norway came under Danish rule for more than 400 years, until the Danes took the wrong side in the Napoleonic Wars. The Treaty of Kiel forced Denmark to cede Norway to Sweden in 1814. Sweden's rule of Norway lasted until 1905, when Norway voted to dissolve the union. Like many European countries, Norway was invaded by Germany during World War II. April 9, 1940, marked the start of five years of Nazi occupation, during which a strong resistance movement developed, hindering some of the Nazi war efforts.

Each year on May 17, Norwegians celebrate their idealistic 1814 constitution with fervor and plenty of flag-waving. Men and women wear folk costumes *(bunads)*, each specific to a region of Norway. Parades are held throughout the country. The parade in Oslo marches past the Royal Palace, where the royal family waves to the populace from their balcony. While the king holds almost zero political power (Norway's parliament is chaired by a prime minister), the royal family is still highly revered and respected.

High taxes contribute to Norway's high standard of living. Norwegians receive cradle-to-grave social care: university education, health care, nearly yearlong paternity leave, and an annual six weeks of vacation. Norwegians feel there is no better place than home: Norway regularly shows up in first place on the annual UN Human Development Index.

Norwegians are mainly of Nordic and Germanic heritage, with a small population of indigenous Sami people in the north.

The growing immigrant population is primarily from Sweden, Poland, Lithuania, Pakistan, and Somalia, with a recent wave from Syria. And though church attendance is way down, the vast majority of Norwegian Christians consider themselves Lutheran.

Visitors enjoy the agreeable demeanor of the Norwegian people—friendly but not overbearing, organized but not uptight, and with a lust for adventure befitting their gorgeous landscape. Known for their ability to suffer any misfortune with an accepting (if a bit pessimistic) attitude, Norwegians are easy to get along with.

Norwegians are proud of their rich folk traditions—from handmade sweaters and folk costumes to the small farms that produce a sweet brown cheese called *geitost*. Less than 7 percent of the country's land is arable, resulting in numerous small farms. The government recognizes the value of farming, especially in the remote reaches of the country, and provides rich subsidies to keep this tradition alive.

With countless fjords and waterfalls, Norway is known for its pristine water. Norwegian-bottled artisanal water has an international reputation for its crisp, clean taste. Although the designer Voss water—the H2O of choice for Hollywood celebrities—comes with a high price tag, the blue-collar Olden is just as good. (Tap water here is actually wonderful, too—and much cheaper.)

While Norwegians speak a collection of mutually understandable dialects, the two official forms of Norwegian are *bokmål* (book language) and *nynorsk* (New Norse). During the centuries of Danish rule, people in Norway's cities and upper classes adopted a Danish-influenced style of speech and writing (called Dano-Norwegian), while rural language remained closer to Old Norse. After independence, Dano-Norwegian was renamed *bokmål*, and the rural dialects were formalized as *nynorsk*, as part of a nationalistic drive for a more purely Norwegian language. Despite later efforts to combine the two forms, *bokmål* remains the most common, especially in urban areas, books, newspapers, and government agencies. Some Sami- and Finnish-speaking minorities are found in the far north.

Most Norwegians also speak English, but a few words in Norwegian will serve you well. If you visit a Norwegian home, be sure to leave your shoes at the door; indoors is usually meant for stocking-feet only. At the end of a meal, it's polite to say *"Takk*

for maten" (tahk for MAH-ten); "Thanks for the food"). Norwegians rarely feel their guests have eaten enough, so be prepared to say *"Nei, takk"* (nay tahk; "No, thanks"). You can always try *"Jeg er mett"* (yay ehr met; "I am full"), but be careful not to say *"Jeg er full"*—"I am drunk." See the next page for more Norwegian survival phrases.

Norwegian Survival Phrases

Norwegian can be pronounced quite differently from region to region. These phrases and phonetics match the mainstream Oslo dialect, but you'll notice variations. Vowels can be tricky: å sounds like "oh," æ sounds like a bright "ah" (as in "apple"), and u sounds like the German ü (purse your lips and say "u"). To pronounce the letter Ø, purse your lips together and say "uh." Certain vowels at the ends of words (such as d and t) are sometimes barely pronounced (or not at all). In some dialects, the letters sk are pronounced "sh." In the phonetics, ī sounds like the long i in "light," and bolded syllables are stressed.

Hello. (formal)	God dag.	goo dahg
Hi. / Bye. (informal)	Hei. / Ha det.	hī / hah deh
Do you speak English?	Snakker du engelsk?	**snahk**-kehr dew **eng**-ehlsk
Yes. / No.	Ja. / Nei.	yah / nī
Please.	Vær så snill.	vayr soh sneel
Thank you (very much).	(Tusen) takk.	(**tew**-sehn) tahk
You're welcome.	Vær så god.	vayr soh goo
Can I help you?	Kan jeg hjelpe deg?	kahn yī **yehl**-peh dī
Excuse me.	Unnskyld.	**ewn**-shuld
(Very) good.	(Veldig) fint.	(**vehl**-dee) feent
Goodbye.	Farvel.	fahr-**vehl**
zero / one / two	null / en / to	newl / ayn / toh
three / four	tre / fire	treh / **fee**-reh
five / six	fem / seks	fehm / sehks
seven / eight	syv / åtte	seev / **oh**-teh
nine / ten	ni / ti	nee / tee
hundred	hundre	**hewn**-dreh
thousand	tusen	**tew**-sehn
How much?	Hvor mye?	voor **mee**-yeh
local currency: (Norwegian) crown	(Norske) kroner	(**norsh**-keh) **kroh**-nehr
Where is...?	Hvor er...?	voor ehr
...the toilet	...toalettet	toh-ah-**leh**-teh
men	menn / herrer	mehn / **hehr**-rehr
women	damer	**dah**-mehr
water / coffee	vann / kaffe	vahn / **kah**-feh
beer / wine	øl / vin	uhl / veen
Cheers!	Skål!	skohl
The bill, please.	Regningen, takk.	**rī**-ning-ehn tahk

OSLO

Though Oslo is the smallest of the Scandinavian capitals, this brisk little city offers more sightseeing thrills than you might expect. Get ready to be inspired—Oslo simply has its act together.

Situated at the head of a 60-mile-long fjord, surrounded by forests, and populated by more than a half-million people, Oslo is Norway's cultural hub. For 300 years (1624-1924), the city was called Christiania, after Danish King Christian IV. With independence, it reverted to the Old Norse name of Oslo. As an important port facing the Continent, Oslo has been one of Norway's main cities for a thousand years and the de facto capital since around 1300. Still, Oslo has always been small by European standards; in 1800, Oslo had just 10,000 people—one-fiftieth the size of Paris or London.

But Oslo experienced a growth spurt with the Industrial Age, and in 50 years (from 1850 to 1900) its population exploded upward to about 250,000. Most of "old Oslo" dates from this period, when the city's many churches and grand buildings were built of stone in the Historicism styles (neo-Gothic and neo-Romanesque) of the late 19th century.

Today the city sprawls out from its historic core to encompass nearly a million people in its metropolitan area, about one in five Norwegians. Oslo's onetime industrial area, along the Akers River, has been reclaimed as a

lush green zone, filled with spiffed-up brick warehouses and (on a sunny day) hundreds of sunbathing Norwegians. The city's port hums with international shipping and a sizeable cruise industry. Its waterfront, once traffic-congested and slummy, has undergone an extreme urban makeover, and today sports ultramodern yet people-friendly residential zones and the Havnepromenaden—a pedestrian walkway stretching the length of the harbor.

Sights of the Viking spirit—past and present—tell an exciting story. Prowl through the remains of ancient Viking ships, and marvel at more peaceful but equally gutsy modern boats (the *Kon-Tiki, Ra II, Fram,* and *Gjøa*). Dive into the traditional folk culture at the Norwegian open-air folk museum and get stirred up by the country's heroic spirit at the Norwegian Resistance Museum. For a look at modern Oslo, tour the striking City Hall, peek at sculptor Gustav Vigeland's people pillars, ascend the exhilarating Holmenkollen Ski Jump, wander futuristic promenades, walk all over the Opera House, and celebrate the world's greatest peacemakers at the Nobel Peace Center.

Even with all this modernization, it's delightfully easy to escape the urban downtown and harbor area to a sprawling, green, and pastoral countryside—dotted with parks and lakes, and surrounded by hills and forests. For the visitor, Oslo is an all-you-can-see smorgasbord of historic sights, nature, art, and Nordic fun.

PLANNING YOUR TIME

Oslo offers an exciting slate of sightseeing thrills. Ideally, spend two days here. Keep in mind that the Vigeland Museum (next to Vigeland Sculpture Park) is closed on Monday. The National Museum may also be closed Monday (check ahead). Spend the two days like this:

Day 1: Take my self-guided Oslo Walk. Tour the Akershus Fortress and the Norwegian Resistance Museum, then catch a free City Hall tour (likely offered June-Aug only; off-season, tour it on your own). Spend the afternoon at the National Museum (for Norwegian art, opening in 2022), Munch Museum, or Holmenkollen Ski Jump and museum (to enjoy some wilderness).

Day 2: Ferry across the harbor to Bygdøy and tour the *Fram, Kon-Tiki,* and Viking Ship museums. Spend the afternoon at the Norwegian Folk Museum. Finish the day at Vigeland Sculpture Park, enjoying Gustav Vigeland's statues.

With More Time: You could easily fill a third day: Slow things down, go for a lazy hike along the Akers River (and eat at the trendy Mathallen Oslo food hall), and/or head out to the islands in the Oslofjord.

In the evening, you could enjoy a pricey dinner by the harbor or near Karl Johans Gate. Or venture to the appealing, affordable,

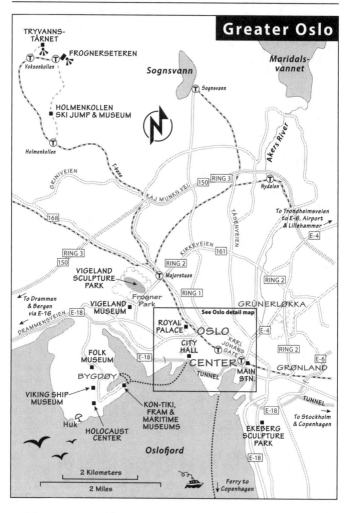

and less touristy dining zones around Youngstorget, Mathallen, and Olaf Ryes Plass.

Orientation to Oslo

Oslo (pop. 680,000) is easy to manage. Most sights are contained within the city center. Much of what you'll want to see clusters in three easy-to-connect zones: **downtown,** around the harbor and the main boulevard, Karl Johans Gate (with the Royal Palace at one end and the train station at the other); in the **Bygdøy** (big-duhy) district, a 10-minute ferry ride across the harbor; and **Frogner Park** (with the Vigeland Sculpture Park), about a mile behind the palace.

With more time, head out of the core to see the more colorful neighborhoods: Majorstuen and Frogner feel "uptown," with chic boutiques, elegant homes, and lots of parks. Grünerløkka and the adjacent Akers River greenbelt is hipster central, with the foodie-paradise Mathallen and plenty of bohemian cafés. Youngstorget, a quick walk north of Karl Johans Gate, is mostly residential and packed with tempting restaurants. And Grønland, behind the train station, is the multiethnic immigrants' zone.

TOURIST INFORMATION

The big, high-tech Visit Oslo office is in the Østbanehallen—the traditional-looking building next to the central train station. Standing in the square (Jernbanetorget) by the tiger statue and facing the train station, you'll find the TI's entrance in the red-painted section between the station and the Østbanehallen. You can also enter the TI from inside the train station (generally July-Aug Mon-Sat 8:00-19:00, Sun 9:00-18:00; May-June and Sept daily 9:00-18:00; slightly shorter hours Oct-April; +47 23 10 62 00, www.visitoslo.com).

At the TI, pick up these freebies: an Oslo city/transit map; the annual *Oslo Guide* (overview of museums, eating, and nightlife); *U.F.O.* (guide to current museum exhibits); and the *What's On Oslo* monthly (museum and event listings). The TI also sells the handy Oslo Pass (described later, under "Sights in Oslo"). If you're traveling beyond Oslo, you can purchase domestic train and Norway in a Nutshell tickets here. Consider picking up the *Bergen Guide* and information for the rest of Norway, including the useful, annual *Fjord Norway Travel Guide*.

ARRIVAL IN OSLO
By Train

The central train station (Oslo Sentralstasjon, or "Oslo S" for short) is slick and helpful. You'll find ATMs, two exchange desks, and luggage storage. The station is plugged into a lively modern shopping mall called Byporten (Mon-Fri 10:00-20:00, Sat until 18:00, closed Sun), where just inside the entrance you'll find a cheap Bit sandwich shop. Inside the station is a well-stocked Co-op Prix grocery store (long hours Mon-Sat, closed Sun), a small Joker supermarket (long hours daily), and a Vinmonopolet liquor store (Oslo's most central place to buy wine or liquor—which is sold only at Vinmonopolet stores, Mon-Fri 10:00-18:00, Sat until 15:00, closed Sun).

For tickets and train info, head to the station's ticket office between tracks 8 and 9 (Mon-Fri 7:30-20:00, Sat-Sun 10:00-18:00 plus summer weekends from 7:45). Here, you can buy domestic and Norway in a Nutshell tickets, get information on the Flåm and Bergen Railway (Bergensbanen), and buy international train tick-

OSLO

ets. Domestic train tickets (but not international tickets) can also be bought at ticket machines. Tickets to Sweden are available at the blue machines marked *SJ*.

By Plane or Boat

For details on arriving in Oslo by plane or boat, see the end of this chapter.

HELPFUL HINTS

Theft Alert: Pickpockets are a problem in Oslo, particularly in crowds on the street and on subways and buses. Oslo's street population loiters around the train station; you may see aggressive panhandlers there and along Karl Johans Gate.

Pharmacy: Jernbanetorgets Vitus Apotek is open 24 hours daily (across from train station on Jernbanetorget, +47 23 35 81 00).

Laundry: Billig Vask & Rens ("Cheap Wash & Clean") is near Vår Frelsers Cemetery, a half-mile north of the train station (self-serve open daily 8:00-21:00; full-serve Mon-Fri 9:00-18:00, Sat 10:00-15:00, closed Sun; on the corner of Wessels Gate and Ullevålsveien, Ullevålsveien 15, bus #37 from train station, +47 41 64 08 33).

Bike Rental: Oslo's near-complete ban on cars in the city core and the addition of bike lanes have made it an increasingly good city for cycling, despite its hills. A public bike-rental system lets you grab basic **city bikes** from locked racks at various points around town (first hour free, then 15 NOK/15 minutes; requires smartphone app, www.oslobysykkel.no). If you're traveling with a group, you can reserve bikes in advance with **Viking Biking** (no walk-up rentals, daily flat rate of 2,000 NOK for 1-10 bikes; includes helmet, lock, and map; daily 10:00-18:00, Nedre Slottsgate 4, +47 41 26 64 96, www.vikingbikingoslo.com; see "Tours in Oslo," later, for their guided bike tours).

Movies: The domed Colosseum Kino in Majorstuen, with 1,500 seats, is a fun place to catch a big-time spectacle. Originally built in 1928, this now high-tech, four-screen theater shows first-run films in their original language (Fridtjof Nansens Vei 6, a short walk west from Marjorstuen T-bane station, www.oslokino.no).

OSLO

Sightseeing by Public Transit

With a transit pass or an Oslo Pass, take full advantage of the T-bane and the trams. Spend just five minutes getting a grip on the system, and you'll be in command. Here are some handy stops and stations.

T-bane Stations

Jernbanetorget (central station, bus and tram hub, express train to airport)

Stortinget (top of Karl Johans Gate, near Akershus Fortress)

Nationaltheatret (National Theater, also a train station, express train to airport; near City Hall, National Museum, Aker Brygge, Royal Palace)

Majorstuen (walk to Vigeland Sculpture Park, trendy shops on Bogstadveien, Colosseum cinema)

Grønland (cheap and fun restaurant zone, bottom of Grünerløkka district; the underground mall in the station is a virtual trip to Istanbul)

Holmenkollen (famous ski jump, city view)

Frognerseteren (highest point in town, jumping-off point for forest walks and bike rides)

Sognsvann (idyllic lake in forest outside of town)

Tram and Bus Stops

Trams #11 and **#12** ring the city (stops at central station, fortress, harborfront, City Hall, National Museum, Aker Brygge, Vigeland Sculpture Park, Bogstadveien, and Stortorvet)

Trams #11, #12, and **#18** to Olaf Ryes Plass (center of Grünerløkka district)

Trams #13 and **#19**, and **bus #32** (south and parallel to Karl Johans Gate to central train station; stops near Opera House and Munch Museum)

Bus #30 (Olaf Ryes Plass in Grünerløkka, train station, near Karl Johans Gate, National Theater, and Bygdøy, with stops at each Bygdøy museum)

GETTING AROUND OSLO
By Public Transit

Oslo is a big city, and taxi fares are exorbitant. Take advantage of the excellent transit system, made up of buses, trams, ferries, and a subway (*Tunnelbane*, or T-bane for short; see the "Sightseeing by Public Transit" sidebar). The system is run by Ruter, which has a transit-information center below the skinny glass tower in front of the central train station (Mon-Fri 7:00-20:00, Sat-Sun 8:00-18:00, www.ruter.no).

Schedules: The system runs like clockwork, with schedules clearly posted and followed. Download the RuterReise app for schedules at your fingertips, or check reader boards at stops for the next tram's arrival time (usually every 10 minutes).

Tickets: A different app—called RuterBillett—lets you buy tickets with your mobile phone (credit card or PayPal). **Individual tickets** work on buses, trams, ferries, the T-bane, and Vy trains (within Oslo) for one hour (37 NOK via RuterBillett app and at the transit office, ticket machines, transit office, Narvesen kiosks, and convenience stores; 57 NOK from driver; note that boats to Bygdøy require a separate, more expensive ticket). Other options include a **24-hour ticket** (111 NOK; buy on RuterBillett app or at ticket machines or the transit office; good for unlimited rides in 24-hour period) and the **Oslo Pass** (free run of entire system, including Bygdøy boats; described later under "Sights in Oslo"). Validate your ticket by holding it next to the card reader when you board.

By Taxi or Uber

Taxis come with a 150-NOK drop charge (yes, that's nearly $20 just to get in the car) that covers you for three or four kilometers—about two miles (more on evenings and weekends). Taxis are a good value only if you're with a group. If you use a minibus taxi, you can negotiate an hourly rate. To get a taxi, wave one down, find a taxi stand, or call +47 22 38 80 90. Uber works in Oslo just like in the US.

Tours in Oslo

Local Guides

You can hire a private guide for around 2,000 NOK for a two- to three-hour tour. I had a good experience with **Oslo Guideservice** (2,000 NOK/2 hours, +47 22 42 70 20, www.guideservice.no); my guide, Aksel, had a passion for both history and his hometown of Oslo. The easy-to-work-with **Oslo Guidebureau** will tailor a tour to meet your interests (+47 22 42 28 18, www.osloguidebureau.no).

Bike Tours

Viking Biking gives several different guided tours in English, including a three-hour Oslo Highlights Tour that includes Bygdøy beaches and a ride up the Akers River (425 NOK, May-Sept daily at 14:00, Nedre Slottsgate 4, +47 41 26 64 96, www.vikingbikingoslo.com). They also rent bikes to groups; see "Helpful Hints," earlier. If you'd rather walk, check out their forest-to-fjord and island nature walks.

Bus Tours

While a bus tour can help you get your bearings, most of Oslo's sightseeing is concentrated in a few discrete zones and well-

OSLO

West Cemetery

To Holmenkollen
Ski Jump

SØRKEDALSVEIEN

SKØYENVEIEN

GULDBERGS VEI

SLEMDALSVEIEN
KIRKEVEIEN

Majorstuen
#11, 12
& 19

See Frogner Park detail map

VIGELAND
SCULPTURE
PARK

WHEEL OF
LIFE

MONOLITH

Frogner

FOUNTAIN

MIDDELTHUNS

SOKGENFRI

MAJORSTUEN

Skøyen-
parken

BRIDGE

Park

VISITORS
CENTER

GATE

BOGSTADVEIEN

#11

#12

VEIEN

OSLO CITY
MUSEUM

MAIN
GATE

#12

PROF. DAHLS GATE

SKØYENVEIEN

G. VIGELANDS VEI

H. SVARTES GATE

VIGELAND
MUSEUM

ECKERS. BERGS GATE

KIRKE

#12

Frogner
Plass

GLYDEN.

DRISKEVEIEN

To
Drammen
& Bergen

161

ODINS

FROGNER

ODINS

FROGNERVEIEN

LØVES GATE

OSCARS GATE

URANIEN-
BORG

INKOGNITO-

See Oslo Center detail maps

E-18

NOBELS GATE

BYGDØY

#30

THOMAS HEFTYES

#30

ALLE

#12
#30

SKOV.VEIEN

Solli
Plass

#12

US
EMBASSY

B
#30

DRAMMENSVEIEN

STANGS GATE

GABELS GATE

IBSENS GATE

NIELS JUELS GATE

C. ADLERS GATAN

MUNKEDAMSVEIEN

E-18

VIKA

See Bygdøy detail map

DRONNING BLANCAS VEI

FROGNERSTRANDA

Frognerkilen

KONGEN
PIER

DRONNINGEN
PIER

TJUV-
HOLMEN

MUSEUMS

FOLK
MUSEUM

#30

HUK AVENY

FILIPSTAD
CRUISE BERTH

ASTRUP
FEARNLEY
MUSEUM

VEIEN

#30

VIKING
SHIP
MUSEUM

BYGDØY

KON-TIKI
MUSEUM

#30

FRAM
MUSEUM

#30

To Norwegian
Holocaust
Center &
Huk Beach

BYGDØYNESVEIEN

MARITIME
MUSEUM

Oslo-

N

1,000 Meters

1,000 Yards

--T-- Oslo Tram Tour
T T-bana Station
.... Boat

To Kiel,
Germany

To Copenhagen,
Denmark

OSLO

Oslo

See Grünerløkka detail map

BEYER BRIDGE

#11 & 12

RINGNES BREWERY

ULLEVÅLSVEIEN

VALLEGATA

THERESES GATE

COLLETTS GATE

UELANDS GATE

MARIDALSVEIEN

SANNERGATA

THORVALD MEYERS GATE

(B) #30

SCHLEPPEGRELLS GATE

VIBES GATE

ROSENBORGGATA

ST. HANS-HAUGEN

ÅMOT BRIDGE

MARKVEIEN

FOSSVEIEN

HELGESENS GATE

JOSEFINES

PILESTREDET

GAMLE AKER CHURCH

Akers River

Olaf Ryes Plass #11 & 12

GRÜNERLØKKA

To E-4, E-6 & Airport

(T) #11

AKERSBAKKEN

ULLE VALSVEIEN

NORDRE GATE

SOFIENBERG

(T) #11

GATA

PARKVEIEN

SVENSBERG

Vår Frelsers Cemetery

ST. OLAF'S CHURCH

HAUSMANNS GATE

#11 & 12

(B) #30

TRONDHEIMSVEIEN

SARS GATE

Slotts-parken

TREFOLDIGHETS CHURCH

Youngs-torget

Botanic Garden

ROYAL PALACE

HIST. MUSEUM

#11

KRISTIAN IVs GATE

National-theatret

NAT'L GALL.

GRUBBEGATA

MØLLERGATA

TORGGATA

STORGATA

HAMMERS

BORGGATA

#11, 12 & 17

BRUGATA

C. KROHGS GATE

TØYEN

NYLANDSVEIEN

TØYENGATA

NAT'L THEATER STN.

NAT'L THEATER (B) #30

KARL JOHANS GATE

Stor-torvet

#11 & 17

OSLO CATHEDRAL

OSLO SPEKTRUM

(B) #30

(T) Grønland

PARL.

Stortinget

CENTER

GRØNLAND

NAT'L MUS.

NOBEL PEACE CTR.

#12

CITY HALL

Rådhus-plassen

#12

#12 (T)

Jernbane-torget

#11 & 12

BISKOP GUNNERUS GATA

AKER BRYGGE MALL

FDR STATUE

TOLLBUGATA

PRINSENS GATE

KIRKE

DRON.

RÅDHUSGATA

STRAND

(i)

TRAIN STATION

(B) #30

SCHWEIGAARDS

Pipervika

NORWEGIAN RESISTANCE MUSEUM

MYNTGATA

LANGKAIA

BARCODE PROJECT

162

DRON. EUPHEMIAS GATE

OPERA HOUSE

OPERAGATAN

AKERSHUSSTRANDA

AKERSHUS FORTRESS

REVIERKAIA CRUISE BERTH

MUNCH MUSEUM

SØNDRE AKERSHUSKAIA CRUISE BERTH

Bjørvika

Bispevika

RUINS OF MEDIEVAL OSLO

KONG HAKON 5S. GATE

fjord

VIPPETANGEN (AKERSHUS) CRUISE BERTH

DFDS TICKET OFFICE

SØRENGKAIA

162

To E-6

OSLO

GRESSHOLMEN

EKEBERG SCULPTURE PARK

(B)

KONGSVEIEN

E-18

To Gothenburg & Stockholm

HOVEDØYA

Oslo at a Glance

▲▲▲**City Hall** Oslo's artsy 20th-century government building, lined with vibrant municipal-themed murals, best visited with included tour. **Hours:** Daily 9:00-16:00, June-Aug until 18:00; generally 3 tours/day (may not run off-season). See page 33.

▲▲▲**National Museum** Norway's cultural and natural essence, captured on canvas. **Hours:** Opens in 2022; likely Tue-Fri 10:00-18:00, Thu until 19:00, Sat-Sun 11:00-17:00, closed Mon. See page 36.

▲▲▲**Vigeland Sculpture Park and** ▲▲**Vigeland Museum** Set in sprawling Frogner Park, with tons of statuary by Norway's greatest sculptor, Gustav Vigeland, and the studio where he worked. **Hours:** Sculpture park—always open; Vigeland Museum—Tue-Sun 10:00-16:00, closed Mon year-round. See pages 45 and 50.

▲▲▲**Fram Museum** Captivating exhibit on two Arctic exploration ships. **Hours:** Daily June-Aug 9:00-18:00, May and Sept 10:00-18:00, Oct-April until 17:00. See page 57.

▲▲**Norwegian Resistance Museum** Gripping look at Norway's tumultuous WWII experience. **Hours:** Daily 10:00-17:00; Sept-April until 16:00. See page 40.

▲▲**Norwegian Folk Museum** Norway condensed into 150 historic buildings in a large open-air museum. **Hours:** Daily 10:00-17:00—grounds open until 20:00; Sept-May park open daily 11:00-16:00, but most historical buildings closed. See page 54.

▲▲**Viking Ship Museum** Impressive trio of ninth-century Viking ships, with exhibits on the people who built them. **Hours:** Tue-Sun 10:00-16:00, closed Mon. See page 55.

▲▲**Kon-Tiki Museum** Adventures of primitive *Kon-Tiki* and *Ra II* ships built by Thor Heyerdahl. **Hours:** Daily 10:00-17:00, June-Aug from 11:00, Nov-Feb until 16:00. See page 59.

OSLO

connected by public transit. Consider my self-guided tram tour (later) instead. If a bus tour appeals, **HMK** does a daily city tour (350 NOK/3 hours, 500 NOK/4 hours, departs from the DFDS cruise terminal, Akershusstranda 31, +47 48 08 31 02, https://sightseeingoslo.com).

Oslofjord Cruises

A fascinating world of idyllic islands sprinkled with charming vacation cabins is minutes away from the Oslo harborfront. For

▲**Aker Brygge and Tjuvholmen** Oslo's harborfront promenade and nearby arty Tjuvholmen neighborhood with Astrup Fearnley Museum, upscale galleries, shops, and cafés. See page 38.

▲**Akershus Fortress Complex and Tours** Historic military base and fortified old center, with guided tours, ho-hum castle interior, and excellent Norwegian Resistance Museum (listed earlier). **Hours:** Park generally open daily 6:00-21:00—until 18:00 in winter; fortress tours run 2/day July-mid-Aug, 1/day Sat-Sun only off-season. See page 39.

▲**Oslo Opera House** Stunning performance center that's revitalized the harborfront. **Hours:** Foyer and café/restaurant open daily roughly 11:00-18:00; Opera House tours—1-2/day year-round. See page 43.

▲**Munch Museum** Works of Norway's famous Expressionistic painter. **Hours:** Daily 10:00-17:00, Oct-May until 16:00. See page 44.

▲**Norwegian Maritime Museum** Briny voyage through Norway's rich seafaring heritage. **Hours:** Daily 10:00-17:00; Oct-April 11:00-16:00. See page 61.

▲**Grünerløkka** Oslo's popular former working-class district, bustling with cafés, pubs, and shops. See page 62.

▲**Ekeberg Sculpture Park** Hilly, hikeable 63-acre forest park with striking contemporary art and city views. See page 67.

▲**Holmenkollen Ski Jump and Ski Museum** Dizzying vista and a schuss through skiing history, plus a zip line off the top. **Hours:** Daily 9:00-20:00, May and Sept 10:00-17:00, Oct-April until 16:00. See page 69.

OSLO

locals, the fjord is a handy vacation getaway. Tourists can get a glimpse of this island world by public ferry or tour boat. Cheap ferries regularly connect the nearby islands with downtown (covered by public transit tickets and Oslo Pass).

Several tour boats leave regularly from pier 3 in front of City Hall. **Båtservice** has a relaxing and scenic 1.5-hour hop-on, hop-off service, with recorded multilingual commentary. It departs from the City Hall dock (235 NOK, discount with Oslo Pass; daily at 10:15, 11:45, 13:15, and 14:45; departs 30 minutes earlier from

the Opera House and 30 minutes later from Bygdøy; +47 23 35 68 90, www.boatsightseeing.com). They also offer two-hour fjord tours with dull live commentary (355 NOK, 3/day late March-mid-Oct, additional departures in summer, 2/day on winter weekends), a dinner cruise on a sailing ship (485 NOK, no narration; "shrimp buffet" is just shrimp, bread, and butter; daily mid-June-Aug 19:00-22:00), and jazz and blues-themed cruises.

Oslo Walk

This self-guided stroll, worth ▲▲, covers the tourist-friendly walking zone in the heart of Oslo—from the train station, up the main drag, and past City Hall to the harborfront. Allow a brisk 45 minutes without stops.

❶ **Central Train Station:** Start at the plaza just outside the main entrance of Oslo's central train station (Oslo Sentralstasjon),

near the statue of the **tiger** prowling around out front. This alludes to the town's nickname of Tigerstaden ("Tiger Town"), and commemorates the 1,000th birthday of Oslo's founding, celebrated in the year 2000. In the 1800s, Oslo was considered an urban tiger, leaving its mark on the soul of simple country folk who ventured into the wild and crazy New York City of Norway.

In the middle of the plaza, look for the tall, skinny, glass **Ruter tower** that marks the public transit office. From here, trams zip to City Hall (harbor, boat to Bygdøy), and the T-bane subway (look for the *T* sign to your right) goes to Vigeland Sculpture Park and Holmenkollen. Tram #12—described in my self-guided tram tour, later—leaves from directly across the street.

The green building behind the Ruter tower is a shopping mall called **Byporten** (literally, "City Gate," see big sign on rooftop), built to greet those arriving from the airport on the shuttle train. Oslo's 37-floor pointed-glass **skyscraper,** the Radisson Blu Plaza Hotel, pokes up behind that. The hotel's 34th-floor SkyBar welcomes the public with air-conditioned views and pricey drinks. The tower was built with reflective glass so that, from a distance, it almost

Oslo's Most Strollable Spots

Oslo's pulse is best felt by strolling. Three good areas are 1) along and near the central Karl Johans Gate, which runs from the train station to the palace (follow my self-guided Oslo Walk); 2) in trendy harborside Aker Brygge, a glass-and-chrome collection of sharp cafés, fine condos, and polished produce stalls (really lively at night, tram #12 from train station); and 3) along Bogstadveien, a bustling shopping street with no-nonsense modern commerce, lots of locals, and no tourists (T-bane to Majorstuen and follow this street back toward the palace and tourist zone).

While most tourists never get out of the harbor/Karl Johans Gate district, the real, down-to-earth Oslo is better seen elsewhere, in places such as Bogstadveien. The bohemian, artsy Grünerløkka district, is also good for a daytime wander. And the new Havnepromenaden stretches all the way along the harbor, from the marina at Frognerkilen to the Sørenga neighborhood to the east. The 5.5-mile pedestrian route is marked by orange towers (get info at TI or see www.visitoslo.com/en/articles/the-harbour-promenade for route).

disappears. The area behind the Radisson—the lively and colorful "Little Karachi," centered along a street called Grønland—is where many of Oslo's immigrants settled. It's become a vibrant nightspot, offering a fun contrast to the predictable Norwegian cuisine and culture.

Oslo allows hard-drug addicts and sex workers to mix and mingle in the station area. (While it's illegal to buy sex in Norway, those who sell it are not breaking the law.) The cameras near the top of the Ruter tower monitor drug deals. Signs warn that this is a "monitored area," but keep your valuables close.

• *Note that you are near the Opera House and the Munch Museum, if you'd like to side-trip there now. (The Opera House is through the park to the right of the station, and the Munch Museum is just a few minutes' walk beyond that.) Otherwise, turn your back to the station. You're now looking (across the street) up Norway's main drag, called...*

Karl Johans Gate: This grand boulevard leads directly from the train station to the Royal Palace. The street is named for the French general Jean-Baptiste Bernadotte, who took the Swedish name Karl Johan when he was elected the crown prince of Sweden in 1810. He ruled as a popular king (1818-1844) during the period after Sweden took Norway from Denmark.

Walk three blocks up Karl Johans Gate. This people-filled stretch is crowded with street musicians, sidewalk artists, and shops greedily devouring tourists' money. Even if you're visiting in

OSLO

Oslo Walk

Oslo Walk

1 Central Train Station
2 Oslo Cathedral
3 Stortorvet (Square)
4 Crest of Karl Johans Gate
5 Freia Sign

6 Grand Hotel & Café
7 Parliament Building
8 Statue of Wergeland
9 National Theater
10 City Hall

11 Harbor View
12 Nobel Peace Center

OSLO

Shopping & Services
- **13** Norway Designs
- **14** Paleet
- **15** Dale of Norway
- **16** Heimen Husfliden
- **17** GlasMagasinet & Heimen Husfliden
- **18** Oslo Sweater Shop
- **19** Byporten Mall
- **20** To Bogstadveien Shops & Flea Market
- **21** Oslo Flaggfabrikk
- **22** Vinmonopolet (2)
- **23** To Laundry
- **24** Bike Rental

OSLO

the snowy winter, you'll walk on bare concrete: Most of downtown Oslo's pedestrian streets are heated.

• *Hook right around the curved old brick structure of an old market and walk to the...*

❷ **Oslo Cathedral** (Domkirke): This Lutheran church is the third cathedral Oslo has had, built in 1697 after the second one burned down. It's where Norway commemorates its royal marriages and deaths, and national tragedies. In the grass in front of the cathedral, you may see a memorial to the victims of the 2011 bombing and mass shooting.

Look for the cathedral's cornerstone (near the base of the steeple), a thousand-year-old carving from Oslo's first and long-gone cathedral showing how the forces of good and evil tug at each of us. Look high up on the tower. The tiny square windows midway up the copper cupola were once the lookout quarters of the fire watchman.

Step inside (daily 10:00-16:00, Fri until late) beneath the red, blue, and gold seal of Oslo and under an equally colorful ceiling (late Art Deco from the 1930s). The box above on the right is for the royal family. The fine Baroque pulpit and altarpiece date from 1700. The chandeliers are from the previous cathedral (which burned in the 17th century). The colorful windows in the choir (leading up to the altar) were made in 1910 by Emanuel Vigeland (Gustav's less famous brother).

The church courtyard (to the right as you face the entrance) is lined by a circa-1850 circular row of stalls from an **old market.** Rusty meat hooks now decorate the lamps of a peaceful café, which has quaint tables around a fountain. The atmospheric **$$$$ Café Bacchus,** at the far left end of the arcade, serves food outside and in a classy café downstairs (sandwiches, salads, full meals, good cakes, coffee, Mon-Sat 11:30-22:30, closed Sun, +47 90 51 52 64).

• *The square that faces the cathedral is called...*

❸ **Stortorvet:** In the 17th century, when Oslo's city wall was located about here, this big square was the point where farmers entered and sold their goods. Today it's still lively as a flower and produce market (Mon-Fri). The statue shows Christian IV, the Danish king who ruled Norway around 1600, dramatically gesturing at some geraniums. He named the

city, rather immodestly, Christiania. (Oslo took back its old Norse name only in 1925.) Christian was serious about Norway. During his 60-year reign, he visited it 30 times (more than all other royal visits combined during 300 years of Danish rule). The big GlasMagasinet department store is a landmark on this square.

• *Return to Karl Johans Gate, and continue up the boulevard past street performers, cafés, shops, and throngs of people. At the next corner, Kongens Gate leads left, past the 17th-century grid-plan town to Akershus Fortress (described in "Sights in Oslo," later). But we'll continue hiking straight up to the crest of the hill, enjoying some of the buskers along the way.*

Pause at the wide spot in the street (near the T-bane stop) to appreciate the...

❹ Crest of Karl Johans Gate (Egertorget): Look back at the train station. A thousand years ago, old Oslo was located at the foot of the wooded hill behind the station. Now look ahead to the **Royal Palace** in the distance, which was built in the 1830s "with nature and God behind it and the people at its feet." If the flag flies atop the palace, the king is in the country.

Karl Johans Gate, a parade ground laid out in about 1850 from here to the palace, is now the axis of modern Oslo. Each May 17, Norway's Constitution Day, an annual children's parade turns this street into a sea of marching student bands and young costumed flag-wavers, while the royal family watches from the palace balcony. Since 1814, Norway has preferred peace. Rather than celebrating its military on the national holiday, it celebrates its children.

In the middle of the small square, the *T* sign marks a stop of the T-bane subway. W. B. Samson's bakery is a good place for a quick, affordable lunch, with a handy cafeteria line (WC in back)—duck inside and be tempted by the pastries. Two traditional favorites are *kanelboller* (cinnamon rolls) and *skolebrød* ("school bread," with an egg and cream filling).

High overhead, the big neon **❺ Freia sign** (dating from 1911) trumpets another sweet Norwegian treat. Norway's answer to Cadbury, the Norwegian chocolatier Freia is beloved...or it was, until an American company bought it. Still, the local factory is partly operational, and nostalgic Norwegians will always think of Freia as "a little piece of Norway."

Continuing down Karl Johans Gate: People-watching is great along Karl Johans Gate. If it's summer, half of the city's population is gone—vacationing in their cabins or farther

away—and the people you'll see in the city center are mostly visitors.

Hike two blocks farther down Karl Johans Gate. The street called **Akersgata,** on your right, kicks off a worthwhile stroll past the site of the July 2011 bombing, the national cemetery, and through a parklike river gorge to the popular Grünerløkka quarter (an hour-long walk, described later, under "Sights in Oslo").

Pass the big brick **Parliament** building (on the left, described later). On your right, seated in the square, is a bearded, tubby statue of the 19th-century painter Christian Krohg.

If you'd like to get a city view (and perhaps a pricey refreshment), enter the glass doors facing the street at #27 (not the bank entrance at the corner) and take the elevator to the eighth-floor rooftop bar, aptly named Eight.

A few doors farther down Karl Johans Gate, just past the Freia shop (selling that favorite Norwegian chocolate), the venerable **Grand Hotel** (Oslo's celebrity hotel—Nobel Peace Prize winners sleep here) overlooks the boulevard.

• *Politely ask the waiter at the Grand Café—part of the Grand Hotel— if you can pop inside for a little sightseeing (he'll generally let you).*

❻ **Grand Café:** This historic café was for many years the meeting place of Oslo's intellectual and creative elite (playwright Henrik Ibsen was a regular here). It still has some beautiful old artwork—including (at the far back) a wall-length **mural** showing Norway's literary and artistic clientele from a century ago enjoying this fine hangout. On the far left, find Ibsen, coming in as he did every day at 13:00. Behind the waiter on the right, Edvard Munch leans against the window, apparently dozing. Names are on the sill beneath the mural.

• *Continue to the next corner (at the intersection of Karl Johans Gate and Rosenkrantz Gate). To your left, a little park faces Norway's...*

❼ **Parliament Building** (Stortinget): Norway's parliament meets here (along with anyone participating in a peaceful protest outside). *Stortinget*—from an old Viking word—basically means "Big Gathering." Built in 1866, the building seems to counter the Royal Palace at the other end of Karl Johans Gate. If the flag's flying, parliament's in session. Today the king is a figurehead, and Norway is run by a unicameral parliament and a prime minister. Guided tours of the Stortinget are offered for those interested in Norwegian government (free, 1 hour, typically Sat mornings, may be more frequent in summer—check schedule at www.stortinget. no, enter on Akersgata—on the back side of the building).

• *Cross over into the long median park. On your left, notice the red, white, and blue coin-op public WCs. (Free WCs are inside the Paleet shopping mall, on the right side of the boulevard).*

Enjoying the park, stroll toward the palace, past the fountain. Pause at the...

❽ **Statue of Wergeland:** The poet Henrik Wergeland helped inspire the national resurgence of Norway during the 19th century. Norway won its independence from Denmark in 1814 but within a year lost its freedom to Sweden. For nearly a century, until Norway regained independence in 1905, Norwegian culture and national spirit was stoked by artistic and literary patriots like Wergeland. In the winter, the pool here is frozen and covered with children happily ice-skating.

Across the street behind Wergeland stands the ❾ **National Theater** and statues of Norway's favorite playwrights: Ibsen and Bjørnstjerne Bjørnson.

Across Karl Johans Gate, the pale yellow building is the first university building in Norway, dating from 1854. A block behind that is the National Gallery building (reopening with a new collection in 2021 or later).

Take a moment here to do a 360-degree spin to notice how quiet and orderly everything is. People seem content—and, according to most surveys, Norwegians are among the happiest people on earth. If you ask them why, their hunch is that it's because they live collectively. The Vikings would famously share one large bowl of mead, passing it around the circle. Nobody—no matter how big, angry, hairy, or smelly—gulped more than his share. They all made sure that everyone got some.

In modern times, Norwegians at the dinner table are still mindful when helping themselves not to take too much: They mentally ration enough for the people who come after them. It's a very considerate—and a very Norwegian—way of thinking. (Similarly, upper midwesterners in the US are familiar with the "Minnesota Slice": The Scandinavian-American tendency to carve off a little sliver of the last slice of pie, rather than take the entire thing.)

• *Facing the theater, turn left and follow Roald Amundsens Gate to the towering brick...*

❿ **City Hall** (Rådhuset): Built mostly in the 1930s with contributions from Norway's leading artists, City Hall is full of great art and is worth touring (see listing later, under "Sights in Oslo"). The mayor has his office

here (at the base of one of the two 200-foot towers), and every December 10, this building is where the Nobel Peace Prize is presented. The semicircular square facing the building, called Fridtjof Nansens Plass, was designed to evoke Il Campo, the iconic main square in Siena, Italy, that's also dominated by its City Hall.

To see the City Hall's best exterior art, step up into the U-shaped courtyard and circle it clockwise, savoring the colorful woodcuts in the arcade. Each shows a scene from Norwegian mythology, well explained in English: Thor with his billy-goat chariot, Ask and Embla (a kind of Norse Adam and Eve), Odin on his eight-legged horse guided by ravens, the swan maidens shedding their swan disguises, and so on.

Facing City Hall, circle around its right side (through a lovely garden) until you reach the front. Like all of the statues adorning the building, the **six figures** facing the waterfront—dating from a period of Labor Party rule in Norway—celebrate the nobility of the working class. Norway, a social democracy, believes in giving respect to the workers who built their society and made it what it is, and these laborers are viewed as heroes.

• *Walk to the...*

❶ Harbor: Over a decade ago, you would have dodged several lanes of busy traffic to reach Oslo's harborfront. Today, the traffic passes beneath your feet in tunnels. In addition, the city has made its town center relatively quiet and pedestrian-friendly by levying a toll on every car entering town. (This system, like in other European capitals, subsidizes public transit and the city's infrastructure.)

At the water's edge, find the shiny metal plaque (just left of center) listing the contents of a sealed time capsule planted in 2000 in the little Kavringen lighthouse, straight ahead out in the harbor (to be opened in a thousand years).

Head to the end of the stubby pier (just to the right). This is the ceremonial "enter the city" point for momentous occasions. One such instance was in 1905, when Norway gained its independence from Sweden, and a Danish prince, elected by referendum, sailed in from Copenhagen to become the first modern king of Norway. Another milestone event occurred at the end of World War II, when the king returned to Norway after the country was liberated from the Nazis.

• *Stand on that important pier and give the harbor a sweeping counterclockwise look.*

Harborfront Spin-Tour: Oslofjord is one big playground, with 40 city-owned, parklike islands. Big cruise ships—a large part of the local tourist economy—dock just under the Akershus Fortress on the left. (The big, boxy building clinging to the top of the fortress—just under the green steeple—is the excellent Norwegian Resistance Museum.) Just this side of the fort's impressive

13th-century ramparts, a **statue of FDR** grabs the shade. He's here in gratitude for the safe refuge the US gave to members of the royal family (including the young prince, Harald, who is now Norway's king) during World War II—while the king and his government-in-exile waged Norway's fight against the Nazis from London.

The next **pier** over is the launchpad for harbor boat tours and the shuttle boat to the Bygdøy museums. At the base of this pier, the glassy box is a fish market, serving locals and tourists alike. You may see a fisherman mooring his boat near here, selling shrimp from the back. Nearby, look for a bright-orange container box—an info point for Oslo's impressive **Havnepromenaden,** the 5.5-mile promenade that runs the entire length of the city's harborfront.

Panning left, enjoy the grand view of **City Hall.** The yellow building farther to the left, formerly a train station, today houses the ⓬ **Nobel Peace Center,** which celebrates the work of Nobel Peace Prize winners. Just to the left and behind that is the new **National Museum**, with an impressive collection of Norwegian and international art within its sleek walls (opening 2022).

Turning to facing the harbor, look to the right side, where **Aker Brygge**, Oslo's thriving restaurant/shopping/nightclub zone, has replaced the shipyard buildings that were once the heart of Norway's once-important shipbuilding industry. Just past the end of Aker Brygge is **Tjuvholmen,** an arts district and housing development with some of Norway's most expensive real estate. With outdoor installations, water sculptures, and plentiful galleries, it's anchored by the Astrup Fearnley Museum, a modern art complex designed by renowned architect Renzo Piano (most famous for Paris' Pompidou Center).

These flourishing urban spaces are all part of Oslo's ambitious Fjord City (Fjordbyen) urban renewal project, which kicked off years ago with Aker Brygge and Oslo's dramatic Opera House. The city has made remarkable progress in turning the formerly industrial waterfront into an inviting people zone.

• *From here, you can stroll out Aker Brygge and through Tjuvholmen to a tiny public beach at the far end; tour City Hall; visit the Nobel Peace Center; hike up to Akershus Fortress; take a harbor cruise (see "Tours in Oslo," earlier); or catch a boat across the harbor to the museums at Bygdøy (from pier 3).*

OSLO

Oslo Tram Tour

Tram #12, which becomes tram #11 halfway through its loop (at Majorstuen), circles the city from the train station, lacing together many of Oslo's main sights (see the "Oslo" map on page 19 to trace the route). Apart from the practical value of being able to hop on and off as you sightsee your way around town (trams come by at least every 10 minutes), this 40-minute trip gives you a fine look at parts of the city you wouldn't otherwise see.

This tour starts at the central train station, at the traffic-island tram stop located immediately in front of the Ruter transit office tower. The route makes almost a complete circle and finishes at Stortorvet (the cathedral square), dropping you off a three-minute walk from where you began the tour. Ongoing construction work may disrupt trams occasionally, but the route I've outlined here should still be doable.

Starting out, you want tram #12 as it leaves from the second set of tracks, going toward Majorstuen. Confirm with your driver that the particular tram #12 you're boarding becomes tram #11 and finishes at Stortorvet; some turn into tram #19 instead, which takes a different route. If yours becomes #19, simply hop out at Majorstuen and wait for the next #11.

Here's what you'll see and places where you might want to hop out:

From the **station,** you'll go through the old grid streets of 16th-century Christiania, King Christian IV's planned Renaissance town. After the city's 17th fire, in 1624, the king finally got fed up. He decreed that only brick and stone buildings would be permitted in the city center, with wide streets to serve as fire breaks.

You'll turn a corner at the **fortress** (Christiana Torv stop; get off here for the fortress and Norwegian Resistance Museum), then head for **City Hall** (Rådhus stop). Next comes the harbor and upscale **Aker Brygge** waterfront neighborhood (jump off at the Aker Brygge stop for the National Museum, harbor, and restaurant row). Passing the harbor, you'll see on the left a few old shipyard buildings that still survive. Then the tram goes uphill into a district of ugly 1960s buildings (when elegance was replaced by "functionality"). The tram then heads onto the street Norwegians renamed **Henrik Ibsens Gate** in 2006 to commemorate the centenary of Ibsen's death, honoring the man they claim is the greatest playwright since Shakespeare.

After Henrik Ibsens Gate, the tram follows Frognerveien

through the chic **Frogner neighborhood.** Behind the fine old facades are fancy shops and spendy condos. Here and there you'll see 19th-century mansions built by aristocratic families who wanted to live near the Royal Palace; today, many of these house foreign embassies. Turning the corner, you roll along the edge of **Frogner Park** (which includes **Vigeland Sculpture Park**), stopping at its grand gate (hop out at the Vigelandsparken stop).

Ahead on the left, a statue of 1930s ice queen Sonja Henie marks the arena where she learned to skate. Turning onto Bogstadveien, the tram usually becomes #11 at the Majorstuen stop. **Bogstadveien** is lined with trendy shops, restaurants, and cafés—it's a fun place to stroll and window-shop. (You could get out here and walk along this street all the way to the Royal Palace park and the top of Karl Johans Gate.) The tram veers left before the palace, passing the **Historical Museum** and stopping at the red-brick **National Gallery** building (Tullinløkka stop). As you trundle along, you may notice that lots of roads are ripped up for construction. It's too cold to fix the streets in winter, so, when possible, the work is done in summer. Jump out at **Stortorvet** (the big square filled with flower stalls and fronted by the cathedral and the big GlasMagasinet department store). From here, you're a three-minute walk from the station, where this tour began.

Sights in Oslo

SIGHTSEEING PASS

The **Oslo Pass** covers the city's public transit, ferry boats, and entry to nearly every major sight—all described in a useful handbook (445 NOK/24 hours, 655 NOK/48 hours, 820 NOK/72 hours, big discounts for kids ages 6-17 and seniors 67 and over). It's best to buy the pass from the TI upon arrival in Oslo. Some included sights sell the 24-hour adult pass, but they may not sell the kids or senior pass. Students with an ISIC card may be better off without the pass.

NEAR THE HARBORFRONT
▲▲▲City Hall (Rådhuset)

City halls, rather than churches, are the dominant buildings in Scandinavian capitals. In 1931, Oslo tore down a slum and began constructing its richly decorated City Hall. It was finally finished—after a WWII delay—in 1950 to celebrate the city's 900th birthday. Norway's leading artists all contributed to the building, which was an avant-garde thrill in its day. The prominence of this building on the harborfront makes sense in this most humanistic, yet least churchgoing, northern end of the Continent. Up here, people pay high taxes, have high expecta-

OSLO

tions, and are generally satisfied with what their governments do with their money.

Cost and Hours: Free, daily 9:00-16:00, June-Aug until 18:00, free and fine WC in basement, +47 23 46 12 00, www.oslo. kommune.no/radhuset.

Tours: Free 45-minute guided tours generally run daily at 10:00, 12:00, and 14:00. Tours may not operate Sept-May, so check ahead.

⊘ Self-Guided Tour: For descriptions of the building's exterior features and symbolism, see the City Hall section of my Oslo Walk, earlier. This tour focuses on the interior.

The visitor entrance is on the Karl Johans Gate side (away from the harbor). You'll step into a cavernous **main hall,** which feels like a

temple to good government, with its altar-like murals celebrating "work, play, and civic administration." It's decorated with 20,000 square feet of bold and colorful murals celebrating a classless society, with everyone—town folk, country folk, and people from all walks of life—working harmoniously for a better society. The huge murals take you on a voyage through the collective psyche of Norway, from its simple rural beginnings through the scar tissue of the Nazi occupation and beyond. Filled with significance and symbolism—and well described in English—the murals become even more meaningful with the excellent guided tours.

First, turn around and face the mural over the door you came in, which celebrates the **traditional industries** of Norway (from left to right): the yellow-clad fisherman (standing in his boat, glancing nervously at a flock of seagulls), the factory worker (with his heavy apron), the blue-clad sailor (he's playing with exotic beads acquired through distant trade), the farmer (in a striped dress, with a bushel under her arm), and the miner (lower right, lifting a heavy rock). Flanking these figures are portraits of two important Norwegians: On the far right is Bjørnstjerne Bjørnson (1832-1910), a prominent poet and novelist whose works pluck the patriotic heartstrings of Norwegians. And on the far left is Fridtjof Nansen (1861-1930), the famous Arctic explorer (you can learn more about him at the Fram Museum on Bygdøy). Here Nansen sheds the heavy coat of his most famous endeavor—polar exploration—as he embarks on his second act: Once retired from seafaring, he advocated for the dissolution of Norway's union with Sweden—which took place in 1905, making Norway fully independent.

Now turn 180 degrees and face the hall's main mural, which emphasizes **Oslo's youth** participating in community life—and re-

building the country after Nazi occupation. Across the bottom, the slum that once cluttered up Oslo's harborfront is being cleared out to make way for this building. Above that, scenes show Norway's pride in its innovative health care and education systems. Left of center, near the top, Mother Norway stands next to a church—reminding viewers that the Lutheran Church of Norway (the official state religion) provides a foundation for this society. On the right, four forms represent the arts; they illustrate how creativity springs from children. And in the center, the figure of Charity is surrounded by Culture, Philosophy, and Family.

The **Mural of the Occupation** lines the east side of the hall, tucked under the balustrade. Scan it from left to right to see the

story of Norway's WWII experience: First, the German blitzkrieg overwhelms the country. Men head for the mountains to organize a resistance movement. Women huddle around the water well, traditionally where news is passed, while Quislings (traitors named after the Norwegian fascist who ruled the country as a Nazi puppet) listen in. While Germans bomb and occupy Norway, a family gathers in their living room. As a boy clenches his fist (showing determination) and a child holds the beloved Norwegian flag, the Gestapo steps in. Columns are toppled to the ground, symbolizing how Germans shut down the culture by closing newspapers and the university. Two resistance soldiers stand up against a wall—about to be executed by firing squad. A cell of resistance fighters (wearing masks and using nicknames, so if tortured they can't reveal their compatriots' identities) plan a sabotage mission. Finally, prisoners are freed, the war is over, and Norway celebrates its happiest day, May 17, 1945: the first Constitution Day after five years under Nazi control.

While gazing at these murals, keep in mind that the Nobel Peace Prize is awarded in this central hall each December (though the general Nobel Prize ceremony occurs in Stockholm's City Hall). You'll see photos of this event in the little foyer with the strollers (on the right from where you entered). You can see videos of the ceremony and acceptance speeches in the adjacent Nobel Peace Center (listed later).

At the base of the grand marble staircase is a mural of the 11th-century **St. Hallvard,** the patron saint of Oslo. Above his head, he holds his symbol—three arrows—and he rests a millstone on his knee. As the story goes, Hallvard took pity on a pregnant woman

OSLO

(the naked woman in front of him) who had been wrongly accused of theft by three men. They attempted to escape, but the accusers killed the woman, shot Hallvard with three arrows, tied a millstone around his neck, and tossed him into the fjord. Miraculously, he survived (or perhaps rose from the dead). This story of compassion in the face of injustice swayed Norwegians at a time when Christianity was making its bid to be the country's main religion.

In front of the mural is a **bell** from the ship that brought Norway's royal family back home after World War II—landing at the pier right in front of City Hall.

Now head up the stairs and explore several **ceremonial rooms,** each well described in English. The wood-paneled Munch Room is dominated by the artist's oil painting *Life.* Circle around the gallery to the City Council Assembly Room, where Oslo's leadership steers the agenda of this impressive city. Notice the "three arrows and millstone" motif, recalling St. Hallvard. The city council acts collectively as a virtual "mayor"—a system, originating here in Oslo in 1986, called "parliamentary metropolitan government." Notice how this room evokes the semicircular shape of the square where you entered. Out in the hall, you'll pass gifts from visiting heads of state (*gave fra* means "gift from").

Nearby: Fans of the explorer Fridtjof Nansen might enjoy breaking for a bite or drink across the street at **Fridtjof,** an atmospheric bar filled with memorabilia from Nansen's Arctic explorations. A model of his ship, the *Fram,* hangs from the ceiling, and 1894 photos and his own drawings are upstairs (Mon-Sat 12:00-late, Sun 14:00-22:00, Nansens Plass 7, +47 93 25 22 30).

▲▲▲National Museum (Nasjonalmuseet)

Just steps off the waterfront is Oslo's strikingly modern National Museum building, opening in 2022. The new museum boasts extensive collections of fine art, decorative arts and design, and contemporary art that once had been scattered across three city museums. A tour of these galleries gives travelers bound for the mountains and fjord country a chance to pack along a little of Norway's cultural soul. Don't miss the roof terrace with its dramatic views of Akershus Fortress, Rådhusplassen, and the inner Oslo fjord.

Cost and Hours: Opening in 2022—call ahead or check website for admission price and hours; café and restaurant; Brynjulf Bulls Plass 3, +47 21 98 20 00, www.nasjonalmuseet.no.

Visiting the Museum: The permanent collection is installed

Edvard Munch (1863-1944)

Edvard Munch (pronounced "moonk") is Norway's most famous and influential painter. His life was rich, complex, and

sad. His father was a doctor who had a nervous breakdown. His mother and sister both died of tuberculosis. He knew suffering. And he gave us the enduring symbol of 20th-century pain, *The Scream.*

Munch was also Norway's most forward-thinking painter, a man who traveled extensively through Europe, soaking up the colors of the Post-Impressionists and the curves of Art Nouveau. Living in Germany in the years before World War I, he helped pioneer a radical new style—Expressionism—in which raw emotion was the subject. Jarring colors and wavy lines "expressed" inner turmoil and the angst of the modern world.

After a nervous breakdown in late 1908, followed by eight months of rehab in a clinic, Munch emerged less troubled—but a less powerful painter. His late works were as a colorist: big, bright, less tormented...and less noticed.

Munch painted several versions of *The Scream:* You can see the 1910 version and much more of the artist's work at the Munch Museum (see page 44); another version of *The Scream,* from 1893, is at the National Museum.

in an ambitious chronology over two floors. The collection is international in scope, but to make the most of a visit here, focus on what's uniquely Norwegian—you're sure to see plenty that showcases the harsh beauty of Norway's landscape and the resourcefulness of the Norwegian people.

Displays on the ground floor focus on design and decorative objects, including ancient Roman artifacts, imperial Chinese porcelain, the treasured medieval Baldishol Tapestry (the oldest in Norway), Norwegian glass, and contemporary crafts.

The first floor showcases art from the 15th century to the present. Highlights are 17th-century Dutch landscapes and still lifes, early 19th-century landscapes by the Norwegian Romantic painter Johan Christian Dahl, modern classics by Impres-

OSLO

sionists and international 20th-century mas-
ters, and the moody canvases of Norway's
most renowned artist, Edvard Munch—including the 1893 version of his iconic *Scream*.
In response to early criticism of the painting, Munch himself added a barely visible
inscription to the canvas: "Could only have
been painted by a madman!"

The boxy top floor of the musem is
dubbed the Light Hall (Lyshallen) for its
translucent, illuminated profile. This vast
space is reserved for special exhibits of Norwegian and international art.

Nobel Peace Center (Nobels Fredssenter)

This museum, housed in a former train station, celebrates the
800-some past and present Nobel Peace Prize winners and poses
the question, "What is the opposite of conflict?" The ground
floor is dominated by temporary exhibits on themes related to the
Peace Prize ideals. The permanent collection upstairs is modest:

 First you'll step into the
Nobel Field, a sea of lights
and touchscreens profiling
various past prizewinners
(from Teddy Roosevelt to
Mother Theresa). Next,
the Nobel Chamber has
a big virtual book that
invites you to learn more
about the life and work of
Alfred Nobel, the Swedish inventor of dynamite, who initiated
the prizes.

Cost and Hours: 100 NOK; daily 10:00-18:00, closed
Mon Sept-mid-May; includes English guided tours at 14:00 and
15:00—off-season weekends only at 14:00; Brynjulfs Bulls Plass 1,
+47 48 30 10 00, www.nobelpeacecenter.org.

▲Aker Brygge and Tjuvholmen

Oslo's harborfront was dominated by the **Aker Brygge** shipyard
until it closed in 1986. In the late 2000s, it became the first finished part of the Fjordbyen (Fjord City) urban renewal project,
which has converted part of Oslo's harborfront into a people-
friendly park and culture zone. Today's Aker Brygge is a stretch
of overpriced waterfront restaurants facing a fine promenade—just
the place to join in on a Nordic stroll on a balmy summer's eve.

The far end of Aker Brygge is marked by a big black anchor
from the wreck of the German warship *Blücher,* sunk by Norwe-

gian forces near Drøbak while heading for Oslo during the Nazi invasion on April 9, 1940. From there a bridge crosses over onto **Tjuvholmen** (Thief Island, where Oslo hung thieves back in the 17th century). This planned community boasts the

costliest apartments in town, private moorings for luxury jet boats, boardwalks with built-in seating to catch the sun, elegant shops and cafés, and the striking, wood-clad, glass-roofed **Astrup Fearnley Museum of Modern Art** (good temporary exhibits, closed Mon, www.afmuseet.no). On the harbor side of the museum, find the grassy little knob of land with an appealing sculpture park. This area is well worth a wander, including the back lanes away from the water. As you stroll here, admire how, while the entire complex feels cohesive, each building has its own personality.

Eating: Dining here is appealing but be prepared to pay royally for the experience. Choose from a slew of restaurants, or picnic on a budget at one of the many public benches, tables, or lounge chairs that offer the best seats of all (grocery stores are a block away from the harborfront views). For recommendations, see "Eating in Oslo," later.

AKERSHUS FORTRESS COMPLEX

This parklike complex of sights, worth ▲, is scattered over Oslo's fortified old center. It's also a military base, and you'll see

uniformed members of the Royal Guard keeping watch over the royal mausoleum here. But the public is welcome, and as you dodge patrol guards and vans filled with soldiers, you'll see the castle, war memorials, the Norwegian Resistance Museum,

OSLO

and cannon-strewn ramparts affording fine harbor views and picnic perches. Expect bumpy cobblestone lanes and steep hills.

Hours: The park is generally open daily 6:00-21:00 (until 18:00 in winter). There's an unimpressive changing of the guard—that's singular "guard," as in just one—daily at 13:30 (at the parade ground, deep in the castle complex).

Getting There: It's a sprawling complex. From the harbor, you

can hike up the stairs by the FDR statue or (less steeply) from the grid of streets just east of City Hall. As you hike up toward the ramparts, go through the gate smack in the middle of the complex (rather than hooking up around to the right). You'll pop out into an inner courtyard. The visitors center (described next) is to the left, and the other sights are through the gate on the right. Heading through this gate, you'll curl up along a tree-lined lane, then pass the Norwegian Resistance Museum on your right (capping the ramparts). The entrance to the castle is dead ahead. There are terrific harbor views from the rampart alongside the Resistance Museum.

Fortress Visitors Center: Stop here to pick up the fortress trail and site map, quickly browse through a modest exhibit tracing the story of Oslo's fortifications from medieval times, use the free WCs, and consider catching a tour (daily May-Aug 10:00-17:00, shorter hours off-season, +47 23 09 39 17, www.akershusfestning. no).

Fortress Tours: Hour-long English walking tours of the grounds help you make sense of the most historic piece of real estate in Oslo (100 NOK, July-mid-Aug daily in English at 11:00 and 15:00, off-season Sat-Sun only at 13:00; departs from Fortress Visitors Center, call ahead to confirm tour is running).

▲▲Norwegian Resistance Museum (Norges Hjemmefrontmuseum)

This fascinating museum tells the story of Norway's WWII experience: appeasement, Nazi invasion (they made Akershus one of their headquarters), resistance, libera-
tion, and, finally, the return of the king. This is an inspirational look at how the national spirit can endure total occupation by a malevolent force. While the exhibit grows a bit more old-fashioned with each passing year, for those with an appetite for WWII history and the patience
to read the displays, it's both riveting and stirring. Norway had the fiercest resistance movement in Scandinavia, and this museum shows off their (hard-earned) pride.

Cost and Hours: 60 NOK; daily 10:00-17:00, Sept-April until 16:00; next to castle, overlooking harbor, +47 23 09 31 38, www.forsvaretsmuseer.no.

Visiting the Museum: It's a one-way, chronological route. As you enter the exhibit, you're transported back to 1940, greeted by an angry commotion of rifles aimed at you. A German notice

proclaiming "You will submit or die" is bayonetted onto a gun in the middle. A **timeline** on the right wall traces the brief history of skirmishes between Nazi and improvised Norwegian forces following the invasion on April 9, 1940. This ends abruptly on June 10, when the Norwegian government officially capitulates.

On the left, you'll see the German ultimatum to which King Haakon VII gave an emphatic "No." A video screen nearby plays the radio address by Vidkun Quisling, the fascist Nasjonal Samling (National Union Party) politician who declared himself ruler of Norway on the day of the invasion. (Today, Quisling's name remains synonymous with "traitor"—the Norwegian version of Benedict Arnold.)

Head **downstairs** to explore the in-depth exhibits. Various displays show secret radios, transmitters, and underground newspapers. The official name for the resistance was Milorg (for "Military Organization")—but Norwegians affectionately referred to the ragtag, guerilla force as simply *gutta på skauen* ("the boys in the forest"). Look for the display case explaining wartime difficulty and austerity in Norway. Red knit caps were worn by civilians to show solidarity with the resistance—until the hats were outlawed by Nazi officials. In the same case, notice the shoes made of fish skin, and the little row of *erstatning* (ersatz, or replacement) products. With the Nazi occupation, Norway lost its trade partners, and had to improvise.

You'll also learn about the military actions against the occupation. British-trained special forces famously blew up a strategic heavy water plant (a key part of the Nazis' atomic bomb program). The event is immortalized in the not-so-accurate 1965 Kirk Douglas film *The Heroes of Telemark*. Nearby, see the case of crude but effective homemade weapons and the German machine used to locate clandestine radio stations. Exhibits explain how the country coped with 350,000 occupying troops; how airdrops equipped a home force of 40,000 so they were ready to coordinate with the Allies when liberation was imminent; and the happy day when the resistance army came out of the forest, and peace and freedom returned to Norway. Liberation day was May 8, 1945...but it took a few days to pull together the celebration, which coincided neatly with the 17th of May—Constitution Day. (That's partly why May 17 is still celebrated so fiercely today.)

Back **upstairs,** notice the propaganda posters trying to recruit Norwegians to the Nazi cause and "protect the eastern border" from the Soviets and communism. A more recent addition to the museum (downstairs) considers the many Norwegians who did choose to cooperate with (and profit from) the Nazis.

The museum is particularly poignant because many of the patriots featured inside were executed by the Germans right out-

side the museum's front door; a
stone memorial marks the spot.
(At war's end, the traitor Vidkun Quisling was also executed
at the fortress, but at a different
location.)

Akershus Castle
(Akershus Slott)
One of Oslo's oldest buildings,
the castle overlooking the harbor, with big, empty rooms, recalls
Norway's medieval poverty. Norwegians built the first fortress here
in 1299; later, in 1649, the Danes made it stronger so the Danish
king Christian IV would have a suitable and safe place to stay dur-

ing his many visits. When
Oslo was rebuilt in the
17th century, many of the
stones from the first Oslo
cathedral were reused
here, in the fortress walls.

Cost and Hours: 100
NOK, includes audio-
guide; Mon-Sat 10:00-
16:00, Sun from 12:00;
Sept-April Sat-Sun 12:00-17:00 only, closed Mon-Fri; +47 23 09
35 53. The castle has been closed for renovation but should reopen
by the time you visit—check locally.

Visiting the Castle: From the old kitchen, where the ticket
desk and gift shop are located, you'll follow a one-way circuit of
rooms open to the public. Descend through a secret passage to the
dungeon, crypt, and royal tomb. Emerge behind the altar in the
chapel, then walk through echoing rooms including the Daredevil's Tower, Hall of Christian IV (with portraits of Danish kings of
Norway on the walls), and Hall of Olav V.

Old Christiania
In the mid-1600s, the ruling Danes had the original Oslo leveled and built a more modern grid-planned city named Christiania, after their king. They located it just below the castle for easier
control and defense, and built with stone so it wouldn't burn. The
checkerboard neighborhood between the castle and the cathedral
today—aptly called Kvadraturen—marks that original Christiania
town. There's little to see, but curious tourists can wander through
this sleepy zone (between the castle and Karl Johans Gate) and
look for some 17th-century buildings. Bits of Christiania's original
Dutch Renaissance-style buildings survive. (Norwegian builders,
accustomed to working with wood, lacked skill with stone, so the

Danes imported Dutch builders.) The area's main square, Christiania Torv (near the recommended Café Skansen), is marked by a modern fountain called "The Glove." The sculpture of Christian IV's glove points as if to indicate, "This is where we'll build my city." The old City Hall, now the Gamle Raadhus restaurant, survives.

ON THE WATERFRONT, NEAR THE TRAIN STATION
▲Oslo Opera House (Operahuset Oslo)
Oslo's striking Opera House angles up from the water on the city's

eastern harbor, across from the train station. Its boxy, low-slung, glass center holds a state-of-the-art 1,400-seat main theater with a 99-piece orchestra "in the pit," which can rise to put the orchestra "on the pedestal." The season is split between opera and ballet.

Cost and Hours: Foyer and café/restaurant open daily roughly 11:00-18:00, open longer hours during performances.

Tours: Fascinating 50-minute guided tours of the stage, backstage area, and architecture run year-round (120 NOK; usually 1-2 tours/day in English—generally at 12:00 and 13:00; reserve online at www.operaen.no, +47 21 42 21 00).

Daytime Mini-Concerts: For a few weeks in the summer, the Opera House offers sporadic one-hour daytime concerts (70 NOK, many days in late July at 14:00).

Getting There: You'll find it on Bjørvika, the next harbor over from City Hall and Akershus Fortress—just below the train station.

Visiting the Opera House: Information-packed tours explain what makes this one of the greenest buildings in Europe and why Norwegian taxpayers helped foot its half-billion-dollar construction cost—to make high culture (ballet and opera) accessible to the younger generation and a stratum of society who normally wouldn't care. You'll see a workshop employing 50 people who hand-make costumes, and learn how a foundation of 700 pylons set some 150 feet deep support the jigsaw puzzle of wood, glass, and 36,000 individual pieces of marble. The construction masterfully integrates land and water, inside and outside, nature and culture.

The jutting white marble planes of the Opera House's roof double as a public plaza. You feel a need to walk all over it. The

Opera House is part of a larger harbor-redevelopment plan that included rerouting traffic into tunnels and turning a once-derelict industrial zone into an urban park. If you hike all the way to the top of the building (watch your footing—it's slippery when wet), you can peek over the back railing to see the high-rise development known as the Barcode Project. This sleek and distinctive collection of high-rise office buildings resembles the bars in a universal product code. The new Munch Museum resides in the futuristic building on the adjacent pier.

▲Munch Museum (Munchmuseet)

The only Norwegian painter to have had a serious impact on European art, Edvard Munch (pronounced "moonk") developed an international reputation during the 16 years he lived and worked in Germany (1892-1908)—an especially prolific period during which he created many of his most well-regarded works. But a breakdown in 1908 sent him back to Oslo, where he would live out his life working quietly at his property just outside the city. At his death in 1944, he left all the artwork still in his possession—thousands of paintings, drawings, photographs, and prints—to the city of Oslo.

These collections are now stretched over the 11 galleries and 13 floors of a new modernistic building sitting on the harbor, not far from the Opera House. This is the place to appreciate in depth the emotional, disturbing, and powerfully Expressionistic work of this strange and perplexing man, including one version of his most famous painting, *The Scream* (for more on Munch, see page 37). Works by other modernist and contemporary artists round out the exhibits.

Cost and Hours: 160 NOK, daily 10:00-20:00, café and restaurant, on the harbor at Edvard Munchs Plass 1, +47 23 49 35 00, www.munchmuseet.no.

IN THE CITY CENTER
Royal Palace (Slottet)

Set at the top of Karl Johans Gate, the Neoclassical Royal Palace is home to Norway's King Harald V and Queen Sonja. Completed in 1849, it was extensively (and expensively) renovated in 2001. To quell controversy the public is now invited inside each summer with a one-hour guided tour that includes the king's Council Chamber, the Great Dining Room (seating for 220), and the palace's finest guest room, the King Haakon suite.

Cost and Hours: 135 NOK, English tours 4/day late June-mid-Aug, tickets go on sale in March and fill fast—it's smart to book in advance at www.ticketmaster.no, limited number of tickets are available at the entrance, www.kongehuset.no.

OSLO

Historical Museum (Historisk Museum)

Just below the Royal Palace is a fine Art Nouveau building offering exhibits about the history of humankind—and an easy peek at Norway's history, from the Stone Age to modern times. Skip over the ancient Egypt, Greek, and Roman displays to focus on the country's top collection of Viking artifacts.

Cost and Hours: 100 NOK, same ticket covers Viking Ship Museum on Bygdøy for 48 hours; open Tue-Sun 10:00-17:00, mid-Sept-mid-May 11:00-16:00; closed Mon year-round; Frederiks Gate 2, +47 22 85 19 00, www.khm.uio.no.

Visiting the Museum: The ground floor has medieval and Viking Age artifacts from around Norway. Ogle the gorgeous carved doors with their filigreed details from stave churches. Look for the little door to the easy-to-miss Viking section, where you'll find the museum's hidden highlight: the only intact, authentic Viking helmet ever found in Scandinavia (with an eye mask; it's unceremoniously jammed into a crowded display case). Upstairs is an exhibit about life for the far northern Sami people and other Arctic cultures. It's fun to peek in the cutaway igloo for a glimpse at Inuit lifestyles. There's also a modest anthropological exhibit about indigenous peoples of the Americas. A few Egyptian mummies and Norwegian coins through the ages are tossed in for good measure.

National Gallery (Nasjonalgalleriet)

Part of the National Museum, Oslo's National Gallery is temporarily closed. When it reopens, visitors can expect art collections, workshops, and rotating exhibitions (backing up to the Historical Museum at Universitetsgata 13, +47 21 98 20 00, www.nasjonalmuseet.no).

FROGNER PARK

The sprawling Frogner Park anchors an upscale neighborhood of the same name, 1.5 miles west of the city center. Here you'll find the breathtaking Vigeland Sculpture Park, the Vigeland Museum, and the Oslo City Museum. The Frognerbadet swimming pool is nearby.

Getting There: Tram #12—which leaves from the central train station, Rådhusplassen in front of City Hall, Aker Brygge, and other points in town—drops you off right at the park gate (Vigelandsparken stop). Tram #19 (with stops along Karl Johans Gate) takes you to Majorstuen, a 10-minute walk to the gate (or you can change at Majorstuen to tram #12 and ride it two stops to Vigelandsparken).

▲▲▲Vigeland Sculpture Park (Vigelandsparken)

Within Oslo's vast Frogner Park is Vigeland Sculpture Park, containing a lifetime of work by Norway's greatest sculptor, Gustav

OSLO

Frogner Park

Note: Vigeland Sculpture Park is the shaded area within Frogner Park—from the Main Entrance Gate to the Wheel of Life

100 Meters
100 Yards

West Cemetery

MONOLITVEIEN

WHEEL OF LIFE

TOUR ENDS

MONOLITH
❹

MALE GATE

FEMALE GATE

MADSERUD ALLE

VIGELAND SCULPTURE PARK

Frogner   FOUNTAIN ❸   Park

ROSE GARDEN

Pond

VIGELAND MUSEUM

ANGRY BOY →

❷

BRIDGE

FROGNER-BADET (POOL)

NOBELS GATE

HALVDAN SVARTES GATE

OSLO CITY MUSEUM

CAFÉ

TOUR BEGINS

VISITORS CENTER CAFETERIA, & WC

FROGNER STADIUM

SONJA HENIE STATUE

MIDDELTHUNS GATE

To Majorstuen

Frogner #12

MAIN ENTRANCE GATE

❶

#12 Vigelands-parken

KIRKEVEIEN

❺

THOMAS HEFTYES GATE

GYLDENLØVES GATE

MUNTHES GATE

PROF. DAHLS GATE

MARIES GATE

Frogner Stadion #12

❻

FROGNERVEIEN

To Oslo Center

Vigeland Sculpture Park Tour
❶ Gustav Vigeland Statue
❷ Bridge
❸ Fountain
❹ Monolith

Eateries
❺ Lofotstua Restaurant
❻ Curry and Ketchup Indian Restaurant

Vigeland (see sidebar). In 1921, he made a deal with the city. In return for a great studio and state support, he'd spend his creative life beautifying Oslo with this sculpture garden. From 1924 until his death in 1943 he worked on-site, designing 192 bronze and granite statue groupings—600 figures in all, each

nude and unique. Vigeland even planned the landscaping.

Today the park is loved and respected by the people of Oslo (no police, no fences—and no graffiti). At once majestic, hands-on,

entertaining, and deeply moving, I find this park to be one of Europe's top artistic sights. In summer, this is a tempting destination in the late afternoon—after the museums have closed and there's still plenty of daylight. (Note that the nearby Vigeland Museum closes at 16:00.) The sculpture park is more than great art: It's a city at play. Appreciate its urban Norwegian ambience.

Cost and Hours: The garden is always open and free. The park is safe and lit in the evening.

Visitor Information and Services: For an illustrated guide and fine souvenir, consider the 120-NOK book in the visitors center *(besøkssenter)* on your right as you enter. The modern **$$** cafeteria has sandwiches and light meals (indoor/outdoor seating, daily 9:00-20:30 in summer, shorter hours off-season), plus books, gifts, and pay WCs.

● Self-Guided Tour: Frogner Park is huge, but this visit to its central spine, the Vigeland Sculpture Park, is a snap. Here's a quick, four-stop, straight-line, gate-to-monolith tour.

• *Begin by entering the park through the grand gates, from Kirkeveien (with the tram stop). In front of the visitors center, look at the...*

❶ Gustav Vigeland Statue: Vige-
land has his hammer and chisel in hand...and is drenched in pigeon poop. Consider his messed-up life. He lived with his many models. His marriages failed. His children entangled his artistic agenda. He didn't age gracefully. He didn't name his statues, and he refused to explain their meanings. While those who know his life story can read it clearly in the granite and bronze, I'd forget Gustav's troubles and see his art as observations on the bittersweet cycle of life in general—from a man who must have had a passion for living.

• *Now walk 100 yards toward the fountain and the pillar.*

❷ Bridge: The 300-foot-long bridge is bound by four granite columns: Three show a man fighting a lizard, and the fourth shows a woman submitting to the lizard's embrace. Hmmm. (Vigeland was familiar with medieval mythology, where dragons represent man's primal—and sinful—nature.)

But enough lizard love; the 58 bronze statues along the bridge are a general study of the human body. They capture the joys of life (and, on a sunny day, so do the Norwegians and tourists filling the park around you). Many deal with relationships between people. In the middle, on the right, find the circular statue of a man and woman going round and round—perhaps the eternal attraction and love between the sexes. But directly opposite, another circle feels

OSLO

Gustav Vigeland (1869-1943)

Gustav Vigeland's father was a carpenter in the city of Mandal, in southern Norway. Vigeland grew up carving wood and showed promise. As a young man, he went to Oslo to study sculpture, then supplemented his education with trips abroad to Europe's art capitals. Back home, he carved out a successful, critically acclaimed career feeding newly independent Norway's hunger for homegrown art.

During his youthful trips abroad, Vigeland had frequented the studio of Auguste Rodin, admiring Rodin's naked, restless, intertwined statues. Like Rodin, Vigeland explored the yin/yang relationship of men and women. Also like Rodin, Vigeland did not personally carve or cast his statues. Rather, he formed them in clay or plaster, to be executed by a workshop of assistants. Vigeland's sturdy humans capture universal themes of the cycle of life—birth, childhood, romance, struggle, child-rearing, growing old, and death.

like a prison—man against the world, with no refuge.

On your left, see the famous *Angry Boy (Sinnataggen)*, the hot-headed little boy and a symbol of the park. (Notice his left hand is worn shiny from too many hand-holdings.) It's said Vigeland gave a boy chocolate and then took it away to get this reaction. Look below the angry toddler, to the lower terrace—with eight bronze infants circling a head-down fetus.

• *Continue through a rose garden to the earliest sculpture unit in the park.*

❸ **Fountain:** Six giants hold a fountain, symbolically toiling with the burden of life, as water—the source of life—cascades steadily around them. Twenty tree-of-life groups surround the fountain. Four clumps of trees (on each corner) show humanity's relationship to nature and the seasons of life: childhood, young love, adulthood, and winter.

Take a quick swing through life, starting on the right with youth. In the branches you'll see a swarm of children (Vigeland called them "geniuses"): A boy sits in a tree, boys actively climb while most girls stand by quietly, and a girl glides through the branches wide-eyed and ready for life...and love. Circle clockwise to the next stage: love scenes. In the third corner, life becomes more complicated: a sad woman in an animal-like tree, a lonely child, a couple plummeting

OSLO

downward (perhaps falling out of love), a man desperately clinging to his tree, and finally an angry man driving away babies. The fourth corner completes the cycle, as death melts into the branches of the tree of life and you realize new geniuses will bloom.

The 60 bronze reliefs circling the basin develop the theme further, showing man mixing with nature and geniuses giving the

carousel of life yet another spin. Speaking of another spin, circle again and follow these reliefs.

The pattern in the pavers surrounding the basin is a maze—life's long and winding road with twists, dead ends, frustrations, and, ultimately, a way out. If you have about an hour to spare, enter the labyrinth (on the side nearest the park's entrance gate, there's a single break in the black border) and follow the white granite path until (on the monolith side) you finally get out. (Tracing this path occupies older kids, affording parents a peaceful break in the park.)

• *Or you can go straight up the steps to the...*

❹ **Monolith:** The centerpiece of the park—a teeming monolith of life surrounded by 36 groups of granite statues—continues Vigeland's cycle-of-life motif.

The figures are hunched and clearly earthbound, while Vigeland explores a lifetime of human relationships. At the center, 121 figures carved out of a single block of stone rocket skyward. Three stone carvers worked daily for 14 years, cutting Vigeland's full-size plaster model into the final 180-ton, 50-foot-tall erection.

Circle the plaza, once to trace the stages of life in the 36 statue groups, and a second time to enjoy how Norwegian kids relate to the art. The statues—both young and old—seem to speak to children. Note the two wrought iron gates flanking each side of the plaza with their themes of male and female.

Vigeland lived barely long enough to see his monolith raised. Covered with bodies, it seems to pick up speed as it spirals skyward. Some people seem to naturally rise. Others struggle not to fall. Some help others. Although the granite groups around the

monolith are easy to understand, Vigeland left the meaning of the monolith itself open to interpretation. Like life, it can be experienced many different ways.

From this summit of the park, look a hundred yards farther, where four children and three adults are intertwined and spinning in the *Wheel of Life* sculpture. Now, look back at the entrance. If the main gate is at 12 o'clock, the studio where Vigeland lived and worked—now the Vigeland Museum—is at 2 o'clock (see the green copper tower poking above the trees). His ashes sit in the top of the tower in clear view of the monolith. If you liked the park, visit the Vigeland Museum (described next), a delightful five-minute walk away, for an intimate look at the art and how it was made.

▲▲Vigeland Museum

This palatial city-provided studio was Gustav Vigeland's home and workplace for the last two decades of his life. The high south-facing windows provided just the right light. Vigeland, who had a deeply religious upbringing, saw his art as an expression of his soul. He once said, "The road between feeling and execution should be as short as possible." Here, immersed in his work, Vigeland supervised his craftsmen like a father, from 1924 until his death in 1943.

Today it's filled with plaster casts and studies of many of the works you'll see in the adjacent park—shedding new light on that

masterpiece and allowing you to see familiar pieces from new angles. It also holds a few additional works and explains Vigeland's creative (and technical) process. While his upstairs apartment is usually closed to the public, it may be open for guided tours—check the website.

Cost and Hours: 100 NOK; Tue-Sun 10:00-16:00, closed Mon year-round; bus #20 or tram #12 to Frogner Plass, Nobels Gate 32, +47 23 49 37 00, www.vigeland.museum.no.

Visiting the Museum: It's all on one floor, roughly arranged chronologically, which you'll see in an easy clockwise loop. **Rooms I-III** explain Vigeland's development, including his early focus on biblical themes. In *Accused* (1891), Cain flees with his family, including their dog. But gradually, Vigeland grew more interested in the dynamics between families, and those between men and women. In these first rooms, look for two particularly touching sculptures in marble (a medium you won't often see used by Vigeland): *Mother and Child* (1909) and *Young Man and Woman* (1906).

Room IV is a long hall of portrait busts, which Vigeland often

created without payment—he considered this task an opportunity to practice. While most of the busts don't depict famous people, you will see King Oscar II and Arctic explorer Fridtjof Nansen. **Room V** continues this theme, with a few portraits (mostly full-body) of more recognizable figures: Beethoven, Ibsen, Wergeland, Bjørnson.

Room VI, with a 1942 self-portrait, explains the process by which Vigeland created his statues. See his tools displayed in a case and read the explanation: Using the "sand casting" method, Vigeland would make a small plaster model, which guided his workers in creating a metal "skeleton." Vigeland would then bring the skeleton to life with soft clay—which he enjoyed using because its pliability allowed him to be spontaneous in his creativity. Once the clay piece was finished, plaster and sand were used to create a cast, used for the final bronze piece. For his stone works, they used a "pointing machine" to painstakingly measure the exact nuances of Vigeland's contours. Examples of using both methods (including five different versions of the famous "angry baby" bronze) are displayed around the room.

Room VII holds temporary exhibits, while **Room VIII** features the full-sized plaster models for the park's bronze fountain. The large **Room IX** has more pieces from the park, including a one-fifth-scale model of the fountain (used to win the Oslo City Council's support for the project) and the four dragon statues that top the bridge's pillars (high up and difficult to see in the park, but fascinating up close).

Room X is the dramatic climax of the museum, with a model of the entire park, and the life-size plaster models for the Mono-

lith—in three pieces, making it easy to scrutinize the details. You'll also see wrought-iron chained dragons—originally designed as a feature for the park gates—and several plaster models for the statues that surround the Monolith. Notice the

many little "freckles" on these statues, left behind by the pointer used by craftsmen to replicate Vigeland's work. The museum finishes with more temporary exhibits (in Rooms XI and XII).

Oslo City Museum (Oslo Bymuseum)

This modest, hard-to-be-thrilled-about exhibit tells the story of Oslo. For a quick overview of the city, watch the 15-minute English video (90 NOK, includes audioguide, Tue-Sun 11:00-16:00,

closed Mon, across street from the Vigeland Museum in Frogner Manor Farm, +47 23 28 41 70, www.oslomuseum.no).

Frognerbadet
Located near Vigeland Sculpture Park, the Frognerbadet has three outdoor pools, a waterslide, high dives, a cafeteria, and lots of young families (open mid-May-late Aug, closed off-season, Middelthunsgate 28, +47 23 27 54 50).

BYGDØY NEIGHBORHOOD
This thought-provoking and exciting cluster of sights, worth ▲▲, is on a parklike peninsula just across the harbor from down-town Oslo. It provides a busy and rewarding half-day (at a minimum) of sightseeing.

Here, within a short walk, are six major sights (listed in order of importance): the **Nor-wegian Folk Museum,** an open-air museum with tradi-tional wooden buildings from all corners of the country, a stave church, and a collection of 20th-century urban buildings; the **Vi-king Ship Museum,** showing off the best-preserved Viking ships in existence; the **Fram Museum,** showcasing the modern Viking spirit with the *Fram,* the ship of Arctic-exploration fame, and the *Gjøa,* the first ship to sail through the Northwest Passage; the **Kon-Tiki Museum,** starring the *Kon-Tiki* and the *Ra II,* in which Norwegian explorer Thor Heyerdahl proved that early civilizations could have crossed the oceans; the **Norwegian Maritime Muse-um,** interesting mostly to old salts; and the **Norwegian Holocaust Center,** memorializing the Holocaust in Norway.

Getting to Bygdøy: Sailing from downtown to Bygdøy is fun, fast, and gets you in a seafaring mood. Ride the Bygdøy **ferry**—marked *Public Ferry Bygdøy Museums*—from pier 3 in front of City Hall (52 NOK one-way at the ticket desk, 62 NOK on board; 78 NOK round-trip at the ticket desk; covered by Oslo Pass—but not by individual Ruter transit tickets; 3/hour, 10-15 minutes; May-Sept daily 8:55-20:55, fewer sailings spring and fall, no boats off-season). Boats generally leave from downtown at :05, :25, and :45 past each hour. In summer, avoid the nearby (much more expen-sive) tour boats.

For a less memorable approach, you can take **bus** #30 (from train station, National Theater, or in front of City Hall, direction: Bygdøy; 20-minute trip).

Returning to Oslo: Note that after 17:00, bus and boat depar-

OSLO

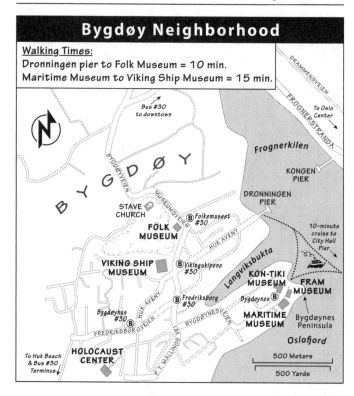

Bygdøy Neighborhood

<u>Walking Times:</u>
Dronningen pier to Folk Museum = 10 min.
Maritime Museum to Viking Ship Museum = 15 min.

tures back to downtown are sparse. If returning by ferry, get to the dock a little early—otherwise the boat is likely to be full, and you'll have to wait for the next sailing.

Getting Around Bygdøy: The Norwegian Folk and Viking Ship museums are a 10-minute walk from the ferry's first stop (Dronningen). The other boating museums (Fram, Kon-Tiki, and Maritime) are at the second ferry stop, in an area called Bygdøynes. The Holocaust Center is off Fredriksborgveien, about halfway between these two museum clusters. All Bygdøy sights are within a pleasant (when sunny) 15-minute walk of each other. The walk gives you a picturesque taste of suburban Oslo.

City bus #30 connects the sights four times hourly in this order: Norwegian Folk Museum, Viking Ship Museum, Kon-Tiki Museum, Norwegian Holocaust Center. (For the Holocaust Center, you'll use the Bygdøyhus stop a long block away; tell the bus driver you want the stop for the "HL-Senteret.") The bus turns around at its final stop (Huk), then passes the sights in reverse order on its way back to the city center.

Planning Your Day: If the weather's good, hit the folk museum first (before it gets too hot). If it's ugly out, begin with the

mostly indoor boat museums at Bygdøynes. The marginally interesting Holocaust Center is a bit of a detour, and skippable if you're
short on time. The Bygdøynes museums offer a 10 percent discount
if you buy tickets for all three at the same time; decide before you
buy your first ticket and save a few bucks.

Eating at Bygdøy: Each museum area has **$** food options. At
the boat museum cluster (Bygdøynes), you'll find the **Framheim
Café** inside the Fram Museum; a little **café window** with hot dogs
and ice cream outside the Kon-Tiki Museum; and two more-sub-
stantial eateries at the Maritime Museum: the indoor **Kafe Fjord**
with sandwiches and soup, and the outdoor **Fjordterrassen Café,**
with hot dogs and deep-fried fish and veggie burgers, and tables
overlooking the harbor (open May-Aug). The Norwegian Folk
Museum houses the decent **Kafe Arkadia** at its entrance, but picnics are also encouraged. A fun little **farmers market** stall across
the street sells produce, drinks, and yogurt—just enough to forage
a healthy lunch). The Viking Ship Museum has an outdoor **snack
window** selling shrimp and salmon sandwiches in summer. The
Holocaust Center has a small **café** upstairs (closed Mon).

Beach at Bygdøy: A popular beach is located at Huk, on the
southwest tip of the peninsula.

Museums on Bygdøy
▲▲Norwegian Folk Museum (Norsk Folkemuseum)
Brought from all corners of Norway, 150 buildings have been re-
assembled here on 35 acres. While Stockholm's Skansen was the
first museum of this kind to open to the public, this collection is
a bit older, started in 1881 as the king's private collection (and the
inspiration for Skansen). The folk museum is most lively (and worth
▲▲▲) June through mid-August, when buildings are open and
staffed with attendants in period clothing (who'll happily answer
your questions). You'll also see artisans working at traditional crafts
and barnyard animals roaming about. In the off-season, the indoor
museum is fine, but the park is just a pleasant place to stroll past
lots of locked-up log cabins. Be prepared for an uphill walk to reach
the Gol stave church.

Cost and Hours: 160 NOK, daily 10:00-17:00—grounds
open until 20:00; Sept-May park open daily 11:00-16:00, but most
historical buildings closed; Museumsveien 10, bus #30 stops immediately in front, +47 22 12 37 00, www.norskfolkemuseum.no.

Tours and Activities: Upon arrival, pick up the site map and
review the list of the day's events, concerts, and guided tours (on a
video screen near the ticket desk). In summer, there are usually two
guided tours in English per day; the Telemark Farm hosts a small
daily fiddle-and-folk-dance show; and a folk music-and-dance
show is held each Sunday. If you don't take a tour, invest in a guide-

OSLO

book and ask questions of the informative attendants stationed in buildings throughout the park.

Visiting the Museum: Think of the visit in three parts: the park sprinkled with old buildings, the re-created old town, and the folk-art museum. As you enter, you'll cut through the courtyard with the museum to reach the open-air sections.

The **park** is loaded with mostly log-built, sod-roofed cabins from various parts of Norway (arranged roughly geographically). Be sure to go inside the buildings. The evocative Gol stave church, at the top of a hill at the park's edge, is worth the climb. Built in 1212 in Hallingdal and painstakingly reconstructed here, it has a classic design and, inside, beautiful yet primitive wood paintings on the apse walls (c. 1452). If you won't make it to a stave church elsewhere on your trip, this is a must. (For more on stave churches, see page 116.)

Back near the entrance building, the **old town** has a variety of homes and shops that focus on urban lifestyles. It's worth exploring the tenement building, in which you can explore intimate, fully furnished apartments from various generations and lifestyles—1905, 1930, 1950, 1979, and even a Norwegian-Pakistani apartment.

In the **museum,** the ground floor beautifully presents woody, colorfully painted, and exactingly carved folk art; traditional Norwegian knitting; and weapons. Upstairs are exquisite-in-a-peasant-kind-of-way folk costumes. I'd skip the sleepy collection of Norwegian church art (in an adjoining building). But don't miss the best Sami culture exhibit I've seen in Scandinavia (across the courtyard in the green building, behind the toy exhibit). The museum's newest exhibit traces the evolution of Norway's culture and identity from 1600 to 1914.

▲▲Viking Ship Museum (Vikingskiphuset)

This impressive museum is undergoing a multiyear expansion, and exhibits will ultimately move into the new Museum of the Viking Age (scheduled to open on the same site by 2025). In the meantime, some of the ships described here may not be on display, and the building itself may be closed from time to time—check locally.

Even if the main attractions aren't on display during your visit, this museum still offers a fine look at Viking culture. You'll see finely crafted, majestic oak Viking ships dating from the 9th and 10th centuries alongside the bones of Vikings buried with these

vessels and remarkable artifacts that may cause you to consider these notorious raiders in a different light. Over a thousand years ago, three things drove Vikings on their far-flung raids: hard economic times in their bleak homeland, the lure of prosperous and vulnerable communities to the south, and a mastery of the sea. There was a time when most frightened Europeans closed every prayer with, "And deliver us from the Vikings, Amen." Gazing up at the prow of one of these sleek, time-stained vessels, you can almost hear the shouts of those redheads on the rampage.

Cost and Hours: 120 NOK, ticket also covers the Historical Museum in downtown Olso for 48 hours; Tue-Sun 10:00-16:00, closed Mon; Huk Aveny 35, +47 22 85 19 00, www.khm.uio.no.

Tours: The museum doesn't offer tours, but you can use the free Wi-Fi to download an informative audioguide.

Visiting the Museum: If they're on display, focus on the two well-preserved ships, starting with the *Oseberg*, from AD 834. With its ornate carving and impressive rudder, it was likely a royal pleasure craft. It seems designed for sailing on calm inland waters during festivals, but not in the open ocean.

The *Gokstad*, from AD 950, is a practical working boat capable of sailing the high seas. A ship like this brought settlers to the west of France (Normandy was named for the Norsemen). And in such a vessel, explorers such as Erik the Red hopscotched from Norway to Iceland to Greenland and on to what they called Vinland—today's Newfoundland in Canada. Imagine 30 men hauling on long oars out at sea for weeks and months at a time. In 1892, a replica of this ship sailed from Norway to America in 44 days to celebrate the 400th anniversary of Columbus *not* discovering America.

You'll also see the ruins of a third vessel, the **Tune Ship** (c. AD 910), which saw service only briefly before being used as the tomb for an important chieftain. In this hall, every 20 minutes, the lights dim and a wrap-around film plays on the walls around the ship for five minutes—with dramatic virtual footage of the Vikings and their fleet.

The ships tend to steal the show, but don't miss the **jewelry and personal items** excavated along with the ships. The ships and related artifacts survived so well because they were buried in clay as part of a gravesite. Many of the finest items were not actually Viking art, but goodies they brought home after raiding more advanced (but less tough) people. Still, there are lots of actual Viking items, such as metal and leather goods, that give insight into their

culture. Highlights are the cart and sleighs, ornately carved with scenes from Viking sagas.

▲▲▲Fram Museum (Frammuseet)

Under its distinctive A-frame roof, this museum holds the 125-foot, steam- and sail-powered ship that took modern-day Vikings Roald Amundsen and Fridtjof Nansen deep into the Arctic and Antarctic, farther north and south than any vessel had gone before. In an adjacent A-frame is Amundsen's *Gjøa*, the first ship to sail through the Northwest Passage. Together, the ex-

hibit spins a fascinating tale of adventure, scientific exploration, and human determination...all at subzero temperatures.

Cost and Hours: 120 NOK; daily June-Aug 9:00-18:00, May and Sept 10:00-18:00, Oct-April until 17:00; Bygdøynesveien 36, +47 23 28 29 50, www.frammuseum.no.

Visiting the Museum: Stepping into the museum, you're immediately bow-to-bow with the 128-foot *Fram*. Before diving in, remember that there are two parts to the museum: The *Fram*, which you're looking at, and to the left through a tunnel, the smaller *Gjøa*. I'd see the *Gjøa* first, because it's a better lead-up to the main event, and because it features a short film that's a fine introduction to the entire museum.

Crossing through the tunnel to the ***Gjøa***, you'll learn about the search for the Northwest Passage (that long-sought-after trade route through the Arctic from the Atlantic to the Pacific). Exhibits tell the story of how Roald Amundsen and a crew of six used this motor- and sail-powered ship to successfully navigate the Northwest Passage (1903-1906). Exhibits describe their ordeal as well as other Arctic adventures, such as Amundsen's 1925 flight to 88 degrees north (they had to build a runway out of ice to take off and return home); and his 1926 airship (zeppelin) expedition from Oslo over the North Pole to Alaska. This section also features a 100-seat cinema showing an excellent 15-minute film about the exploration of the earth's polar regions (shows every 15 minutes).

Now return to the ***Fram*** and peruse the exhibits—actual artifacts and profiles of the brave explorers and their crew. The upper floor focuses on Nansen's voyages to the North Pole on the *Fram*, including an early kayak, a full-size stuffed polar bear, and a model of the ship. Here you can cross a gangway to explore the *Fram*'s claustrophobic but fascinating interior. A simulated Northern

The Fram Museum: From Pole to Pole

The Fram Museum tells the tale of two great Norwegian explorers, Fridtjof Nansen and Roald Amundsen.

Early polar explorers focused on the Northwest Passage, believing the Arctic could hold a highly lucrative trade route between the Atlantic and the Pacific oceans. Englishman John Franklin famously led a failed expedition looking for the Northwest Passage in 1845; two ships and 129 men were never seen again. Many others attempted and failed—more than a thousand sailors were lost in the search.

A generation later, with the Northwest Passage conquered by Amundsen, explorers (inspired by tales of Franklin and his ilk) became determined to reach the North Pole.

Fridtjof Nansen (1861-1930) prepared for his North Pole expedition by crossing the inland ice of Greenland in six weeks in 1888—hand-pulling sledges all the way—and then spent the winter learning from Inuit people he met. Nansen also commissioned the *Fram,* which was purpose-built for Arctic exploration with a rounded hull, designed to withstand being stuck in ice without being crushed. (The downside was that it got tossed around in fierce waves.) It even had a windmill that could power electric lights. In the end, the *Fram* went on three major expeditions. In each one, the crew set out knowing they'd be living in subzero temperatures for three to five years.

The *Fram's* maiden voyage was Nansen's search for the North Pole (1893-1896). He believed that, due to the natural drifting of the northern ice cap, a ship encased in ice would simply be carried by currents to the North Pole. For three years, the *Fram* drifted, trapped in the Arctic ice. While he didn't reach the North Pole, Nansen made better progress than anyone before him.

Then, **Otto Sverdrup** (1854-1930) took the helm of the *Fram* and advanced Nansen's progress (riding icebergs from 1898 until 1902), but he didn't make it all the way, either.

Finally, **Roald Amundsen** (1872-1928)—who had already successfully sailed the Northwest Passage—made plans to reach the North Pole in the *Fram* in 1910. Amundsen's crew (and financiers) believed he was heading north. But when word came that American explorer Frederick Cook had beaten him to the North Pole, Amundsen sailed the *Fram* to Antarctica instead and set out to reach the South Pole (1910-1912). Amundsen and his team were in a race to the pole with Englishman Robert Falcon Scott and his men, who had arrived aboard the ship *Terra Nova*. Amundsen beat Scott to the South Pole by about a month. And, unlike Scott, Amundsen made it home alive.

The *Fram* expeditions coincided with the nascent Norwegian independence movement and became a proud patriotic symbol of the Norwegian people.

Lights show, best viewed from the *Fram*'s main deck, is presented every 20 minutes.

Exhibits on the middle floor focus on Admundsen, who picked up where Nansen left off and explored the South Pole. You'll see an actual dogsled Admundsen's team used and a small model of the motorized sled from the rival Scott expedition. Also featured are a tent like the one Amundsen used, reconstructed shelves from his Arctic kitchen, models of the *Fram*, and a "polar simulator" plunging visitors into a 15° Fahrenheit environment.

▲▲Kon-Tiki Museum (Kon-Tiki Museet)

Next to the *Fram* is a museum housing the *Kon-Tiki* and the *Ra II*, the ships built by the larger-than-life anthropologist, seafarer, and adventurer Thor Heyerdahl

(1914-2002). Heyerdahl and his crew used these ships—constructed entirely without modern technology—to undertake tropical voyages many had thought impossible. Both ships are well displayed and described in English. This museum—more lighthearted than the other boat-focused exhibits—puts you in a castaway mood.

Cost and Hours: 120 NOK, daily 10:00-17:00, June-Aug from 11:00, Nov-Feb until 16:00, Bygdøynesveien 36, +47 23 08 67 67, www.kon-tiki.no.

Background: Thor Heyerdahl believed that early South Americans could have crossed the Pacific to settle Polynesia. To prove his point, in 1947 Heyerdahl and five crewmates constructed the *Kon-Tiki* raft from balsa wood, using only premodern tools and techniques, and adorned its sail with a giant image of the sun god Kon-Tiki. They set sail from Peru on the tiny craft, surviving for 101 days on fish, coconuts, and sweet potatoes (native to Peru). About 5,000 miles later, they arrived in Polynesia. (While Heyerdahl proved that early South Americans *could* have made this trip, anthropologists doubt they did.) The *Kon-Tiki* story became a best-selling book and award-winning documentary (and helped spawn the "Tiki" culture craze in the US). Funded by the *Kon-Tiki* success, Heyerdahl went on to explore Easter Island (1955) and then turned his attention to another voyage—this time across the Atlantic. In 1970, Heyerdahl's *Ra II* made a similar 4,000-mile journey from Morocco to Barbados—on a vessel made of reeds—to prove that Africans could have populated the Americas.

Visiting the Museum: You'll see both the *Kon-Tiki* and the *Ra II* and learn about Heyerdahl's other adventures (including

In Cold Blood

Norway likes to think of itself as a quiet, peaceful nation on the edge of Europe—after all, its legislators award the Nobel Peace Prize. So the events of July 22, 2011 had a profound effect on the country's psyche. On that day, an anti-immigration fanatic named Anders Behring Breivik set off a car bomb in Oslo, killing eight. He then traveled to a summer camp where he hunted down, shot, and killed 69 young people and counselors.

Until Breivik's attack Norway had largely escaped 21st-century terrorism. When the public learned that the man behind the violence was a native Norwegian, they reacted with a huge outpouring of grief. Bouquets flooded the square in front of Oslo Cathedral.

Arrested after the shootings, Breivik was described by police as obsessed with what he saw as the "threat" of multiculturalism and immigration to Norwegian values. It's true that Norway has a big and growing immigrant community. More than 15 percent of the population is not ethnic Norwegian, and a quarter of Oslo's residents are immigrants. These "new Norwegians" provide a much-needed and generally appreciated labor force, filling jobs that wealthy natives would rather not do.

Horrified by Breivik's actions, after the attack many Norwegians went out of their way to make immigrants feel welcome. Even though the country strengthened its immigration laws in 2014, Norway seems determined not to let the July 22 massacre poison its peaceful soul. Calls for police to start carrying weapons or to reinstate the death penalty were quickly rejected. "Breivik wanted to change Norway," an Oslo resident told me. "We're determined to keep Norway the way it was."

Easter Island and the *Ra I*, which sank partway into its journey). Everything's well-described in English and very kid-friendly. In the basement, you'll see the bottom of the *Kon-Tiki* vessel with a life-size model of a whale shark (the largest fish on earth) and other marine life that the crew observed at sea. Nearby, a small theater continuously plays a 10-minute documentary about the voyage; every day at 12:00, they show the full-length (67-minute), Oscar-winning 1950 documentary film *Kon-Tiki*.

▲Norwegian Maritime Museum (Norsk Maritimt Museum)

If you're into the sea and seafaring, this museum is a salt lick, providing a wide-ranging look at Norway's maritime heritage through exhibits, art, and a panoramic film soaring over Norway's long and varied coastline.

Cost and Hours: 120 NOK; daily 10:00-17:00, Oct-April 11:00-16:00; two cafés—one with city views; Bygdøynesveien 37, +47 22 12 37 00, www.marmuseum.no.

Visiting the Museum: The core of the museum is the Boat Hall (Båthallen), where you'll see a collection of traditional boats, fishing gear, clothing, and household goods that capture the challenges and hardships of 19th-century coastal Norway. In another display, artifacts recently recovered from some of the many shipwrecks in Oslo's old harbor illustrate international shipping, trade, and communications in the 16th and 17th centuries. The exhibit *At Sea* takes a personal look at seafarers' lives from Viking days to the present. If you appreciate maritime art, the painting collection in the gallery should float your boat. If it's still showing, watch the wrap-around, 20-minute movie *The Ocean: A Way of Life* (look for *Supervideografen* signs), which swoops you scenically over Norway's diverse coast, showing off fishing townscapes, shiplap villages, industrial harbors, and breathtaking scenery from here all the way to North Cape.

Norwegian Holocaust Center (HL-Senteret)

Located in the stately former home of Nazi collaborator Vidkun Quisling—whose name is synonymous with "complicit in atrocities"—this museum and study center offers a high-tech look at the racist ideologies that fueled the Holocaust. It's designed primarily for Norwegians, but you can borrow a tablet with English translations of the exhibits. The ground floor displays historical documents about the rise of anti-Semitism and personal effects from Holocaust victims. The exhibits continue downstairs, where the names of 760 Norwegian Jews killed by the Nazis are listed in a bright, white room. Out front, the *Innocent Questions* glass-and-neon sculpture shows an old-fashioned punch card, reminding viewers of how the Norwegian puppet government collected seemingly innocuous information before deporting its Jews.

Cost and Hours: 70 NOK; daily 10:00-17:00, mid-Sept-mid-May until 16:00; Huk Aveny 56—take bus #30 to the Bygdøyhus stop and follow brown *HL-Senteret* signs, +47 22 84 21 00, www.hlsenteret.no.

GRÜNERLØKKA AND GRØNLAND DISTRICTS

Oslo's Grünerløkka district, bisected by the Akers River, is lively, and workaday Grønland is emerging as a fun spot. You can connect

OSLO

it all together by following the self-guided Up Akers River and Down Grünerløkka Walk (described below).

Akers River

The source of the Akers River (and Oslo's drinking water) is the pristine Lake Maridal, situated at the edge of the Nordmarka wilderness. The idyllic recreation scenes along Lake Maridal are a favorite for nature-loving Norwegians.

Though only about five miles long, the Akers River powered Oslo's early industry: flour mills in the 1300s, sawmills in the 1500s, and Norway's Industrial Revolution in the 1800s. Today the river valley becomes a park as it winds past decent-size waterfalls and red-brick factories that now house shops and apartments. The bottom of the river —bordered by the high-rise Radisson Blu Plaza Hotel and the gritty "Little Pakistan" neighborhood of Grønland (where my walk doesn't go)—has its share of drunks and drugs, reflecting a new urban reality in Oslo.

▲Grünerløkka

The Grünerløkka district, built in the latter half of the 1800s to house the legions of workers employed at factories powered by the Akers River, has reinvented itself as a one-stop neighborhood for shopping, street life, and food. Old-style buildings have found new life as restaurants, bars, and coffeehouses. Vintage shops rub elbows with indie boutiques. Grünerløkka lies just east of the Akers River, offering welcome green spaces and urban park life.

Getting There: Grünerløkka can be reached from the center of town by a short ride on tram #11, #12, or #18, or by taking the interesting walk described next.

▲Up Akers River and Down Grünerløkka Walk

Once housing poor workers, the Grünerløkka neighborhood now attracts Norwegian hipsters and foodie tourists. This hike up the Akers River, finishing in stylish Grünerløkka, shines a different and more appealing light on Oslo than the touristy central zone. Allow about an hour at a brisk pace, including a fair bit of up and down and a 20-minute detour en route.

While there are a few sights along this walk, they're all skippable—making this a fun experience on a sunny early evening, after the museums have closed, when Oslo's young people are out enjoying their riverside park. (Several excellent dining opportunities are along or near this walk.)

Begin the walk by leaving Karl Johans Gate near where it crests (alongside the Parliament building, by the T-bane stop), and head up ❶ **Akersgata**—Oslo's "Fleet Street," lined with major newspaper companies.

After two blocks, at **Apotekergata,** you'll notice stout barriers

Grünerløkka/Grønland Area

Walk
1. Akersgata
2. July 2011 Bombing Site
3. Vår Frelsers Cemetery
4. Gamle Aker Church
5. Telthusbakken Road
6. Mathallen Oslo & Vulkan Depot
7. Åmotbrua (Bridge)
8. Big Waterfall
9. Fabrikkjentene Statue & Honse-Lovisas Hus
10. Thorvald Meyers Gate
11. Olaf Ryes Plass
12. Vaterlands Bridge

Eateries & Nightlife
13. Olaf Ryes Plass Eateries
14. Tim Wendelboe Coffee
15. Südøst Asian Crossover Rest.
16. Punjab Tandoori & Asylet
17. Istanbul & Dattera Til Hagen
18. Olympen Brown Pub

OSLO

blocking car traffic, and may see some construction work to the right. Continue into the big plaza. ❷ Behind the tall, blocky building, on Grubbegata, was where a car bomb went off on July 22, 2011 (see the "In Cold Blood" sidebar, earlier). Four buildings in the area suffered structural damage—including the long, low-lying one to the left, known as Y-Block. Locals are divided on the fate of the damaged building (and its two Picasso murals that decorated the building's facade and lobby).

Also on this square, you may see (on the right as you face the tall building) a small visitors center marked *22. juli-senteret*, with

photos and information about the terror event. Along the street, notice the row of newspaper headlines under shattered glass. These were displayed in a newspaper office's window just down Akersgata, and have been preserved here—symbolizing how, for Oslo residents, time stood still on that fateful Friday morning.

Continuing straight past this somber site, you'll approach the massive brick Trefoldighets Church. Passing that, angle right onto the uphill street called **Akersveien,** along the side of the pointy-steepled St. Olav's Church. Hiking up this quiet street, you'll pass some traditional wooden houses. This is what much of "Christiania" (as Oslo was then called) looked like in the early 20th century; after World War II, most of this classic architecture was torn down in favor of modern construction.

After passing a square with a big pool, watch on the left for the entrance gate to the ❸ **Vår Frelsers (Our Savior's) Cemetery.**

Stop at the big metal map just inside the gate to chart your course through the cemetery: You'll go through the light-green Æreslunden section—with the biggest plots and VIP graves (including Munch, Ibsen, Bjørnson, and many of the painters whose works you can see in the National Gallery)—then veer right to return to Akersveien, using the exit at the far end (#13).

Once oriented, head into the cemetery and bear right into the elevated, walled area. The tall, green, canopied grave belongs to **Henrik Wergeland** (1808-1845), Norway's national poet who

OSLO

helped to create its May 17th celebrations (including the children's parade). Wergeland is beloved not only for his poetry, but as a champion of civil rights: He spent his life fighting a clause in the Norwegian constitution that denied the rights of citizenship to Jews. A few years after his death, it was removed.

Go up the path to the right of Wergeland, into the uppermost part of the cemetery. Bear left with the path, then turn left again. You'll pass the grave of painter Christian Krohg on your left, then reach the grave of the great Expressionist painter, **Edvard Munch** (1863-1944).

At Munch's 10 o'clock, walk under the drooping tree to the tall, obelisk-topped tomb of **Henrik Ibsen** (1828-1906), the great Norwegian playwright. Notice the hammer engraved in his tomb, an allusion to an Ibsen poem that spoke of a man chipping away inside a cave. This represents the determination of Ibsen the artist—who would walk the streets of Oslo, lost in thought, painstakingly crafting his next masterpiece in his mind.

Facing Ibsen's grave, turn left and walk toward the yellow house, exiting through the nearby gate. Turn left and walk 100 yards up Akersveien to the Romanesque ❹ **Gamle Aker Church** (from the 1100s)—the oldest building in Oslo. The church, which fell into ruins and has been impressively rebuilt, is rarely open and is pretty bare inside except for a pulpit and baptismal font from the 1700s.

On the little terrace just below the church, notice the **stone marker** indicating 639 kilometers to Nidaros Cathedral in Trondheim—the burial place of the great Norwegian king/saint, Olav II (995-1030). Olav was instrumental in Christianizing Norway, and his tomb in Trondheim was the focus of Norway's main medieval pilgrimage route. Walking half the length of Norway by foot offered forgiveness of sins. Like the Camino de Santiago in northern Spain, this pilgrimage route—long forgotten—is again in vogue, not only for spiritual reasons, but for anyone who simply wants a long walk with time to think. If you're up for a slightly longer walk than this one, the modern pilgrimage office is in the pink, half-timbered building across the street.

From the church, backtrack 20 yards, head left at the red hydrant, and go downhill on the steep ❺ **Telthusbakken** road toward the huge, gray former grain silos (now student housing). This delightful lane is lined with colorful old wooden houses, built here outside the city limits by people

OSLO

too poor to meet the no-wood fire-safety building codes within the city proper. Take a peek at the little neighborhood garden patches on the right (through the fence).

At the bottom of Telthusbakken, you'll reach busy **Maridalsveien** street. Cross it and head down to the right about 40 yards, then turn left down the driveway next to the modern **Vulkan shopping center.** Follow the driveway just in front of Vulkan as it curls around and behind the building to the recommended ❻ **Mathallen**—a foodie paradise, with more than a dozen stalls selling every kind of cuisine imaginable, and lots of outdoor tables filling an inviting plaza.

Find the **bridge** over the river at the near end of Mathallen (just follow the sound of the waterfall). You'll pop out into a beautiful little square. Turn left just before the playground and walk along the river (with the silo housing on your right). At the waterfall, look down on your left to see fish ladders—which allow salmon and sea trout to make their way upstream to spawn. Farther along, enjoy a little stretch of **boardwalk** that's cantilevered to stick out over the waterfall.

The lively **Grünerløkka** district is just to your right. But if you have 20 minutes and a little energy, detour upstream first, then hook back down. Continuing along the river, you'll pass a log bridge on your left, then a few rusty *lur* horns on your right, before you come to yet another **bridge**—this one loaded down with "love locks." Cross this bridge, turn right, and continue following the riverside path uphill.

Just above the next waterfall, cross ❼ **Åmotbrua** (Åmot Bridge), a big white springy suspension footbridge from 1852 (moved here in 1958). Keep hiking uphill along the river. At the base of the next ❽ **big waterfall,** cross over again to the large brick buildings, hiking up the stairs to the **Beyer Bridge** (above the falls) and ❾ *Fabrikkjentene,* a statue of four women laborers. They're pondering the textile factory where they and

700 others toiled long and hard. This gorge was once lined with the water mills that powered Oslo through its 19th-century Industrial Age boom.

Look back (on the side you just left) at the city's two biggest former textile factories. Once you could tell what color the fabric was being dyed each day by the color of the river. Just beyond them, between the two old factories, is a small light-gray building housing the **Labor Museum** (Arbeidermuseet, free; Wed-Sun

11:00-16:00, closed Mon-Tue; mid-Aug-late June Sat-Sun only; borrow English handout). Inside you'll see old photos that humanize the life of laborers there, and an 1899 photo exhibit by Edvard Munch's sister, Inger Munch.

The tiny red house just over and below the bridge—the **Honse-Lovisas Hus** cultural center—makes a good rest-stop (Tue-Sun 11:00-17:00, closed Mon, coffee and waffles). Continue past the red house to the red-brick Ringnes Brewery and follow ❿ **Thorvald Meyers Gate** downhill directly into the heart of Grünerløkka. First you'll go through a few blocks of modern, tidy apartment buildings. Then you'll pass a park (Birkelunden) with a tram stop and a gazebo. The next stretch of Thorvald Meyers Gate is lined with inviting bars and cafés with outdoor seating. And a few short blocks farther is Grünerløkka's main square, ⓫ **Olaf Ryes Plass**—a lively place to grab a meal or drink. Trams take you from here back to the center.

• *To continue exploring, you could keep going straight past Olaf Ryes Plass and continue walking until you reach a T-intersection with a busy road (Trondheimsveien). From there (passing the recommended Südøst Asian Crossover Restaurant) you can catch a tram back to the center, or drop down to the riverside path and follow it downstream to* ⓬ **Vaterlands bridge** *in the* **Grønland** *district. From here the train station is a five-minute walk down Stenersgata.*

Grønland

The T-bane's Grønland stop deposits you in the center of an old working-class neighborhood of Industrial Age Oslo (if you look down side streets, you'll see fine 19th-century facades). Today it's a bit shabby, like working-class and immigrant neighborhoods in other cities. But Grønland is emerging as a trendy place for eating out and after-dark fun. Locals know you'll get double the food and lots more beer for the kroner here. If you'd enjoy a whiff of Istanbul, make a point to wander through the underground commercial zone at the Grønland station (easy to visit even if you're not riding the T-bane).

SOUTHEAST OF DOWNTOWN
▲Ekeberg Sculpture Park (Ekebergparken)

In 2013, this piece of wilderness—on a forested hill over town, with grand city views—was transformed from a long-neglected public green space into a modern sculpture park. In 2013, real estate tycoon and art collector Christian Ringnes (grandson of Norwegian brewery tycoons) paid to turn the wooded area into a park. Ringnes wanted his creation to be an homage to women. To that end, the park is filled with modern and contemporary sculptures

OSLO

ranging from the ample nudes of Rodin, Renoir, and Botero to the evocative abstractions of Bourgeois, Turrell, and Holzer.

Getting There: The park, always open and free, is a 10-minute tram ride southeast of the center (at the train station, catch tram #18 from platform E, or #19 from platform C; take either one in the direction of Ljabru). Ride just a few stops to Ekebergparken, right at the park's entrance.

Background: This location (literally "Oak Hill") is historic: There's evidence that Stone Age people lived here 7,000 years ago; a spot in this park is said to be where Edvard Munch was inspired to paint *The Scream* (the viewpoint is marked *Utsiktspunkt Skrik* on maps), and in World War II, it held a Nazi military cemetery. Today the people of Oslo are embracing this lovely 63-acre mix of forest and contemporary art.

Visiting the Park: A visit here involves lots of climbing on trails through the trees. While some people come for the statues (at this point 35 in all, but with plans to expand to 80), others simply enjoy a walk in nature...and most agree that the views of Oslo's harbor scene (the Opera House, Munch Museum, and Barcode Project) may be the highlight. From the tram stop, hike up to the little cluster of buildings (including the visitors center, where you can pick up a map and join a 1.5-hour guided walk in English—see schedule at www.ekebergparken.com). In this area, you can see the first of the sculptures. For views and more art, keep heading up the hill to the restaurant...and beyond. Maps, suggesting various walking routes, are posted throughout the park.

Nearby: The faint **ruins of medieval Oslo** (free, always open) are between the harbor and Ekeberg Park—you can get a peek of them as you rumble past on the tram. History buffs can spend a few minutes wandering a park with a few scant foundations of the 11th-century town—back when it was 3,000 people huddled around a big stone cathedral, seat of the Norwegian bishop. The arcade of a 13th-century Dominican monastery still stands (office of today's Lutheran bishop). To get there, hop off at the Oslo Hospital tram stop; the ruins are across Ekebergveien street from the tram stop.

ESCAPES FROM THE CITY

Oslo is surrounded by a vast forest dotted with idyllic little lakes, huts, joggers, bikers, and sun-worshippers. One of the easiest escapes is simply to grab a beach towel and ride T-bane line #5 to its last stop, Sognsvann, and join the lakeside scene of Norwegians at play. A pleasant trail leads around the lake. To go farther afield, consider these options.

▲Holmenkollen Ski Jump and Ski Museum

The site of one of the world's oldest ski jumps (from 1892), Holmenkollen has hosted many championships, including the 1952 Winter Olympics. To win the privilege of hosting the 2011 World Ski Jump Championship, Oslo built a bigger jump to match modern ones built elsewhere—futuristic, cantilevered, and Olympic-standard. For skiers and winter-sports fans, a visit here is worth ▲▲.

Cost and Hours: 150-NOK ticket includes museum and viewing platform at top of jump; zipline-680 NOK, ski simulator-110 NOK; daily 9:00-20:00, May and Sept 10:00-17:00, Oct-April until 16:00; +47 22 92 32 64, www.skiforeningen.no.

Getting There: T-bane line #1 gets you out of the city, through the hills, forests, and mansions that surround Oslo, and to the jump (4/hour, 25 minutes, direction: Frognerseteren). From the Holmenkollen station, you'll hike steeply up the road 15 minutes to the ski jump. (Getting back down is more like 10 minutes. Note T-bane departure times before you leave.) For more details—including a slightly longer, but more scenic, approach—see "Near the Ski Jump," later.

Visiting Holmenkollen: You'll enter the complex directly under the ramp. First you'll tour the **ski museum,** which traces the evolution of the sport, from 4,000-year-old rock paintings to crude 1,500-year-old wooden sticks to the slick and quickly evolving skis of modern times, including a fun exhibit showing the royal family on skis. You'll see gear from Roald Amundsen's famous trek to the South Pole, including the stuffed remains of Obersten ("The Colonel"), one of his sled dogs. Exhibits show off lots and lots of historic skis, gear, and video clips of great moments in skiing. Kids love the downhill ski-breeze simulator...basically a superpowered fan that blasts you in the face with fierce wind.

Near the end of the museum exhibits, look for the sign up to the **ski jump.** The tilted elevator takes you up to the top (on a sunny day, you may have to wait your turn for the elevator). Stand right at the starting gate, just like an athlete, and get a feel for this daredevil sport. The jump empties into a 30,000-seat amphitheater. Climb the stairs up to the rooftop deck; when it's clear, you'll see one of the best possible views of Oslo. While the view is exciting from the top, even more thrilling is the **zip-line** ride that sends daredevils

OSLO

screaming (literally) down over the jump to the landing area at the very bottom in 30 heart-stopping seconds.

As you ponder the jump, consider how modern athletes continually push the boundaries of their sport. The first champion here in 1892 jumped 21 meters (nearly 69 feet). In 1930 it took a 50-meter jump to win. In 1962 it was 80 meters, and in 1980 the champ cracked 100 meters. And, most recently, a jump of 140 meters (459 feet) took first place.

To cap your Holmenkollen experience, you can step into the **simulator** (or should I say stimulator?) and fly down the ski jump and ski in a virtual downhill race. My legs were exhausted after the five-minute terror. It's located at the lower level of the complex, near the entry of the ski museum. Outside, have fun watching a candid video of those shrieking inside.

Near the Ski Jump

For an easy downhill jaunt through the Norwegian forest, with a woodsy coffee or meal break in the middle, stay on the T-bane past Holmenkollen to the end of the line at Frognerseteren. From there, follow signs five minutes downhill on the gravel path to the recommended **Frognerseteren Hovedrestaurant,** a fine traditional eatery with a sod roof, reindeer meat on the griddle, an affordable cafeteria, and a city view over more sod rooftops.

From the restaurant, head down to the little sod-roofed village and look for the *Holmenkollen 1.6* sign to the right. Follow the wide, reddish gravel path through the woods (don't be distracted by the many side-paths, which are for mountain bikers—speaking of which, keep an eye out for bicycles zipping across your path). After about 20 minutes, you'll come to a paved roller-ski course (use the gravel path alongside), then pass between the wooden Holmenkollen village church and the top of a different ski jump (Midtstubakken). Soon you'll see the glassy swoop of Holmenkollen on your right; the entrance to the jump is at the base of the ramp.

On your way back to the Holmenkollen T-bane stop, you'll pass the recommended **Holmenkollen Restaurant,** with a similar view, but without Frognerseteren's pewter-and-antlers folk theme—or pretense.

Oslofjord Island Beaches

On a hot day, the busy ferry scene at Oslo's harborfront lures locals out to the cool, green islands across the harbor where they can take a dip in the fjord, enjoy a little beach time, or simply stroll and enjoy views of the city. The larger Hovedøya offers good beaches, the ruins of a Cistercian monastery from 1147, some old cannons from the early 1800s, a marina, and a café. Little Gressholmen has good swimming, easy wandering to a pair of connected islands, and Gressholmen Kro, a rustic café dating to the 1930s.

Getting to the Islands: From Aker Brygge, catch ferry #B1, #B2, or #B3 to Hovedøya, or ferry #B4 to Gressholmen (both routes covered by city transit passes and Oslo Pass, ticket machines at dock, ferries run in summer only). For schedules and fare info, check www.ruter.no.

Beach at Bygdøy: There's also a beach at Huk on the Bygdøy peninsula; take the direct boat from pier 3 in front of City Hall or bus #30. Once there, if you head left, you'll find a clothed beach, and to the right is a nude beach.

Mountain Biking

Mountain-biking possibilities are endless (as you'll discover if you go exploring without a good map). Consider taking your bike on the T-bane (free outside of rush hour, otherwise half the normal adult fare) to the end of line #1 (Frognerseteren, 30 minutes from National Theater) to gain the most altitude possible. Then follow the gravel roads (mostly downhill but with some climbing) past several dreamy lakes to Sognsvann at the end of T-bane line #5. Farther east, from Maridalsvannet, a bike path follows the Akers River all the way back into town. Get biking details at the TI.

Amusement Parks and Wet Fun

The giant **Tusenfryd** amusement complex, just out of town, offers a world of family fun. It's sort of a combination Norwegian Disney-land/Viking Knott's Berry Farm, with more than 50 rides, plenty of entertainment, and restaurants (closed off-season, +47 64 97 66 99, www.tusenfryd.no, ride regional bus #500 from behind Oslo's train station).

Tøyenbadet, a modern indoor/outdoor pool complex with a 330-foot-long waterslide, also has a gym and sauna (northeast of downtown at Helgengate 90, +47 23 30 44 70). Oslo's free botanical gardens are nearby.

NEAR OSLO
▲Eidsvoll Manor

During the Napoleonic period, control of Norway changed from Denmark to Sweden. This ruffled the patriotic feathers of Norway's Thomas Jeffersons and Ben Franklins, and on May 17, 1814, Norway's constitution was written and signed in this stately mansion (in the town of Eidsvoll Verk, north of Oslo). While Sweden still ruled, the constitution gave Norway more autonomy. To mark the 2014 bicentennial of Norway's constitution, the manor building was restored to how it looked in 1814. A visitors center in the nearby Wergeland House uses 21st-century high-tech touches to tell the history of Norway's march to independence (the union with Sweden was dissolved in 1905). Your ticket also includes an English tour, offered daily at 12:30.

OSLO

Cost and Hours: 125 NOK; daily 10:00-17:00; Sept-April Tue-Fri 10:00-15:00, Sat-Sun 11:00-16:00; +47 63 92 22 10, www.eidsvoll1814.no.

Getting There: To get there by public transportation, take the train to the Eidsvoll Verk station (2/hour, 30 minutes). From there, ride bus #430 three stops (direction: Eidsvoll Station, 5 minutes, included with train ticket) or plan on a 20-minute walk. If you're driving from Oslo to Lillehammer and the Gudbrandsdal Valley, the manor is right on the way and worth a stop. It's a 45-minute drive from Oslo: Take road E-6 toward Trondheim, then turn right at the *Eidsvolls Bygningen* sign. Parking is free.

Drøbak

This delightful fjord town is just an hour from Oslo by bus (61 NOK, ticket covers two zones, 2/hour, bus #500 from behind the train station) or ferry from Aker Brygge (109 NOK one-way, ticket covers four zones, 2/day weekends only spring and fall, also 1/day weekdays mid-June-mid-Aug, take ferry #B21 on weekdays or #B22 on weekends, 1.25 hours, no ferry off-season, check at pier 1 or ask at Oslo TI). Consider taking the boat trip down, exploring the town, having dinner, and taking the bus back. Drøbak TI: +47 64 93 50 87, www.visitdrobak.no.

For holiday cheer year-round, stop into **Tregaarden's Julehus** Christmas shop, right off Drøbak's main square (closed Christmas-Feb, +47 64 93 41 78, http://julehus.no). Then wander out past the church and cemetery on the north side of town to a pleasant park. Looking out into the fjord, you can see the old **Oscarsborg Fortress,** where Norwegian troops fired cannons and torpedoes to sink Hitler's warship, *Blücher.* The attack bought enough time for Norway's king and parliament to escape capture and eventually set up a government-in-exile in London during the Nazi occupation of Norway (1940-1945). Nearby, a monument is dedicated to the commander of the fortress, and one of *Blücher*'s anchors rests aground (the other is at Aker Brygge in Oslo). A summer ferry shuttles visitors from the town harbor.

Eating in Drøbak: With outdoor seating, **$$$$ Restaurant Skipperstuen** is a pricey but good option for dinner overlooking the fjord and all the Oslo-bound boat traffic (Mon-Sat 12:00-22:00, Sun until 20:00; off-season closed Mon-Tue; Havnebakken 11, +47 64 93 07 03, www.skipperstuen.no).

Shopping in Oslo

Shops in Oslo are generally open 10:00-18:00 or 19:00. Many close early on Saturday and all day Sunday. Shopping centers have similar hours without the Saturday early closure. Here are a few favorite

shopping suggestions (note all of these are closed on Sunday). For locations, see the "Oslo Walk" map on page 24.

Norway Designs, just outside the National Theater, shows off the country's sleek, contemporary designs in clothing, kitchenware, glass, textiles, jewelry—and high prices (Stortingsgata 12, T-bane: Nationaltheatret, +47 23 11 45 10).

Paleet is a mall in the heart of Oslo, with 30 shops on three levels and a food court in the basement (Karl Johans Gate 37, +47 23 08 08 11).

Dale of Norway, considered Norway's biggest and best maker of traditional and contemporary sweaters, offers its complete collection at their concept store in downtown Oslo (Karl Johans Gate 45, +47 97 48 12 07).

Heimen Husfliden has a superb selection of authentic Norwegian-made sweaters, *bunads* (national costumes), yarn, traditional jewelry, and colorful Norwegian folk crafts (top quality at high prices, Rosenkrantz Gate 8, +47 23 21 42 00).

GlasMagasinet is one of Oslo's oldest and fanciest department stores (top-end, good souvenir shop, near the cathedral at Stortorvet 9, +47 22 82 23 00). In the basement of the GlasMagasinet is another branch of **Heimen Husfliden** (listed earlier, +47 22 42 10 75).

The **Oslo Sweater Shop** has competitive prices for a wide range of Norwegian-made sweaters, including Dale brand (in Radisson Blu Scandinavia Hotel at Tullinsgate 5, +47 22 11 29 22).

Byporten, the big, splashy mall adjoining the central train station, is filled with youthful and hip shops, specialty stores, and eateries (Jernbanetorget 6, +47 23 36 21 60).

The street named **Bogstadveien** is considered to have the city's trendiest boutiques and chic, high-quality shops (stretches from behind the Royal Palace to Majorstuen near Vigeland Sculpture Park).

OSLO

Oslo's Flea Market makes Saturday morning a happy day for those who brake for garage sales (at Vestkanttorvet, March-Nov only, two blocks east of Frogner Park at the corner of Professor Dahl's Gate and Neubergsgate).

Oslo Flaggfabrikk sells quality flags of all shapes and sizes, including the long, pennant-shaped *vimpel,* seen fluttering from flagpoles all over Norway (a 11.5-foot *vimpel* dresses up a boat or cabin wonderfully, near City Hall at Hieronymus Heyerdahlsgate

1, entrance on Tordenskioldsgate—on the other side of the block, +47 22 40 50 60).

Vinmonopolet stores are the only places where you can buy wine and spirits in Norway. The most convenient location is at the central train station. Another location, not far from Stortinget, is at Rosenkrantz Gate 11. The bottles used to be kept behind the counter, but now you can actually touch the merchandise. Locals say it went from being a jewelry store to a grocery store. (Light beer is sold in grocery stores, but strong beer is limited to Vinmonopolet shops.)

Sleeping in Oslo

Oslo's hotel rates are particularly susceptible to supply-and-demand fluctuation. You may find deals on weekends and during some parts of the summer, but even then, conventions or special meetings can cause hotel prices to double overnight.

Beyond standard hotels, Oslo is a good city for rooms in private homes and apartments offered through services such as Airbnb or www.bbnorway.com. When selecting a room, consider that sleeping downtown puts you close to the sights, but may come with noise (many loud nightclubs are in the center). The upscale area behind the Royal Palace (Frogner and Majorstuen neighborhoods) gives you a posh address. And for proximity to the trendy dining scene, look in the part of Grünerløkka near the river.

NEAR THE TRAIN STATION AND KARL JOHANS GATE

These accommodations are within a 15-minute walk of the station. While some streets near the station can feel a bit sketchy, these hotels are secure and comfortable. Parking in a central garage will run you about 250-300 NOK per day.

Thon Hotels

This chain of business-class hotels (found in big cities throughout Norway) offers little character, but provides maximum comfort per *krone* in big, modern, conveniently located buildings. Each hotel has a cheery staff and lobby, tight but well-designed rooms, Wi-Fi, free coffee in the lobby, and a big buffet breakfast. All are nonsmoking and have elevators and central air-conditioning.

Thon's **$$$$** City Hotels are a cut

above their **$$$** Budget Hotels and are generally more expensive. In Budget hotels, all rooms lack phones and minifridges.

Book by phone or online (central booking +47 21 49 69 00, www.thonhotels.no). For the best prices, check the price calendar on the Thon website. Of the more than a dozen Thon Hotels in Oslo, I find the following most convenient:

Thon City Hotel Rosenkrantz Oslo offers 152 comfortable and stylish rooms two blocks off Karl Johans Gate. Its eighth-floor lounge offers views of the Royal Palace park. They offer a free light supper every evening for guests—making this an even better value than it seems. If you want to splurge, this is the place to do it (Rosenkrantz Gate 1, +47 23 31 55 00, www.thonhotels.no/rosenkrantzoslo, rosenkrantzoslo@olavthon.no).

Thon City Hotel Terminus is similar but just a five-minute walk from the station; along with the Rosenkrantz, it offers a free light evening meal for guests (Steners Gate 10, +47 22 05 60 00, www.thonhotels.no/terminus, terminus@olavthon.no).

Thon City Hotel Cecil, ideally located near the Parliament building a block below Karl Johans Gate, has 110 efficient, comfortable rooms ringing a tall, light-filled, breakfast-room atrium (Stortingsgata 8, +47 23 31 48 00, www.thonhotels.no/cecil, cecil@olavthon.no).

Thon City Hotel Spectrum has 187 rooms just behind Oslo Spektrum concert arena. It's on a pedestrianized street, next door to a handy grocery store. Rooms facing the street can be noisy on weekends (Brugata 7; leave station out north entrance toward bus terminal, go across footbridge and down the stairs on the left, pass by tall glass Radisson Blu Plaza Hotel and walk to the other side of the park; +47 23 36 27 00, www.thonhotels.no/spectrum, spectrum@olavthon.no).

Thon Budget Hotel Astoria, with 180 rooms, has the least charm of my recommended Thon Hotels, but it's well-located and perfectly serviceable (2 blocks in front of station, 50 yards off Karl Johans Gate, Dronningens Gate 21, +47 24 14 55 50, www.thonhotels.no/astoria, astoria@olavthon.no).

Thon City Hotel Munch has 180 rooms in a location that's quiet but still relatively central, a few blocks from the National Gallery. Some rooms have hardwood floors, others have carpets. Because it recently transitioned from "Budget" to "City" class, its prices are a bit lower and a good value (Munchs Gate 5, +47 23 21 96 00, www.thonhotels.no/munch, munch@olavthon.no).

Thon City Hotel Oslo Panorama was a 15-story attempt at a downtown condominium building (the condos didn't work, so now it's a 118-room hotel). While higher rooms are more expensive, even those reserving a cheap room often get bumped up. If you request anything higher than the fourth floor, you'll likely

OSLO

Oslo Center Hotels

1. Thon City Hotel Rosenkrantz Oslo
2. Thon City Hotel Terminus
3. Thon City Hotel Cecil
4. Thon City Hotel Spectrum
5. Thon Budget Hotel Astoria
6. Thon City Hotel Munch
7. Thon City Hotel Oslo Panorama
8. Comfort Hotel Karl Johan

GRÜNERLØKKA

Vår Frelsers Cemetery

St. Olav's Church

#30 (B)

To E-6 & Airport

HAMMERSBORG

JACOB'S CHURCH

TØYEN

TREFOLDIGHETS CHURCH

(TUNNEL)

River

Akers

Youngs-torget

#11,12 & 17

#30 (B)

#11,12 & 17

4

Storanad

Oslo Cathedral

Stor-torvet

#11 & 17

Oslo Spektrum

Grønland

GRØNLAND

Pharmacy

Ruter Tower

Radisson

BUS TERMINAL

Johans Gate

Center

Tiger Statue

Jernbane-torget #11 & 12

TRAIN STATION (OSLO S)

#30 (B) Vestlys Plass

Library

Dronning Euphemias Gate

To Moss & Göteborg (Sweden)

Opera House

BARCODE PROJECT

Bjørvika

Munch Museum

Bispevika

REVIERKAIA CRUISE BERTH

OSLO

9 Hotell Bondeheimen

10 Perminalen Hotel

11 Citybox Oslo

12 P-Hotel

13 To Saga Hotel Oslo & Villa Maria

14 Cochs Pensjonat

15 Anker Hotel

enjoy a bigger room, perhaps with a tiny balcony and/or a kitchenette (just off Dronningens Gate at Rådhusgata 7, about 6 blocks from station, +47 23 31 08 00, www.thonhotels.no/oslopanorama, oslopanorama@olavthon.no).

More Hotels near the Train Station

$$$$ Comfort Hotel Karl Johan fills a mod building with 181 tight rooms, across from the cathedral near the train-station end of Karl Johans Gate. It feels new, with sleek, somewhat minimalist decor and a trendy lobby that tries a little too hard to be hip and funky. Light sleepers should request a quiet room (elevator, Karl Johans Gate 12, +47 23 01 03 52, www.nordicchoicehotels.com, co.karljohan@choice.no).

$$$ Hotell Bondeheimen ("Farmer's Home") is a historic hotel run by the farmers' youth league, *Bondeungdomslaget*. It once housed the children of rural farmers attending school in Oslo. Its 145 rooms have all the comforts of a modern hotel (elevator, Rosenkrantz Gate 8, +47 23 21 41 00, www.bondeheimen.com, bookingoffice@bondeheimen.com). This almost-100-year-old building is also home to the Kaffistova cafeteria (see "Eating in Oslo") and one branch of the Heimen Husfliden shop (see "Shopping in Oslo").

$$ Perminalen Hotel, designed for military personnel on leave, also rents 15 rooms to tourists. It's perfectly central, spartan, and inexpensive. Spliced invisibly into a giant office block on a quiet street, they have the same fair prices all year—making it an excellent deal when the city is busy and rates are sky-high. All of the doubles are bunk beds (some seventh-floor rooms have tiny balconies, elevator, tram #12, #13, or #19 from station to Øvre Slottsgate stop, Øvre Slottsgate 2, +47 24 00 55 00, www.perminalen.no, post.perminalen@iss.no). They also have single beds in dorms segregated by sexes (with lockers and breakfast). Its cheap mess hall is open nightly for dinner, and for lunch on weekdays.

$$ Citybox Oslo has 217 simple, basic rooms at a good price, in a nondescript urban zone a short walk from the train station. While services are minimal (self-check-in), the public areas are inviting (breakfast extra, Prinsens Gate 6, +47 21 42 04 80, www.citybox.no, oslo@citybox.no).

$$ P-Hotel rents 93 cheaply designed, well-worn but affordable rooms. It's a lesser value than the polished Thon hotels but may have rooms when others are full (or charging higher rates). You get a basic breakfast delivered each morning. Avoid late-night street noise by requesting a room high up or in the back (some sixth-floor rooms have balconies, Grensen 19, T-bane: Stortinget, +47 23 31 80 00, www.p-hotels.com, oslo@p-hotels.no).

THE WEST END

This pleasant, refined-feeling residential neighborhood is a long walk or a short tram ride from downtown, tucked between the Royal Palace and Frogner Park. The busy main drag of this area is Hegdehaugsveien, lined with tram tracks, busy shops, and restaurants and cafés. The pensions listed here are affordable but are plagued by street and tram noise—try requesting a quiet room. Saga Hotel is quieter and more upscale.

$$$$ Saga Hotel Oslo feels elegant, with a trendy lobby and gold-trim furnishings. The 47 rooms are comfortable, and the location—in a posh residential area—is appealing (Eilert Sundts Gate 39, +47 22 55 44 90, www.sagahotels.no, post.oslo@sagahotels.no).

$$ Villa Marie is four blocks behind the Royal Palace. It rents several bright and cheery rooms—some with shared bathrooms and lower rates (breakfast extra, nonsmoking, tram #19 from central station to Rosenborg stop, near Uranienborg church at Holtegata 25, +47 22 60 03 59, www.villamarie.net).

$ Cochs Pensjonat is cheap and cozy, with 90 dated, simple rooms, many with kitchenettes (cheaper rooms with shared bath, discounted breakfast at nearby cafés, elevator; T-bane: Nationaltheatret, exit to Parkveien, and 10-minute walk through park; or more-convenient tram #11 to Homansbyen or #17 or #18 to Dalsbergstien; Parkveien 25, +47 23 33 24 00, www.cochs.no, booking@cochs.no, Skram family).

HOSTELS

¢ Anker Hotel, a huge student dorm open to travelers of any age, offers 250 rooms, including 34 of Oslo's best cheap doubles. The hostel also offers bunks in dorm rooms. Though it comes with the ambience of a bomb shelter, each of its rooms is spacious, simple, clean, and has a small kitchen (sheets and towels extra, elevator, no breakfast, pay parking; tram #17, or bus #30 or #31 from central station, bus and tram stop: Hausmannsgate; or 15-minute walk from station; Storgata 55, +47 22 99 72 00, www.ankerhostel.no, hostel@anker.oslo.no).

¢ Haraldsheim Youth Hostel (IYHF), a huge, modern hostel open all year, comes with a grand view, 315 beds—most of them in four-bed rooms...and a long commute (2.5 miles out of town). They also offer private rooms (sheets extra; from Oslo's central train station catch bus #31 or tram #17 to Sinsenkrysset, or T-bane lines #4 or #5 to Sinsen, then hike 5 minutes uphill to Haraldsheimveien 4; +47 22 22 29 65, www.haraldsheim.no, oslo.haraldsheim@hihostels.no). Eurailers can train to the hostel with their rail pass (2/hour, to Grefsen and walk 10 minutes).

OSLO

SLEEPING ON A TRAIN OR BOAT

Norway's trains and ferries offer ways to travel while sleeping. The eight-hour night train between Bergen and Oslo leaves at about 23:00 in each direction (nightly except Sat). An overnight cruise is another clever way to avoid a night in a hotel and to travel while you sleep, saving a day in your itinerary (see "Oslo Connections," later).

Eating in Oslo

Dining out is expensive in Oslo. How do average Norwegians afford their high-priced restaurants? They don't eat out much. This is one city in which you might want to settle for simple takeout or international food—you'll save a lot and miss little.

Splurge for a hotel that includes breakfast, or pay for it if it's optional. At around 80 NOK, a Norwegian breakfast fit for a Viking is a good deal. Picnic for lunch or dinner. Department stores often have supermarkets on the basement level, offering plenty of picnic options beyond sandwiches. The little yogurt tubs with cereal come with collapsible spoons. Wasa crackers and meat, shrimp, or cheese spread in a tube are cheap and pack well. The central station has a Joker supermarket with long hours. Some supermarkets have takeout food that is discounted just before closing—showing up just before 20:00 or so to buy some roast chicken could be your cheapest meal in Oslo. My favorite meals in Oslo are picnic dinners harborside.

You'll save by getting takeaway food from a restaurant rather than eating inside. (The tax on takeaway food is 15 percent, while the tax on dine-in food is 25 percent.) Fast-food restaurants ask if you want to take away or not before they ring up your order on the cash register. Even McDonald's has a two-tiered price list.

Oslo is awash with little budget eateries (modern, international, fast food, pizza, department-store cafeterias, and so on). **Deli de Luca,** a cheery convenience store chain that's notorious for having a store on every key corner in Oslo (including a long block off Karl Johans Gate at Universitesgata 20), is a step up from the similarly ubiquitous 7-Elevens and Narvesens. Most are open 24/7, selling sandwiches, pastries, sushi, and to-go boxes of warm pasta or Asian noodle dishes. You can fill your belly here for about 80 NOK. Some outlets have seating on the street or upstairs. Beware: This is still a *convenience* store, so not everything is well-priced.

OSLO

Oslo's One-Time Grills

Norwegians are experts at completely avoiding costly restaurants. "One-time grills," or *engangsgrill,* are the rage for locals on a budget. For about 25 NOK, you get a disposable outdoor cooker consisting of an aluminum tray, easy-to-light charcoal, and a flimsy metal grill. All that's required is a sunny evening, a grassy park, and a group of friends. During balmy summer evenings, the air in Oslo's city parks is thick with the smell of disposable (and not terribly eco-friendly) grills. It's fun to see how prices for this kind of "dining" aren't that bad in the supermarket: Norwegian beer-28 NOK/half-liter, potato salad-30 NOK/tub, cooked shrimp-50 NOK/half kilo, "ready for grill" steak-two for 120 NOK, *grill pølse* hot dogs-75 NOK per dozen, *lomper* (Norwegian tortillas for wrapping hot dogs)-20 NOK per stack, and the actual grill itself (during dry spells, grill sales are sometimes halted).

Bars are also too expensive for the average Norwegian. Young night owls drink at home before *(forspiel)* and after *(nachspiel)* an evening on the town, with a couple of hours, generally around midnight, when they go out for a single drink in a public setting. A beer in a bar costs about $10 for a half-liter, while a six-pack goes for about twice that price in a grocery store.

KARL JOHANS GATE STRIP

Strangely, **Karl Johans Gate**—the most Norwegian of boulevards—is lined with a strip of American chain eateries and sports bars where you can get ribs, burgers, and pizza. **$$ Egon Restaurant** offers a daily 110-NOK all-you-can-eat pizza deal (available Tue-Sat 11:00-18:00, Sun-Mon all day)—though the rest of their menu is overpriced. Each place comes with great sidewalk seating and essentially the same prices.

$$$$ Grand Café is perhaps the most venerable place in town, with genteel decor described on page 28. They have a seasonal menu, with high-end Nordic, French, and international dishes. Reserve a window, and if you hit a time when there's no tour group, you're suddenly a posh Norwegian (Mon-Fri 11:00-23:00, Sat-Sun 12:00-23:00, Karl Johans Gate 31, +47 98 18 20 00, www.grandcafeoslo.no).

$$ Kaffebrenneriet is a good local coffeehouse chain serving quality coffee drinks and affordable sandwiches, salads, and pastries. Convenient locations include in the park along Karl Johans

OSLO

Norwegian Cuisine

Traditional Norwegian cuisine doesn't rank very high in terms of excitement. But the typical diet of meat, fish, and potatoes is evolving to incorporate more diverse products, and the food here is steadily improving. Fresh produce, colorful markets, and efficient supermarkets abound in Europe's most expensive corner.

In this land of farmers and fishermen, traditional recipes are built on ingredients like potatoes, salmon, or beef. A favorite tart-and-sweet condiment is lingonberry jam, which cuts through a heavy, salty meat dish. Some traditional places also serve *lefse*—a soft flatbread made from potatoes, milk, and flour.

Norway's national dish is *Fårikål,* a lamb or mutton stew with cabbage, peppercorns, and potatoes. This dish is so popular that the last Thursday in September is *Fårikål* day in Norway. There's really no need for a recipe, so every stew turns out differently—and every grandma claims hers is the best.

Because of its long, cold winters, Norway relies heavily on the harvesting and preservation of fish. Smoked salmon, called *røkt laks,* is prepared by salt-curing the fish and cold-smoking it, ensuring the temperature never rises above 85°F. This makes the texture smooth and almost raw. *Bacalao* is another favorite: salted and dried cod that is rehydrated and rinsed in water before cooking. You'll often find *bacalao* served with tomatoes and olives. Stockfish *(tørrfisk),* usually cod, is hung on wooden racks to air-dry (rather than salt-cure), creating a kind of "fish jerky" that goes well with beer. *Klippfisk* is yet another variation, which is partly air-dried on rocks along the shoreline, then further cured in salt.

Some Norwegians serve lutefisk around Christmas time, but you'll rarely see this salty, pungent dish on the menu. Instead, try the more pleasant *fiskekake,* a small white fish cake made with cream, eggs, milk, and flour. You can find these patties year-round.

For a break from seafood, try local specialties such as reindeer meatballs, or pork-and-ground beef meat cakes called *kjøttkaker.* True to Scandinavian cuisine, *kjøttkaker* are usually slathered in a heavy cream sauce.

Dessert and coffee after a meal are essential. *Bløtkake,* a popular delight on Norway's Constitution Day (May 17), is a layered cake drizzled with strawberry juice, covered in whipped cream, and decorated with fresh strawberries. The cloudberry *(multe),* which grows in the Scandinavian tundra, makes a unique jelly that tastes delicious on vanilla ice cream, or even whipped into a rich cream topping for heart-shaped waffles. Norwegians are proud of their breads and pastries, and you'll never be too far from a bakery that sells an almond-flavored *kringle* or a cone-shaped *krumkake* cookie filled with whipped cream.

Gate at #24, closer to the cathedral and train station at Karl Johans Gate 7, behind the cathedral at Storgata 2, facing the back of the Parliament building at Akersgata 16, and next to City Hall at Hieronymus Heyerdahls Gate 1. Most have similar hours (typically Mon-Fri 7:00-19:00, Sat 9:00-18:00, closed Sun).

$$ United Bakeries, next to the Paleet mall, is a quiet bit of Norwegian quality among sports bars, appreciated for its 80-NOK sandwiches, salads, light weekday lunches, and fresh pastries (seating inside and out, Mon-Fri 7:30-20:00, Sat 9:00-18:00, Sun 11:00-17:00).

$$$ Kaffistova, a block off the main drag, is where my thrifty Norwegian grandparents always took me. And it remains almost unchanged since the 1970s. This alcohol-free cafeteria still serves simple, hearty, and typically Norwegian meals (including big portions of Norwegian meatballs) for a good price (Mon-Fri 11:00-21:00, Sat-Sun until 19:00, Rosenkrantz Gate 8, +47 23 21 41 00).

$$$$ Theatercaféen, since 1900 the place for Norway's illuminati to see and be seen (note the celebrity portraits adorning the walls), is a swanky splurge steeped in Art Nouveau elegance (Mon-Sat 11:00-23:00, Sun 15:00-22:00, in Hotel Continental at Stortingsgata 24, across from National Theater, +47 22 82 40 50, www.theatercafeen.no).

NEAR AKERSHUS FORTRESS

$$$$ Café Skansen is a delightful spot for a quality meal—especially in good weather, when its leafy, beer garden-like terrace fills with a convivial, mostly local crowd. Or huddle in the old-time interior and dig into classic Norwegian dishes. They serve more affordable lunches until 16:00, and good salads anytime (Mon-Fri 11:00-23:00, Sat-Sun 12:00-22:00, Rådhusgata 32, +47 24 20 13 11, www.cafeskansen.no).

$$$$ Engebret Café is a classic old restaurant in a 17th-century building in the Christiania section of town below the fortress. Since 1857, it's been serving old-fashioned Norse food (reindeer is always on the menu) in a classic old Norwegian setting. In good weather, you can sit out on the delightful square with a gurgling fountain (Mon-Fri 11:30-23:00, Sat from 17:00, closed Sun and most of July, Bankplassen 1, +47 22 82 25 25, www.engebret-cafe.no).

$$$$ Solsiden ("Sunny Side"), filling a glassed-in former warehouse on the embankment just under the fortress, is a local favorite for a harborfront splurge. You'll dig into fish and seafood meals in an open, unpretentious, nautical-themed, blue-and-white interior that doesn't distract from the cooking. Think of this as a less posh-feeling alternative to the Aker Brygge scene across the harbor. Reserve ahead, and ask for a table with a view (May-mid-

Oslo Center Restaurants

1 Egon Restaurant &
   United Bakeries

2 Grand Café

3 Deli de Luca

4 Kaffebrenneriet (3)

5 Kaffistova

6 Theatercaféen

7 Café Skansen

8 Engebret Café

9 Solsiden

GRÜNERLØKKA

Vår Frelsers Cemetery

St. Olav's Church

HAMMERSBORG

Jacob's Church

Trefoldighets Church

(TUNNEL)

Youngstorget

Stortinget

Stor-torvet

JOHANS GATE

CENTER

Oslo Cathedral

Pharmacy

Tiger Statue

Jernbane-torget

Train Station (Oslo S)

Oslo Spektrum

Ruter Tower

Radisson

GRØNLAND

Bus Terminal

Vestlys Plass

Library

Opera House

Bjørvika

Revierkaia Cruise Berth

Barcode Project

Munch Museum

Bispevika

To Mathallen & bridge to Grünerløkka

To E-6 & Airport

TØYEN

Akers River

To Moss & Göteborg (Sweden)

OSLO

⑩ Fenaknoken Deli
⑪ Aker Brygge Eateries
⑫ Grocery (2)
⑬ Youngstorget Eateries
⑭ Illegal Burger Bar
⑮ Torggata North Eateries
⑯ Peloton
⑰ Torggata South Eateries
⑱ To Frogner Park Eateries

Sept daily 16:30-22:00, in peak times they do two dinner seat-
ings—at 20:00 and 22:30, Akershusstranda 13, +47 22 33 36 30,
www.solsiden.no).

Top-End Picnic Shopping: Near City Hall, **Fenaknoken** is a
characteristic deli specializing in gourmet Norwegian products—
from salmon and lefse to moose salami and dried fish. If you value
authentic quality products over price, this is the place to assemble
a blowout Norwegian picnic to enjoy out along the harbor (Mon-
Fri 10:00-17:00, Sat until 13:30, closed Sun, Tordenskioldsgate 12,
+47 22 42 34 57, www.fenaknoken.no).

HARBORSIDE DINING IN AKER BRYGGE

Aker Brygge, the harborfront development near City Hall, is
popular with businesspeople and tourists. While it isn't cheap, its
inviting cafés and restaurants
with outdoor tables make for
a memorable waterfront meal.
Before deciding where to eat,
walk the entire lane (including
the back side), considering both
the brick-and-mortar places
(some with second-floor view
seating) and the various floating options. Nearly all are open
for lunch and dinner.

$$$$ **Lekter'n Lounge,** right on the water, offers the best
harbor view (rather than views of strolling people). This trendy bar
has a floating dining area open only when the weather is warm.
It serves hamburgers, fish-and-chips, salads, mussels, and shrimp
buckets (all outdoors, Stranden 3, +47 21 52 32 31). If you go just
for drinks, the sofas make you feel right at home, and a DJ adds to
the ambience.

$$$$ **Rorbua** ("Fisherman's Cabin") is a lively yet cozy eatery
tucked back into this otherwise modern stretch of restaurants. The
specialty is food from Norway's north, such as whale and reindeer.
Inside, it's extremely woody with a rustic charm and candlelit picnic
tables surrounded by harpoons and old B&W photos. While the à
la carte dinners start at around 300 NOK, a hearty daily special
with coffee for 175 NOK is one of the city's best restaurant deals
(daily 12:30-23:00, Stranden 71, +47 22 83 64 84, www.rorbua.as).

$$$$ **Lofoten Fiskerestaurant** serves fish amid a dressy
yacht-club atmosphere at the end of the strip. While it's beyond
the people-watching action, it's comfortable even in cold and blus-
tery weather because of its heated atrium, which makes a meal here
practically outdoor dining. Reservations are a must, especially for

a harborside window table (daily 11:00-23:00, Stranden 75, +47 22 83 08 08, www.lofoten-fiskerestaurant.no).

Budget Tips: If you're on a budget, try a hot dog from a *pølse* stand or get a picnic from a nearby grocery store and grab a bench along the boardwalk. The **Co-op Mega** grocery store—in the middle of the mall a few steps behind all the fancy restaurants—has salads, warm takeaway dishes (sold by weight), and more (turn in about midway down the boardwalk, Mon-Sat 8:00-22:00, Sun 9:00-20:00). Farther down is a **Joker mini-grocery,** just over the bridge and to the right on Lille Stranden in Tjuvholmen (Mon-Sat 8:00-22:00, Sun from 11:00).

NEAR YOUNGSTORGET

Central Oslo's most appealing dining zone percolates just a 10-minute stroll north of Karl Johans Gate, around the otherwise nondescript urban square named Youngstorget. This aptly named square feels fresh and trendy, although it's tucked between all-business high-rises and Thon hotels. The square itself has several fine options, but the streets leading off it are also worth a browse—especially Torggata, lined with a couple dozen eclectic options more tempting than anything in the touristy downtown.

On Youngstorget

First, check out the hipster **food carts** that are often parked in the middle of the square, which can be a great spot for a quick, afford-able al fresco bite. But to settle in for a more serious meal, you have plenty of choices.

Three good options cluster at the base of the towering, red-brick head-quarters of the Arbei-derpartiet (Labor Party). **$$$$ Fiskeriet** started as a small fish counter (with stacks of dried cod) before expanding into a full-blown restaurant. It has a concise but tempting menu of simple fish-focused dishes, including fish-and-chips, and seating either in the tiled interior or out on the square (Mon-Fri 11:00-21:00, Sat from 12:00, closed Sun, Youngstorget 2b, +47 22 42 45 40, www.fiskeriet.com). Next door, **$$$$ Taverna'n** is an indus-trial-strength eatery with a big, rustic/trendy interior plus outdoor dining, a fun energy, and a menu of pastas, fish dishes, grill meals, and pizza—which they call "skorpe" (Mon-Fri 11:00-late, Sat from 12:00, Sun 13:00-22:00, Youngstorget 1, +47 40 01 74 37, https://tavernan.no). Rounding out the scene is **$$ Internasjonalen,** a bar

OSLO

with a checkerboard-tile-and-red-leather interior, a wall of lit-up liquor bottles, inviting outdoor tables on the square, and cheap sandwiches (Mon-Sat 10:00-late, Sun from 16:00, Youngstorget 2a, +47 46 82 52 40).

From any of the above, you can gaze across the square to the pinkish, crenellated former police station that was headquarters for the notorious Nazi security service during the occupation—and where traitor Vidkun Quisling surrendered to Norwegian police at war's end. Its former stables, in the arcades just below, are filled with more bars and eateries (cozy **Fyret** has a great selection of aquavit and open-face sandwiches, while **Politiker'n** has ample outdoor seating). And finally, if you were to hike up to the old police station and turn right (at the uphill corner of the square), you'd find **$$$ Illegal Burger Bar**—the best-regarded of Oslo's many trendy burger joints, with a long, creative menu of gourmet burgers (daily 14:00-late, Møllergata 23, +47 22 20 33 02).

On Torggata, North of Youngstorget

For even more options, stroll from Youngstorget up Torggata and comparison-shop menus, ignoring the American fast-food chains and keeping an eye out for these places (listed in order as you head north): A short block up Badstugata (on the left) is the high-end **$$$$ Arakataka,** serving refined New Nordic dishes in an elegant setting (650-NOK tasting *menu,* daily from 16:00, Mariboes Gate 7b, +47 23 32 83 00, www.arakataka.no). Nearby is **Tilt Bar,** a pinball-themed dive filling what used to be the old public bathhouse. On the corner of Torggata and Osterhaus Gate, at #30, **$$$ Taco República** has impressively authentic and delicious Mexican food in a tight, lively, colorful, casual setting. As servings are small, you may need several dishes to fill up (Tue-Thu 16:00-22:00, Fri 15:00-24:00, Sat from 12:00, Sun 14:00-22:00, closed Mon, +47 40 05 76 65). Just past that, at #32, **$$ Crowbar** is an industrial-mod microbrewery with an easy-to-miss self-service counter upstairs serving cheap falafel and kebabs (Sun-Fri 15:00-late, Sat from 13:00, +47 21 38 67 57). And finally, up at the corner (at #35), **$$$ Peloton** is a casual and inviting *sykkelcafe*—a bright, cheery "bicycle café" serving pizza and long list of beers, with a bike shop in the back (Mon 8:00-18:00, Tue-Fri until 24:00, Sat 10:00-24:00, Sun 12:00-23:00, +47 92 15 61 81).

On Torggata, South of Youngstorget

The stretch of Torgatta to the south, where it connects Youngstorget to Karl Johans Gate, feels less residential and more shopping-oriented. But it's also lined with a fun variety of eateries as well—most of which double as hard-partying nightspots into the wee hours. **$$$ Cafe Sør,** a few steps south of Youngstorget, has

a cool ramshackle vibe and an affordable menu of salads and sandwiches. It becomes a lively dance club after hours (Mon-Sat 10:00-late, Sun from 12:00, Torggata 11, +47 23 65 46 46). Nearby, the *Stroget* sign marks the entrance to a courtyard that's jammed with lively eateries, bars, cafés, and clubs. This courtyard is a fun place to browse for a meal or drink by day, or to find a lively nightlife scene after hours. In here, **$$$$ Habibi** has an old cafeteria vibe, a menu of Palestinian mezes, and warbling Middle Eastern music. **Angst** is an achingly hip bar with brooding, atmospheric decor and a live DJ after 23:00.

DINING NEAR FROGNER PARK

These options are handy after your visit to the Vigeland Sculpture Park within sprawling Frogner Park. For locations see the "Frogner Park" map on page 46.

$$$$ Lofotstua Restaurant feels transplanted from the far northern islands it's named for. Kjell Jenssen and his son, Jan Hugo, proudly serve up fish Lofoten-style. Evangelical about fish, they will patiently explain to you the fine differences between all the local varieties, with the help of a photo-filled chart. They serve only the freshest catch, perfectly—if simply—prepared. And if you want meat, they've got it: whale or seal (Mon-Fri 15:00-21:30, closed Sat-Sun, generally closed in July, 5-minute walk from Frogner Park's main gate, tram #12, in Majorstuen at Kirkeveien 40, +47 22 46 93 96, https://lofotstua-as.business.site). This place is packed daily in winter for their famous lutefisk.

$$$ Curry and Ketchup Indian Restaurant is filled with locals enjoying hearty, decent meals for under 200 NOK. This happening place requires no reservations and feels like an Indian market, offering a flavorful meal near Vigeland's statues (daily 14:00-23:00, a 5-minute walk from Frogner Park's main gate, tram #12, in Majorstuen at Kirkeveien 51, +47 22 69 05 22).

TRENDY DINING IN GRÜNERLØKKA

For locations, see the map on page 63.

Mathallen and Vulkan

This fast-emerging zone, on the bank of the Akers River (and covered on my Akers River and Grünerløkka Walk), has recently put Oslo on the foodie map. In the appealing Akers River valley, several old brick industrial buildings and adjoining new construction house a busy hive of culinary activity that's an easy walk or tram ride from downtown (it's a 5-minute walk from the tram stop at Olaf Ryes Plass, described later).

The anchor of this area is **Mathallen Oslo**—once a 19th-

OSLO

century factory, now spiffed up and morphed into a riverside market with a mix of produce stalls and enticing eateries all sharing food-circus-type seating in the middle (Tue-Sat 10:00-20:00, Sun 11:00-18:00, closed Mon except in July, some restaurants open longer hours, www.mathallenoslo.no).

Inside, and ringing the perimeter, you'll find a world of options: tapas, Italian, sushi, tacos and tequila, pizza, Asian street food, Paradis gourmet ice cream, and so on. Most places have high-quality meals in the 150-200-NOK range. **$$$ Galopin** is a French wine bar with tasty light meals and cheeses. **$$$ Atelier Asian Tapas** dishes up small plates and full meals. Or browse the market vendors: **Ost & Sånt** is a high-end Norwegian farm cheese counter. **Smelt Ostesmørbrød** sells fresh breads, pastries, and sandwiches. **The Cupcake & Pie Co.** serves sweet and savory pies. Upstairs, don't miss the taco shop and the sprawling **Hitchhiker** wine bar.

More places face the outside of the hall, including—overlooking the bridge—**$$$$ Lucky Bird** fried chicken and ribs (www.luckybird.no), **$$$$ Smelteverket** ("global tapas" with wonderful views over the river, https://smelteverketoslo.no), and more. Still can't decide? For me, the winner may be **$$$$ Vulkanfisk,** with indoor and outdoor seating and a tempting menu of relatively well-priced and elegantly executed fish and seafood dishes: mussels, fish-and-chips, fish soup, garlic scampi, etc. (Mon-Sat 11:00-21:00, Sun until 20:00, +47 21 39 69 58, www.vulkanfisk.no). For just a drink, consider the sun-trap outdoor patio bar in **Dansens Hus** (the national dance theater), facing Vulkanfisk from across the street.

Just uphill is the **Vulkan Depot,** a small shopping mall with a trendy food court including Sapporo Ramen Bar, an Italian grocery store, a florist, a pharmacy, a co-working space (where independent contractors can rent a desk), and a big Rema 1000 supermarket.

Olaf Ryes Plass

Grünerløkka's main square (and the streets nearby) is lined with inviting eateries and has a relaxed, bohemian-chic vibe. To get here, hop on tram #11, #12, or #18. The top edge of the square has several pubs selling beer-centric food to a beer-centric crowd. Before choosing, simply wander and survey your options: Parkteatret (a classic café), Fontés (tapas), Eldhuset (barbecue), Skaal (sophisticated small plates), the charming little Grünerhaven café

kiosk in the park itself, and perhaps the most appealing choice, **$$$ Villa Paradiso Pizzeria.** Youthful and family-friendly, it has

a rustic interior and a popular terrace overlooking the square and people scene (Olaf Ryes Plass 8, +47 22 35 40 60). Just past Villa Paradiso, a block to the west (toward the Mathallen scene described earlier), sits Oslo's most renowned coffee shop, named **Tim Wendelboe** for its celebrity-barista owner. If you're a coffee pilgrim wanting to caffeinate in style...do it here (Mon-Fri 8:30-18:00, Sat-Sun 11:00-17:00, Grüners Gate 1).

The bottom of the leafy square is more focused on nightlife. From here, it's fun to stroll south on lively Thorvald Meyers Gate back toward downtown, passing a few cheap international eateries (**Miss Gin** Vietnamese street food, **Bislett** kebab house, and **Trattoria Popolare,** with affordable pastas and sprawling outdoor seating perfectly situated to catch the sun's final rays). Eventually you'll run into the place described next.

Between Olaf Ryes Plass and Downtown: Originally a big bank, **$$$$ Südøst Asian Crossover Restaurant** now fills its vault with wine (which makes sense, given Norwegian alcohol prices). It's a fine mix of Norwegian-chic, with a woody ambience inside and a big riverside terrace outdoors with a more casual menu. Diners enjoy its setting, smart service, and creative Asian-fusion cuisine. Reservations are wise, especially on weekends. They're particularly popular on Sundays, when they offer an all-you-can-eat buffet for a relatively affordable 200 NOK (daily 11:00-24:00, at bottom of Grünerløkka, tram #11, #12, or #17 to Trondheimsveien 5, +47 23 35 30 70, https://sudost.no/hjem).

CHEAP AND SPICY IN GRØNLAND

The street called Grønland leads through this colorful immigrant neighborhood (a short walk behind the train station or T-bane: Grønland; see the map on page 63). This area is refreshingly diverse compared to the rest of the city, and whether you eat here or not, Grønland is fun to explore. You'll find plenty of street food, plus cheap and tasty *börek* (savory phyllo pastry with feta, spinach, or mushroom) sold hot and greasy to go for 25 NOK.

$$ Punjab Tandoori is friendly and serves hearty meals (lamb and chicken curry, tandoori specials). I like eating outside here with a view of the street scene (daily 11:00-23:00, Grønland 24).

$$ Istanbul Restaurant is clean and simple, with a decora-

tive interior, outdoor seating, cheap kebabs, and affordable plates of Turkish food (Mon-Fri 10:00-24:00, Sat-Sun from 11:00, Grønland 14, +47 23 40 90 22).

$$$ Asylet is more expensive and feels like it was here long before Norway ever saw a Pakistani. This big, traditional eatery—like a Norwegian beer garden—has a rustic, cozy interior and a cobbled backyard filled with picnic tables (burgers, pub food, hearty dinner salads, daily 11:00-23:30, Grønland 28, +47 22 17 09 39).

$$$ Dattera Til Hagen feels like a college party. It's a lively scene filling a courtyard with graffiti, picnic tables, and benches under strings of colored twinkle lights. Locals like it for the tapas, burgers, salads, and Norwegian microbrews on tap (daily 11:00-late, Grønland 10, +47 22 17 18 61). On weekends after 22:00, it becomes a nightclub.

$$$$ Olympen Brown Pub is a dressy dining hall that's a blast from the past. You'll eat in a spacious, woody saloon with big dark furniture, faded paintings of circa-1920 Oslo lining the walls, and huge chandeliers. It's good for solo travelers, because sharing the long dinner tables is standard practice. They serve hearty, pricey plates and offer a huge selection of beers. Traditional Norwegian cuisine is served downstairs, while upstairs on the rooftop, the food is grilled (daily 11:00-late, Grønlandsleiret 15, +47 24 10 19 99).

NEAR THE SKI JUMP, HIGH ON THE MOUNTAIN

You can combine a trip into the forested hills surrounding the city with lunch or dinner and get a chance to see the famous Holmenkollen Ski Jump up close.

Frognerseteren Hovedrestaurant, nestled high above Oslo (and 1,387 feet above sea level), is a classy, sod-roofed old restaurant. Its packed-when-it's-sunny terrace, offering a commanding view of the city, is a popular stop for its famous apple cake and coffee. The **$$ self-service café** is affordable for hearty plates of classic Norwegian dishes, with indoor and outdoor seating (Mon-Sat 11:00-22:00, Sun 11:00-21:00). The elegant view **$$$$ restaurant** is quite expensive and more formal, with reindeer specials on the menu and antler chandeliers overhead. Ideally, reserve ahead for evening dining (Mon-Fri 12:00-22:00, Sat from 13:00, Sun 13:00-21:00, +47 22 92 40 40, www.frognerseteren.no).

$$$$ Holmenkollen Restaurant, below the ski jump and a five-minute hike above the Holmenkollen T-bane stop, is a practical alternative to Frognerseteren. Woody but modern, it's

OSLO

slightly cheaper and also has a grand Oslofjord view, but without the folk charm and affordable self-service option. I'd eat here only if you need a solid meal near the ski jump and aren't heading up to Frognerseteren (Tue-Sat 12:00-21:00, Sun 13:00-19:00, closed Mon, Holmenkollveien 119, +47 22 13 92 00, www.holmenkollenrestaurant.no).

Oslo Connections

BY TRAIN, BUS, OR CAR

Train service in Norway is run by Vy, a government-run outfit. For train information, call +47 61 05 19 10 (press 9 for English; for international trains, press 3) or visit Vy.no. For general information about train travel in Scandinavia, see the "Transportation" section of the Practicalities chapter.

From Oslo by Train to Stockholm: The speedy X2000 train zips from downtown to downtown in about 5.5 hours, runs several times daily, and requires reservations. Ongoing construction on this line may interrupt service. Until X2000 service resumes, you can take a slower train with a change in Göteborg.

By Train to Bergen: Oslo and Bergen are linked by a spectacularly scenic train ride (at least 4/day, 7 hours, overnight possible daily except Sat). Many travelers take it as part of the **Norway in a Nutshell** route, which combines train, ferry, and bus travel in an unforgettably beautiful trip (see the Norway in a Nutshell chapter).

By Train to: Lillehammer (almost hourly, 2.25 hours), **Kristiansand** (5/day, 4.5 hours, overnight possible), **Stavanger** (5/day, 8 hours, overnight possible), **Copenhagen** (2/day, 8.5 hours, transfer at Göteborg, more with multiple changes).

By Bus to Stockholm: Taking the bus to Stockholm is cheaper but slower than the train (3/day, 8 hours, www.flixbus.se).

By Car to the Jotunheimen Mountains: See "Route Tips for Drivers" on page 162.

BY PLANE
Oslo Airport

Oslo Lufthavn, also called Gardermoen, is about 30 miles north of the city center and has a helpful 24-hour information center (code: OSL, +47 91 50 64 00, www.osl.no).

The fastest and cheapest way to get into the city center is by **train.** Exiting the baggage claim, turn left and head to the far end of the building. Here you'll see two options: local trains (Vy) take about 25 minutes to downtown (109 NOK, 2-3/hour, cheaper if you have an Oslo Pass, buy ticket at machines or pay a little extra to buy it at the counter); the private, competing Flytoget train is only a few minutes faster but costs nearly double (199 NOK, 4/hour, runs

roughly 5:00-24:00, www.flytoget.no; swipe your credit card at the gate and choose your destination station). Unless you are in a big hurry or enjoy paying double, I'd stick with the Vy trains. Note that for either type of train, some departures only go as far as the central train station, while others continue—for no extra charge—to the National Theater station (closer to most recommended hotels). Unfortunately, this isn't clearly indicated on the screen; to spare yourself a transfer (or save some extra walking), ask whether your train continues to the National Theater.

Flybuss airport buses stop directly outside the arrival hall and make several downtown stops, including the central train station (199 NOK one-way, 3/hour, 40 minutes, +47 67 98 04 80)—but since it costs more than the train and takes twice as long, it's hard to justify taking the bus.

Taxis take about 45 minutes to downtown and vary in price depending on the company; figure 600-900 NOK on weekdays, more on weekends or after hours. A taxi booking machine at the information center in the arrivals hall lets you comparison-shop prices and order a cab.

Sandefjord Airport Torp
Ryanair, WizzAir, and other discount airlines use this airport 70 miles south of Oslo (code: TRF, +47 33 42 70 00, www.torp. no). You can take a bus into downtown Oslo (269 NOK, www. torpekspressen.no). Buses *to* Sandefjord depart Oslo's central bus terminal (next to the train station) about three hours before all flight departures.

BY CRUISE SHIP
Oslo has three cruise ports: Akershus, right on the harbor below

Akershus Fortress; Revierkaia, around the east side of the Akershus Fortress peninsula; and Filipstad, just west of downtown. For in-depth cruising information, pick up my *Rick Steves Scandinavian & Northern European Cruise Ports* guidebook.

BY OVERNIGHT BOAT
Consider connecting Oslo and **Copenhagen** by DFDS cruise ship. The boat leaves daily from Oslo around 14:00 and arrives in Copenhagen about 9:00 the following morning (return sailing from Copenhagen follows the same schedule; about 19 hours each way). The boat leaves Oslo from the tip of the Akershus Fortress penin-

sula (take bus #60 from the train station to the Vippetangen stop and follow signs to DFDS ticket office at Akershusstranda 31).

You can also take a DFDS cruise ship overnight from Oslo to **Frederikshavn,** on Denmark's Jutland peninsula—a great option for drivers.

Book in advance—online or by phone—for the best prices (www.dfds.com; from Norway, call DFDS's Denmark office: +45 33 42 38 00, closed Sat-Sun).

NORWAY IN A NUTSHELL

A Scenic Journey to the Sognefjord

While urban Oslo and Bergen are big draws for tourists, Norway is first and foremost a place of unforgettable natural beauty. There's a certain mystique about the "land of the midnight sun," but you'll get the most scenic travel thrills per mile, minute, and dollar by going west from Oslo rather than north.

Norway's greatest claims to scenic fame are her deep, lush fjords. Three million years ago, an ice age made this land as inhabitable as the center of Greenland. As the glaciers advanced and cut their way to the sea, they gouged out long grooves—today's fjords. The entire west coast is slashed by these stunning inlets, and the Sognefjord—Norway's longest (120 miles) and deepest (1 mile)—is tops. The seductive Sognefjord has tiny but tough ferries, towering canyons, and isolated farms and villages marinated in the mist of countless waterfalls.

A series of well-organized and spectacular bus, train, and ferry connections—appropriately nicknamed "Norway in a Nutshell"—lays Norway's beautiful fjord country before you on a scenic platter. With the Nutshell, you'll delve into two offshoots of the Sognefjord, which make an upside-down "U" route: the Aurlandsfjord and the Nærøyfjord. You'll link the ferry ride to the rest of Norway with two trains and a bus: The main train is an express route that takes you through stark and icy scenery above the tree line. To link the express train to the ferry, you'll catch the Flåmsbana train one way (passing waterfalls and forests) and a bus the other way (offering fjord views and more waterfalls). At the start of the fjord, you'll go through the town of Flåm (a transit hub), then pass briefly by the workaday town of Aurland and the hamlet of Undredal (by taking the Nutshell trip segments at your own pace, you can visit the lat-

ter two fjord towns on your own). All connections are designed for tourists, explained in English, convenient, and easy.

This region enjoys mild weather for its latitude, thanks to the warm Gulf Stream. (When it rains in Bergen, it just drizzles here.) But if the weather is bad, don't fret. I've often arrived to gloomy weather, only to enjoy sporadic splashes of brilliant sunshine all day long.

The Nutshell route is hugely popular. Completion of the world's longest car tunnel (the 15-mile-long Lærdal Tunnel, between Aurland and Lærdal) in 2005 rerouted the main E-16 road between Bergen and Oslo through this idyllic fjord corner. Now summer comes with a crush of crowds, dampening some of the area's magic. Unfortunately, many tourists are overcome by Nutshell tunnel-vision, and spend so much energy scurrying between boats, trains, and buses that they forget to simply enjoy the fjords. Relax—you're on vacation.

PLANNING YOUR TIME

Even the blitz tourist needs a day for the Norway in a Nutshell trip. With more time, sleep in a town along the fjord, and customize your fjord experience to include sights outside the Nutshell.

Day 1: The Nutshell works well as a single day (one-way between Oslo and Bergen, or as a long day-trip loop from either city). If you're without a

"Norway in a Nutshell" in a Nutshell

The five essential Nutshell segments are listed below (and explained in this chapter). Be sure to confirm times online or locally, as schedules can change. Nutshell travelers originating in Bergen can do this route in reverse.

Oslo to Myrdal Train (Vy Railway): Two departures each morning—6:25 (recommended) and 8:25, 4.5-5.5 hours.

Myrdal to Flåm Train (Flåmsbana): Departures timed with Oslo train arrivals, 1 hour.

Flåm to Gudvangen Fjord Cruise: Almost hourly departures, 2 hours.

Gudvangen to Voss Bus: Departures timed with boat arrivals, 75 minutes.

Voss to Bergen Train: Hourly departures, 75 minutes.

car and want to make efficient use of your time, organize your trip so that it begins in Oslo and ends in Bergen (or vice versa).

Day 2: If you have enough time, spend the night somewhere on the Sognefjord—either along the Nutshell route itself (in Flåm or Aurland; accommodations listed later), or in another, even more appealing fjordside town (such as Balestrand or Solvorn, both described in the next chapter).

With More Time: The Sognefjord deserves more than a day. If you can spare the time, venture off the Nutshell route. You can easily connect to some non-Nutshell towns (such as Balestrand) via ferry or express boat. Drivers can improve on the Nutshell by taking a northern route: From Oslo, drive through the Gudbrandsdal Valley, go over the Jotunheimen Mountains, then along the Lustrafjord to Kaupanger; from there, you can experience the Sognefjord on a car ferry ending in Gudvangen, and drive the remainder of the Nutshell route to Bergen. (Most of these sights, and the ferry connections, are covered in the next two chapters.) For more tips, see the "Beyond the Nutshell" sidebar, later in this chapter.

Orientation to the Nutshell

The most exciting single-day trip you could make from Oslo or Bergen is this circular train/boat/bus/train jaunt through fjord country.

Local TIs (listed throughout this chapter) are well informed about your options, and sell tickets for various segments of the trip.

At TIs, train stations, and hotels, look for souvenir-worthy brochures with photos, descriptions, and exact times.

Route Overview

The basic idea is this: Take a train halfway across the mountainous spine of Norway, make your way down to the Sognefjord for a boat cruise, then climb back up out of the fjord to rejoin the main train line. Each of these steps is explained in the self-guided "Nutshell Tour" in this chapter. Transportation along the Nutshell route is carefully coordinated. If any segment of your journey is delayed, the transportation for the next segment will wait for you (because everyone on board is catching the same connection).

Doing the Nutshell one-way between Oslo and Bergen (or vice versa) is most satisfying—you'll see the whole shebang, and it's extremely efficient if you're connecting the two cities anyway. It's also possible to do most of the route in a round-trip loop from either Bergen or Oslo. Doing the round-trip from Bergen is cheaper, but it doesn't include the majestic train ride between Myrdal and Oslo. The round-trip from Oslo includes all the must-see sights but is a very long day (you'll leave Oslo at 6:25 and arrive back until around 22:30).

When to Go

The Nutshell trip is possible all year. In the summer (June-Aug), the connections are most convenient, the weather is most likely to be good...and the route is at its most crowded. Outside of this time, sights close and schedules become more challenging. Some say the Nutshell is most beautiful in winter, though schedules are severely reduced.

Nutshell Itineraries
Oslo-Bergen

You must take one of two morning departures (6:25 or 8:25) to do the entire trip from Oslo to Bergen in a day. I recommend the earlier departure to enjoy more time in Flåm (2 hours vs. 45 minutes) and generally fewer crowds. This itinerary shows typical sample times for summer travel; confirm exact times before your trip (www.vy.no for trains, https://en-tur.no for buses and ferries):

- Train from Oslo to Myrdal: 6:25-11:37
- Flåmsbana train from Myrdal to Flåm: 12:13-13:00

- Free time in Flåm: 13:00-15:00
- Boat from Flåm (Flåm kai) to Gudvangen (Gudvangen ferjekai): 15:00-17:00
- Bus from Gudvangen to Voss: 17:25-18:45
- Train from Voss to Bergen: 19:37-20:58

If you leave Oslo on the later train, you can either arrive in Bergen at the same time (with less free time in Flåm) or have more time in Flåm and Voss and arrive later (22:20).

Other Options

Here are other one-day options for doing the Nutshell in the summer. Confirm specific times before your trip.

Bergen-Oslo: Train departs Bergen-8:39, arrives Voss-9:53; bus departs Voss-10:10, arrives Gudvangen-11:20; boat departs Gudvangen-12:00, arrives Flåm-14:00; Flåmsbana train departs Flåm-16:55, arrives Myrdal-17:45; train departs Myrdal-17:53, arrives Oslo-22:35.

Day-Trip Loop from Oslo: Train departs Oslo-6:25, arrives Myrdal-11:37; Flåmsbana train departs Myrdal-12:13, arrives Flåm-13:00; boat departs Flåm-14:00, arrives Gudvangen-15:30; bus departs Gudvangen-15:40, arrives Voss-16:55; train departs Voss-17:10, arrives Oslo-22:27.

Day-Trip Loop from Bergen: Train departs Bergen-8:43, arrives Voss-9:53; bus departs Voss-10:10, arrives Gudvangen-11:20; boat departs Gudvangen-12:00, arrives Flåm-14:00; Flåmsbana train departs Flåm-14:35, arrives Myrdal-15:32; train departs Myrdal-16:47, arrives Bergen-18:56.

Buying Tickets

The easiest way to purchase Nutshell tickets is to buy a package from Fjord Tours—it will save you time and the trouble of planning your itinerary. The downside is that you're locked into their schedule and the package price can be more expensive than buying individual tickets.

On your own, you can often find discounts for the train and can choose the cheapest ferry—possibly saving up to 500 NOK. You also have more flexibility—you choose how much time you spend in Flåm and what time you arrive in Bergen or Oslo. The trade-off is that you have to plan your own itinerary and buy tickets for each leg of your journey—that's five separate tickets for a one-way trip between Oslo and Bergen.

If you have a rail pass, or if you're a student or a senior (68 or older), you'll save money by booking the Nutshell on your own.

Whether you are doing a package deal or buying tickets on your own, in summer book well in advance—four to five weeks is best. Train tickets on the Nutshell route from or back to Oslo can

Nutshell Route & Beyond

(Map showing the Nutshell route with locations including: To Skjolden, Urnes, URNES STAVE CHURCH, To Fjærland, To Lom, Solvorn, Dragsvik, Hella, Fjærlandsfjord, Sogndal, Bale-strand, Kaupanger, Årdalsfjord, Mannheller, Vangsnes, Fodnes, Sognefjord, To Bergen, Sognefjord, Vik, Erdal, Lærdal, "SNOW ROAD", To Oslo (by car), E-16, HOPPERSTAD STAVE CHURCH, Nærøyfjord, STEGASTEIN VIEWPOINT, BORGUND STAVE CHURCH, TUNNEL, 10 Kilometers, 10 Miles, Undredal, Aurland, BOAT, Aurlandsfjord, Gudvangen, OTTERNES FARM, Flåm, 50, Tvinde-fossen Waterfall, Vinje, STALHEIM (Hotel & View), TUNNELS, E-16, Kjosfossen Waterfall, To Geilo, FLÅMSBANA TRAIN, BUS, E-16, TRAIN, OSLO-BERGEN SCENIC TRAIN, TRAIN, Voss, Vossevangen, To Bergen, Hardangervidda (Plateau), To Granvin & Hardangerfjord, Myrdal, To Oslo (by train))

sell out in high season (June-Aug), as can some departures on the ferry from Flåm.

Package Deals

Fjord Tours sells the Nutshell package at train stations—including stations in Oslo and Bergen, at TIs in those two cities, and at Fjord Tours offices throughout Norway (+47 55 55 76 60, www.fjordtours.com, booking@fjordtours.com). With these packages, all your departures are fixed. You can choose between two different types of ferries: Classic, about a 2-hour ride on an old car ferry that just carries foot passengers; or Premium, 1.5 hours on a hybrid catamaran. Unless you are in a hurry (but why hurry through the fjords?), take the Classic ferry.

Here are prices (as of press time) for Nutshell packages on the Classic ferry:

- One-way from Bergen or Oslo-2,040 NOK
- Round-trip from Oslo via Voss-2,890 NOK
- Round-trip from Bergen via Myrdal-1,510 NOK

- Round-trip from Flåm-1,510 NOK

Packages on the Premium ferry cost 250-500 NOK extra. Fjord Tours also sells a Nutshell round-trip from Oslo that includes a night train, a "Sognefjord in a Nutshell" tour, and a "Sognefjord and Nærøyfjord in a Nutshell" tour.

On Your Own

Specifics on buying tickets for each leg of the Nutshell route are explained later, under the individual listings. In general, you can buy train tickets (including the Flåmsbana) at train stations in Oslo or Bergen or online at Vy.no. For the best deal, look for nonrefundable "minipris" tickets. You can buy Flåm-Gudvangen ferry tickets with one of two companies: The Fjords (more sailings, www.visitflam.com) or Lustrabaatane (cheaper prices, www.lustrabaatane.no). You can't buy tickets in advance for the Gudvangen-Voss bus; there's always room but you must pay the driver in cash. If you're a student or senior, always ask about discounts.

Rail Pass Discounts: If you have any rail pass that includes Norway, the Oslo-Bergen train is covered (plus a 59-NOK reservation fee for second class; free for first-class passholders); you also get a 30 percent discount on the Flåmsbana train. Rail-pass holders pay full fare for the boat cruise and the Gudvangen-Voss bus. Your total one-way cost between Oslo and Bergen: about 650 NOK with a first-class pass, 700 NOK with a second-class pass.

Travel Tips

Luggage: Transporting luggage on the Nutshell is no big deal, as the connections require almost no walking: At Myrdal, you just cross the platform; in Flåm, you walk 50 yards from the train to the dock; in Gudvangen, the bus meets the ferry at the dock; in Voss, the bus drops you at the train station. If you want to check your bag during your free time in Flåm, use the baggage-check cabin at the head of the train track, across the lane from the boat dock.

An alternative to carrying your luggage is **Porterservice AS.** They pick up your luggage at your hotel, transport it via train between Oslo and Bergen, and drop it off at your next hotel by 21:00 (300 NOK/piece, mobile +47 90 61 00 09, www.porterservice.no).

Eating: Options along the route aren't great—on the Nutshell I'd consider food just as a source of nutrition and forget about fine dining. You can buy some food on the fjord cruises (hot dogs, burgers, and pizza) and the Oslo-Bergen train. Depending on the timing of your layovers, Myrdal, Voss, or Flåm are your best lunch-stop options (the Myrdal and Flåm train stations have decent cafeterias, and other eateries surround the Flåm and Voss stations)—although you won't have a lot of time there if you're making the journey all in one day. Your best bet is to pack picnic meals and munch en route.

Beyond the Nutshell

The Sognefjord is the ultimate natural thrill Norway has to offer, and there's no doubt that the Nutshell route outlined in this chapter is the most efficient way to see it quickly. Unfortunately, its trains, buses, and boats are thronged with other visitors who have the same idea.

Travelers with a bit more time, and the willingness to chart their own course, often have a more rewarding Sognefjord experience. It's surprisingly easy to break out of the Nutshell and hit the northern part of the Sognefjord (for example, using the Bergen-Vik-Balestrand-Aurland-Flåm express boat, described on page 137.

In the next chapter, you'll find some tempting stopovers on the north bank of the Sognefjord, including adorable fjordside villages (such as Balestrand and Solvorn), evocative stave churches (Hopperstad and Urnes), and a chance to get up close to a glacier (at the Nigard Glacier).

Read up on your options, then be adventurous about mixing and matching the fjordside attractions that appeal to you most. Ideally, use the Nutshell as a springboard for diving into the Back Door fjords of your travel dreams.

If catching an early train in Oslo, the station has a handy grocery store open at 5:00 (6:00 on Sun).

Cruise-Ship Passengers: Tiny Flåm—in the heart of Nutshell country—is a popular destination for huge cruise ships. If arriving in Flåm by cruise ship, see my *Scandinavian & Northern European Cruise Ports* book for tips on how to approach the Nutshell during your day in port.

Nutshell Tour

If you only have one day for this region, it'll be a thrilling one—worth ▲▲▲. The following self-guided segments of the Nutshell route are narrated from Oslo to Bergen. If you're going the other way, hold the book upside down.

▲▲Oslo-Bergen Train (Via Myrdal)
The Oslo-Bergen route—called "Bergensbanen" by Norwegians—is simply the most spectacular train ride in northern Europe. The entire railway, an amazing engineering feat completed in 1909, is 300 miles long; peaks at 4,266 feet, which, at this Alaskan latitude, is far above the tree line; goes under 18 miles of snow sheds; trundles over 300 bridges; and passes through 200 tunnels in just under seven hours. To celebrate the Bergensbanen centennial in 2009, Norwegian TV mounted cameras on the outside of the train

and broadcast the entire trip—and more than a million Norwegians tuned in (search for "Bergensbanen" on YouTube and you can watch it too).

Cost and Reservations: Here are the one-way fares for various segments: Oslo-Bergen-890 NOK, Oslo-Myrdal-860 NOK, Myrdal-Voss-146 NOK, Myrdal-Bergen-309 NOK, Voss-Bergen-223 NOK. You can save money on these fares if you book "minipris" tickets in advance at Vy.no. (See "On Your Own," earlier, for rail pass discounts.) If you have difficulty paying for your ticket with a US credit card online, use PayPal or call +47 61 05 19 10—press 9 for English, and you'll be given a web link where you can finish your transaction. In peak season, reserve this train four to five weeks in advance.

Schedule: The train runs three to five times per day, including two morning departures (overnight possible except Sat). The segment from Oslo to Myrdal takes about five hours; going all the way to Bergen takes seven hours.

Route Narration: The scenery crescendos as you climb over Norway's mountainous spine. After a mild three hours of deep woods and lakes, you're into the barren, windswept heaths and glaciers. Here's what you'll see traveling westward from Oslo: Leaving Oslo, you pass through a six-mile-long tunnel and stop in Drammen, Norway's fifth-largest town. The scenery stays low-key and woodsy up Hallingdal Valley until you reach Geilo, a popular ski resort. Then you enter a land of big views and tough little cabins. Finse, at about 4,000 feet, is the highest stop on the line. At several towns, the conductor may announce how many minutes the train will be stopped there. This gives you a few fun moments to get out, stretch, take a photograph, and look around.

Before Myrdal, you enter the longest high-mountain stretch of railway in Europe. Much of the line is protected by snow tunnels. The scenery gets more dramatic as you approach Myrdal (MEER-doll). Just before Myrdal, look to the right and down into the Flåm Valley, where the Flåmsbana branch line winds its way down to the fjord. Nutshell travelers get off at Myrdal.

▲▲Myrdal-Flåm Train (Flåmsbana)

The little 12-mile spur line leaves the Oslo-Bergen line at Myrdal (2,800 feet), which is nothing but a scenic high-altitude train junction with a decent cafeteria. Before boarding, pick up the free, multilingual souvenir pamphlet with lots of info on the trip (or

see www.visitflam.com/flamsbana). Video screens onboard and sporadic English commentary on the loudspeakers explain points of interest, but there's not much to say— it's all about the scenery. If you're choosing seats, you'll enjoy slightly more scenery if you sit on the left going down.

Cost and Reservations: 430 NOK one-way (rail-pass holders pay 301 NOK), 630 NOK round-trip. You can book one-way tickets on Vy.no; the cheapest round-trip tickets are on VisitFlam.com. You also can buy tickets onboard the train or at the Flåmsbana station in Flåm. Train staff in Oslo may tell you that the Flåmsbana is booked—don't worry, it very rarely fills. Even if it's standing-room only, you can usually squeeze in. Simply get to Myrdal and hop on the train.

However, morning trains ascending from Flåm to Myrdal (when there are several cruise ships in port) can sell out. In summer, if you want to leave Flåm in the morning, try buying your ticket the night before or right when the Flåm ticket office opens (around 7:00). The best plan is to buy your Flåmsbana ticket at the same time you buy your other train tickets.

Schedule: The train departs in each direction nearly hourly.

Route Narration: From Myrdal, the Flåmsbana train winds down to Flåm (sea level) through 20 tunnels (more than three miles' worth) in 55 thrilling minutes.

It's party time on board, and the engineer even stops the train for photos at the best waterfall, Kjosfossen. According to a Norwegian legend, Huldra (a temptress) lives behind these falls and tries to lure men to the rocks with her singing...look out for her...and keep a wary eye on your partner.

The train line is an even more impressive feat of engineering when you realize it's not a cogwheel train—it's held to the tracks only by steel wheels, though it does have five braking systems.

▲▲▲Flåm-Gudvangen Fjord Cruise

The Flåmsbana train deposits you at Flåm, a scenic, functional

transit hub at the far end of the Aurlandsfjord. If you're doing the Nutshell route nonstop, follow the crowds and hop on the sightseeing boat that'll take you to Gudvangen. With minimal English narration, the boat takes you close to the goats, sheep, waterfalls, and awesome cliffs.

Cruise Options: There are two boat companies to choose from—The Fjords (www.visitflam.com) and Lustrabaatane (www.lustrabaatane.com). The Fjords has a Classic option that takes more than two hours. It stops at Aurland, Undredal, Dyrdal, and Styvi, which is handy if you want to hop off and on along the way—though you'll need to buy separate tickets for each leg of your trip, and it'll end up costing you more (be sure to notify the ticket seller where you want to get off, to make certain they'll stop). The other option is their Premium ferry, a hybrid catamaran that's faster, silent, and more expensive. It takes about 1.5 hours nonstop between Flåm and Gudvangen.

The cheapest option is the Lustrabaatane ferry—a slow boat that takes about two hours—similar to the Classic ferry, but with no stops.

I much prefer the slower boats because the price is lower, you have more time to savor the scenery, and the bus connection in Gudvangen is immediate and reliable.

Cost and Reservations: For the Flåm-Gudvangen route, you'll pay 250-645 NOK one-way depending on the ferry (435-705 NOK round-trip). Reservations may be necessary on busy days in summer. Buy your ticket in Flåm as soon as you know which boat you want or in advance at each boat company's website. Beware: The ticket desk at the Flåm Visitors Center doubles as The Fjords boat desk, and they'll sell you a boat ticket implying theirs is the only option. Lustrabaatane tickets are sold online, at the dock in summer, and onboard.

Schedule: In summer (June-Aug), boats run multiple times daily in both directions—Classic ferry (2/day), Premium ferry (5/day), Lustrabaatane ferry (2/day). Specific departure times can vary, but generally boats leave Flåm starting at 8:00, with a last departure at 19:00. From Gudvangen, the first

The Facts on Fjords

The process that created the majestic Sognefjord began during an ice age about three million years ago. A glacier up to 6,500 feet thick slid downhill at an inch an hour, following a former river valley on its way to the sea. Rocks embedded in the glacier gouged out a steep, U-shaped valley, displacing enough rock material to form a mountain 13 miles high. When the climate warmed up, the ice age came to an end. The melting glaciers retreated and the sea level rose nearly 300 feet, flooding the valley now known as the Sognefjord. The fjord is more than a mile deep, flanked by 3,000-foot mountains—for a total relief of 9,300 feet. Waterfalls spill down the cliffs, fed by melting snow. In places, powdery sediment tinges the fjords a cloudy green, the distinct color of glacier melt.

Why are there fjords on the west coast of Norway, but not, say, on the east coast of Sweden? The creation of a fjord requires a setting of coastal mountains, a good source of moisture, and a climate cold enough for glaciers to form and advance. Due to the earth's rotation, the prevailing winds in higher latitudes blow from west to east, so chances of glaciation are ideal where there is an ocean to the west of land with coastal mountains. When the winds blow eastward over the water, they pick up a lot of moisture, then bump up against the coastal mountain range, and dump their moisture in the form of snow—which feeds the glaciers that carve valleys down to the sea.

You can find fjords along the northwest coast of Europe—including western Norway and Sweden, Denmark's Faroe Islands, Scotland's Shetland Islands, Iceland, and Greenland; the northwest coast of North America (from Puget Sound in Washington state north to Alaska); the southwest coast of South America (Chile); the west coast of New Zealand's South Island; and on the continent of Antarctica.

boat is generally at 9:30, with a last departure at 17:45. See http://en-tur.no for schedules covering both ferry lines.

Your only concern is that the Nutshell bus from Gudvangen to Voss may not meet the last departure of the day (check locally); the worst-case scenario is that you'd need to catch the regular commuter bus to Voss, which makes more stops and doesn't take the razzle-dazzle Stalheimskleiva corkscrew road.

Route Narration: You'll cruise up the lovely **Aurlandsfjord,**

motoring by the town of **Aurland** (a good home base, but only a few boats stop here), pass the towns of **Undredal, Dyrdal,** and **Styvi** (possible stops here on limited sailings by request), and hang a left at the stunning **Nærøyfjord.** The cruise ends at the apex of the Nærøyfjord, in **Gudvangen.**

The trip is breathtaking in any weather. For the last hour, as you sail down the Nærøyfjord, camera-clicking tourists scurry around struggling to get a photo that will catch the magic. Waterfalls turn the black cliffs into bridal veils, and you can nearly reach out and touch the cliffs of the Nærøyfjord. It's the world's narrowest fjord: six miles long and as little as 820 feet wide and 40 feet deep. On a sunny day, the ride is one of those fine times—like when you're high on the tip of an Alp—when a warm camaraderie spontaneously combusts between the strangers who've come together for the experience.

▲Gudvangen-Voss Bus

Nutshellers get off the boat at Gudvangen and take the 25-mile bus ride to Voss. Gudvangen offers little more than a boat dock, a giant tourist kiosk, and a re-cre-ation of a Viking village. If you want, you can browse through the grass-roofed souvenir stores and walk onto a wooden foot-bridge—then catch your bus. While some buses—designed for commuters rather than sight-seers—take the direct route to Voss, buses tied to the Nutshell

schedule take a super-scenic detour via Stalheim. If you're a water-fall junkie, sit on the left.

Cost: 115 NOK, pay on board, cash only, no rail pass discounts. Reservations are not necessary.

Schedule: Buses meet each ferry, or will show up usually within an hour. (Confirm this in advance if you plan to take the last boat of the day—the ferry crew can call ahead to be sure the bus waits for you.)

Route Narration: First the bus takes you up the **Nærøydal** and through a couple of long tunnels. Then you'll take a turnoff to drive past the landmark **Stalheim Hotel** for the first of many spectacular views back into fjord country. Though the hotel dates from 1885, there's been an inn here since about 1700, where royal mailmen would change horses. The hotel is geared for tour groups (genuine trolls sew the pewter buttons on the sweaters), but the priceless view from the backyard is free. Drivers should be sure to

stop here for the view and peruse the hotel's living room to survey the art showing this perch in the 19th century.

Leaving the hotel, the bus wends its way down a road called **Stalheimskleiva,** with a corkscrew series of switchbacks flanked by a pair of dramatic waterfalls. With its 18 percent grade, it's the steepest road in Norway.

After winding your way down into the valley, you're back on the same highway. The bus goes through those same tunnels again, then continues straight on the main road through pastoral countryside to Voss. You'll pass a huge lake, then follow a crystal-clear, surging river. Just before Voss, look to the right for the wide **Tvindefossen waterfall,** tumbling down its terraced cliff. Drivers will find the grassy meadow and flat rocks at its base ideal for letting the mist fog their glasses and enjoying a drink or snack (be discreet, as "picnics are forbidden").

Voss

The Nutshell bus from Gudvangen drops you at the Voss train station, which is on the Oslo-Bergen train line. This connection is generally not as well-coordinated; you'll likely have 50 minutes or so to kill before the next train to Bergen.

Visiting Voss: A plain town in a lovely lake-and-mountain setting, Voss lacks the striking fjordside scenery of Flåm, Aurland, or Undredal, and is basically a home base for summer or winter sports (Norway's Winter Olympics teams often practice here). Voss surrounds its fine, 13th-century church with workaday streets—busy with both local shops and souvenir stores—stretching in several directions. Fans of American football may want to see the humble monument to player and coach Knute Rockne, who was born in Voss in 1888; look for the metal memorial plaque on a rock near the train station.

Voss' helpful **TI** is on the ground floor of the Gondola building, next to the train station (daily 9:00-18:00, Sat until 20:00; off-season until 16:00 and closed Sat-Sun; Skulegata 14, mobile +47 40 61 77 00, www.visitvoss.no).

Drivers should zip right through Voss, but two miles outside town, you can stop at the **Mølstertunet Folk Museum,** which has 16 buildings showing off farm life in the 17th and 18th centuries (90 NOK; daily 11:00-16:00, Sept-mid-May until 15:00 and closed Sat; Mølstervegen 143, +47 47 47 97 94, www.vossfolkemuseum. no).

▲Voss-Bergen Train

The least exciting segment of the trip—but still pleasantly scenic—this train chugs 60 miles along the valley between the midsize town of Voss and Bergen. For the best scenery, sit on the right side

of the train if coming from Oslo, or the left side if coming from Bergen. Between Voss and Dale, you'll pass several scenic lakes; near Bergen, you'll go along the Veafjord.

Cost: 223 NOK, fully covered by rail passes that include Norway. Reservations aren't necessary for this leg.

Schedule: Unlike the long-distance Oslo-Bergen journey, this line is also served by more frequent commuter trains (about hourly, 75 minutes).

Voss-Oslo Train: Note that if you're doing the Nutshell round-trip loop from Oslo, you should catch the train from Voss (rather than Bergen) back to Oslo. The return trip takes 5.5 hours and costs 953 NOK; reservations are strongly recommended four to five weeks ahead in peak season.

Flåm

Flåm (pronounced "flome")—where the boat and Flåmsbana train meet, at the head of the Aurlandsfjord—feels more like a transit junction than a village. But its striking setting, easy transportation connections, and touristy bustle make it appealing as a home base for exploring the nearby area.

Orientation to Flåm

Most of Flåm's services are in a modern cluster of buildings in and around the train station, including the TI, train ticket desk, public WC, cafeteria, and souvenir shops. Just outside the station, the little red shed at the head of the tracks serves as a **left-luggage desk** (daily 8:00-19:00, on your right as you depart the train, ring bell if nobody's there), and displays a chart of the services you'll find in the station. The **boat dock** for fjord cruises is just beyond the end of the tracks. Surrounding the station are a Co-op Marked **grocery store** (with a basic pharmacy and post office inside, Mon-Fri 8:00-20:00, Sat-Sun 10:00-18:00, shorter hours off-season) and a smattering of hotels, travel agencies, and touristy restaurants. Aside from a few scattered farmhouses and some homes lining the road, there's not much of a town here. (The extremely sleepy old town center—where tourists rarely venture,

Flåm

❶ Heimly Pensjonat
❷ Flåm Marina & Apartments; Boat Rental
❸ Flåm Youth Hostel & Camping Bungalows
❹ Flåmsbrygga Eateries
❺ Ægir Bryggeri Brewpub
❻ Toget Café
❼ Bakkastova Kafe
❽ Grocery/Post Office
❾ Bike Rental

and which you'll pass on the Flåmsbana train—is a few miles up the river, in the valley.)

Tourist Information: Inside the train station you'll find the TI and the Flåm Visitors Center. The **visitors center** sells tickets for Fjord Tours packages and ferries to Gudvangen (but not the Flåm-Gudvangen boats offered by rival Lustrabaatane), the Flåmsbana train, regular train tickets, and other tours in the area (daily 7:00-19:00, shorter hours Sept-April, +47 57 63 14 00, www. visitflam.com).

At the **TI** you can purchase tickets for the express boat to Bergen, FjordSafari, Njord Seakayak Adventures, and other tours. The TI also hands out schedules for buses, boats, and trains; a diagram of the train-station area, identifying services available in each building; and information on Bergen or Oslo (daily 8:30-17:00, Oct-March 9:00-15:00, mobile +47 99 23 15 00, https:// en.sognefjord.no).

Sights and Activities in and near Flåm

I've listed several activities in the village of Flåm. But the main reason people come here is to leave it. Because Aurland and Flåm are close together (10 minutes away by car or bus, or 20 minutes by boat), I've also listed attractions near Aurland.

IN THE VILLAGE

Flåm's village activities are all along or near the pier.

The **Flåm Railway Museum** (Flåmsbana Museet), sprawling through the long old train station building alongside the tracks, has surprisingly good exhibits about the history of the train that connects Flåm to the main line up above. You'll find good English explanations, artifacts, re-creations of historic interiors (such as a humble schoolhouse), and an old train car. It's the only real museum in town and a good place to kill time while waiting for your boat or train (free, daily 9:00-17:00, until 20:00 in summer).

The pleasantly woody **Ægir Bryggeri,** a microbrewery designed to resemble an old Viking longhouse, offers beer tastings and evening meals with a matching beer menu.

The TI hands out a map suggesting several **walks and hikes** in the area, starting from right in town.

Consider renting a **boat** to go out on the peaceful waters of the fjord. You can paddle near the walls of the fjord and really get a sense of the immensity of these mountains. You can rent rowboats, motorboats, and paddleboats at the little marina across the harbor. If you'd rather have a kayak, **Njord Seakayak Adventures** does kayak tours, but won't rent you one unless you're certified (mobile +47 91 32 66 28, www.seakayaknorway.com).

FROM OR NEAR FLÅM
▲▲▲Cruising the Nærøyfjord

The most scenic fjord I've seen anywhere in Norway is about an hour from Flåm (basically the last half of the Flåm-Gudvangen trip). If you've driven to Flåm, didn't book a Nutshell tour, or are staying overnight, here are several ways to cruise it.

The Fjords Tours: This company runs several trips from Flåm; their most popular is a ferry ride to Gudvangen and a bus ride back to Flåm (435-705 NOK, 4-hour round-trip, 4/day May-Sept, fewer off-season, choose slower Classic ferry for best viewing).

In summer, they may also offer their World Heritage Cruise, a hop-on, hop-off trip up the Nærøyfjord, stopping at Bleiklindi, Bakka, Styvi, and Dyrdal—it's possible to hike about four miles between Bleiklindi and Styvi with this option. Or, consider a variation on this trip with a 45-minute stop in the village of Un-dredal for lunch and a goat-cheese tasting; a bus ride up to the thrilling Stegastein viewpoint; and more. These trips don't always run—check at the Flåm Visitors Center or online for details (www. visitflam.com).

FjordSafari to Nærøyfjord: FjordSafari takes little groups out onto the fjord in small, open Zodiac-type boats with an English-speaking guide. Participants wear full-body weather suits, furry hats, and spacey goggles (making everyone on the boat look like crash-test dummies). As the boat rockets across the water, you'll be thankful for the gear, no matter what the weather. Their two-hour Flåm-Gudvangen-Flåm tour focuses on the Nærøyfjord, and gets you all the fjord magnificence you can imagine (890 NOK, several departures daily). Their three-hour tour is the same but adds a stop in Undredal, where you can see goat cheese being made, sample it, and wander that sleepy village (1020 NOK, 1/day May-Aug, fewer off-season, kids get discounts, mobile +47 99 09 08 60, www. fjordsafari.com, Maylene). Skip the 1.5-hour "basic" tour, which just barely touches on the Nærøyfjord.

▲Flåm Valley Bike Ride or Hike

For the best single-day land activity from Flåm, take the Flåms-bana train to Myrdal, then hike or mountain-bike along the road (half gravel, half paved) back down to Flåm (2-3 hours by bike, gorgeous wa-terfalls, great mountain scenery, and a cute church with an evocative grave-yard, but no fjord views).

Walkers can hike the best two hours from Myrdal to Blomheller, and catch the train from there into the valley. Or, without riding the train, you can simply walk up the valley 2.5 miles to the church and a little farther to a waterfall. Whenever you get tired hiking up or down the valley, you can hop on the next train. Pick up the help-ful map with this and other hiking options (ranging from easy to strenuous) at the Flåm TI.

Bikers can rent good mountain bikes from the Flåm Bike Rental cabin next to the train station (around 180 NOK/2-hour minimum, 400 NOK/day, includes helmet; daily May-June 9:00-

18:00, July-Sept 8:00-20:00, closed off-season). You'll pay 100 NOK to take a bike to Myrdal on the train.

Otternes Farms (Otternes Bygdetun)

This humble but magical cluster of four centuries-old farms is about three miles from Flåm (easy for drivers; a decent walk or bike ride otherwise). It's a ghost vil-lage perched high on a ridge, up a twisty gravel road midway between Flåm and Aurland. These traditional time-warp houses and barns date from the time before emigration decimated the workforce, coinage replaced barter, and industrialized margarine became more popular than butter—all of which left farmers to eke out a living relying only on their goats and the cheese they produced. Until 1919 the only road between Aurland and Flåm passed between this huddle of 27 buildings, high above the fjord. First settled in 1522, farmers lived here until the 1990s.

OVER (OR UNDER) THE MOUNTAINS, TO LÆRDAL AND BORGUND

To reach these sights, you'll first head along the fjord to Aurland (described later). Of the sights below, the Lærdal Tunnel, Stegastein viewpoint, and Aurlandsvegen "Snow Road" are best for drivers. The Borgund Stave Church can be reached by car, or by bus from Flåm or Aurland.

Lærdal Tunnel

Drivers find that this tunnel makes connecting Flåm and Lærdal a snap. It's the world's longest road-vehicle tunnel, stretching 15 miles between Aurland and Lærdal as part of the E-16 highway. It also makes the wonderful Borgund Stave Church (described later) less than an hour's drive from Aurland. The downside to the tunnel is that it goes beneath my favorite scenic drive in Norway (the Aurlandsvegen "Snow Road," described next). But with about two hours, you can drive through the tunnel to Lærdal and then return via the "Snow Road," with the Stegastein viewpoint as a finale, before dropping back into Aurland.

▲▲Stegastein Viewpoint and Aurlandsvegen "Snow Road"

With a car, clear weather, and a little nerve, consider twisting up the mountain behind Aurland on route 243 for about 20 minutes to a

magnificent view over the Aurlandsfjord. A viewpoint called Stegastein—which looks like a giant, wooden, sideways number 7—provides a platform from which you can enjoy stunning views across the fjord and straight down to Aurland. Immediately be-yond the viewpoint, you leave the fjord views and enter the beautifully desolate mountaintop world of the Aurlandsvegen "Snow Road." When this narrow ribbon of a road finally hits civilization on the other side, you're a mile from the Lærdal tunnel entrance and about 30 minutes from the fine Borgund Stave Church.

▲▲Borgund Stave Church

About 16 miles east of Lærdal, in the village of Borgund, is Norway's most-visited and one of its best-preserved stave churches.

Dating from around 1180, the interior features only a few later additions, including a 16th-century pulpit, 17th-century stone altar, painted decorations, and crossbeam reinforcements.

Cost and Hours: 100 NOK, buy tickets at mu-seum across street; open daily June-Aug 8:00-20:00, May and Sept 10:00-17:00, closed Oct-April. The museum has a shop and a fine little **$$ cafeteria** serving filling and tasty lunches, +47 57 66 81 09, www.stavechurch.com.

Getting There: It's about a 30-minute **drive** east of Lærdal, on E-16 (the road to Oslo—if coming from Aurland or Flåm, consider taking the scenic route via the Stegastein viewpoint, described earlier). There's also a convenient **bus** connection: The bus departs Flåm and Aurland around midday (direction: Lillehammer) and heads for the church, with a return bus departing Borgund in mid-afternoon (around 200-NOK round-trip, get ticket from driver, about 1 hour each way with about 1 hour at the church, bus runs daily May-Sept, tell driver you want to get off at the church, www.nor-way.no).

Stave Churches:
Norway's Wooden Wonders

Norway's most distinctive architecture is the stave church. These medieval houses of worship—tall, skinny, wooden pagodas with dragon's-head gargoyles—are distinctly Norwegian and palpably historic, transporting you right back to Viking days.

Stave churches are the finest architecture to come out of medieval Norway. Wood was plentiful and cheap, and locals had an expertise with woodworking (from all that boat-building). In 1300, there were as many as 1,000 stave churches in Norway. After a 14th-century plague, Norway's population dropped, and many churches fell into disuse or burned down. By the 19th century, only a few dozen stave churches survived. Fortunately, Norway realized their importance and protected them. Virtually all of Norway's surviving stave churches have been rebuilt or renovated, with painstaking attention to the original details.

A distinguishing feature of the "stave" design is its frame of tall, stout vertical staves (Norwegian *stav,* or "staff"). The churches typically sit on stone foundations, to keep the wooden structure off the damp ground (to prevent rot). Most stave churches were made of specially grown pine, carefully prepared before being felled for construction. As the trees grew, the tips and most of the branches were cut off, leaving the trunks just barely alive to stand in the woods for about a decade. This allowed the sap to penetrate the wood and lock in the resin, strengthening the wood while keeping it elastic. Once built, a stave church was slathered with black tar to protect it from the elements.

Stave churches are notable for their resilience and flexibility. Just as old houses creak and settle over the years, these wooden churches flex to withstand fierce winds and the march of time. When the wind shifts with the seasons, stave churches groan and moan for a couple of weeks before settling in.

Even after the Vikings stopped raiding, they ornamented the exteriors of their churches with warlike, evil spirit-fighting dragons reminiscent of their ships. Inside, the church's structure makes you feel like you're in an overturned ship's hull. Stave churches are dark, with almost no windows (aside from a few small "portholes" high up). Typical decorations include carved X-shape crossbeams, symbolizing the cross of St. Andrew (who was crucified on such a cross). Round, Romanesque arches near the tops of the staves were made from the "knees" of a tree, where the roots bend to

meet the trunk. Overall, these churches are extremely vertical: the beams inside and the roofline outside lead the eye up, up, up to the heavens.

Most surviving stave churches were renovated during the Reformation (16th and 17th centuries), when they acquired more

horizontal elements such as pews, balconies, pulpits, altars, and other decorations to draw attention to the front of the church. In some (such as the churches in Lom and Urnes), the additions make the church feel almost cluttered. But the most authentic (including Hopperstad near Vik) feel truly medieval. These time-machine churches take visitors back to early Christian days: no pews (worshippers stood through the service), no pulpit, and a barrier between the congregation and the priest, to symbolically separate the physical world from the spiritual one. Incense filled the church, and the priest and congregation chanted the service back and forth to each other, creating an atmosphere that likely made worshippers feel close to God.

When traveling through Norway, you'll be encouraged to see stave church after stave church, but there's no point in visiting more than a few of them. Of Norway's 28 remaining stave churches, seven are described in this book. The easiest to see are those that have been moved to open-air museums in Oslo and Lillehammer. But I prefer to appreciate a stave church in its original fjords-and-rolling-hills setting. My two favorites are near Sognefjord: Borgund and Hopperstad. They are each delightfully situated and evocative as can be. Borgund stands in a pristine wooded valley, while Hopperstad is perched above a fjord. Borgund also comes with a good stave church museum.

Other noteworthy stave churches include the one in Lom, near the Jotunheimen Mountains, which is one of Norway's biggest and quite impressive. The Urnes church, across the Lustrafjord from Solvorn, is technically the oldest of them all—but it's been thoroughly renovated in later ages (yet still worth a visit for its exquisite carvings and the fun ferry crossing to reach it; see the More on the Sognefjord chapter). The Fantoft stave church just outside Bergen was torched by an arsonist in 1992, and the 1997 reconstruction lacks the original's magic. The stave church in Undredal (see page 122) advertises itself as the smallest (but it's also the dullest). For more on Norway's stave churches, visit StaveChurch.com.

Visiting the Church: Explore the dimly lit interior, illuminated only by the original, small, circular windows up high. The oldest and most authentic item in the church is the stone baptismal font. In medieval times, priests conducting baptisms would go outside to shoo away the evil spirits from an infant before bringing it inside the church for the ritual. (If infants died before being baptized, they couldn't be buried in the churchyard, so parents would put their bodies in little coffins and hide them under the church's floorboards to get them as close as possible to God.)

Notice the X-shaped crosses of St. Andrew (the church's patron), carvings of dragons, and medieval runes. Borgund's church also comes with one of this country's best stave-church history museums, which beautifully explains these icons of medieval Norway.

Sleeping in Flåm

My recommended accommodations are away from the tacky train-station bustle, but a close enough walk to be convenient. The first two places are located along the waterfront a quarter-mile from the station: Walk around the little harbor (with the water on your left) for about 10 minutes. It's more enjoyable to follow the level, waterfront dock than to hike up the main road.

$$$$ Heimly Pensjonat, with 22 straightforward rooms, is clean, efficient, and the best small hotel in town. Sit on the porch with new friends and watch the clouds roll down the fjord. Prices include breakfast and a three-course dinner (family rooms, doubles are mostly twins, closed off-season, +47 57 63 23 00, post@heimly.no, www.visitflam.com).

$$$ Flåm Marina and Apartments, perched right on the fjord, is ideal for families and longer stays. They offer one standard double and 10 new-feeling, self-catering apartments that each sleep 2-5 people. All units offer views of the fjord with a balcony, kitchenette, and small dining area (no breakfast, café serving lunch and dinner open during high season, boat rental, laundry facilities, next to the guest harbor just below Heimly Pensjonat, +47 57 63 35 55, www.flammarina.no, booking@flammarina.no).

¢-$$ Flåm Youth Hostel and Camping Bungalows, voted Scandinavia's most beautiful campground, is run by the friendly Håland family, who rent the cheapest beds in the area (sheets and towels included in hostel but extra in cabins, showers extra, no meals but kitchen access, laundry, apple grove, mobile +47 94 03 26 81, www.flaam-camping.no, camping@flaam-camping.no). It's a five-minute walk toward the valley from the train station: Cross the bridge and turn left up the main road; then look for the hostel on the right.

Eating in Flåm

Dining options beyond your hotel's dining room or kitchenette are expensive and touristy. Don't aim for high cuisine here—go practical. Almost all eateries are clustered near the train station complex. Hours can be unpredictable, flexing with the season, but you can expect these to be open daily in high season. Places here tend to close pretty early (especially in shoulder season)—don't wait too long for dinner.

The **Flåmsbrygga** complex, sprawling through a long building toward the fjord from the station, includes a hotel, the affordable **$$ Furukroa Caféteria** (daily 8:00-20:00 in season, sandwiches, fast-food meals, and pizzas), and the pricey **$$$$ Flåmstova Restaurant** (breakfast and lunch buffet, sit-down dinner service, www.flamsbrygga.no). Next door is their fun, Viking-longhouse-shaped brewpub, **$$$ Ægir Bryggeri** (daily 17:00-22:00, local microbrews, Viking-inspired meals). **$$ Toget Café,** with seating in old train cars, prides itself on using as many locally sourced and organic ingredients as possible. **$$ Bakkastova Kafe,** at the other end of town, feels cozier. Housed in a traditional Norwegian red cabin just above the Fretheim Hotel, with a view terrace, it serves sandwiches, salads, and authentic Norwegian fare (daily 12:00-16:00).

Aurland

A few miles north of Flåm, Aurland is more of a real town and less of a tourist depot. While it's nothing exciting (Balestrand is more lively and appealing, and Solvorn is cuter— see next chapter), it's a good, easygoing fjordside home base. And thanks to its location—on the main road and boat lines, near Flåm—it's relatively handy for those taking public transportation. For fjord cruising options in this area, see "Cruising the Nærøyfjord," earlier.

Getting There: Aurland is an easy 10-minute drive or bus trip from Flåm. If you want to stay overnight in Aurland, note that every train (except the late-night one) arriving in Flåm connects with a bus or boat to Aurland (in summer: bus-11/day, 10 minutes, 65 NOK; ferry-4/day, 20 minutes, 195 NOK). The Flåm-

Gudvangen Classic ferry doesn't always stop at Aurland, but they will if you ask—so it's possible to continue the Nutshell route from Aurland without backtracking to Flåm. Boat tickets can be bought aboard the ferry in Aurland or at VisitFlam.com. The Bergen-Balestrand-Flåm express boat stops in Aurland (for details, see the "Express Boat Between Bergen and the Sognefjord" sidebar in the next chapter).

Orientation to Aurland

From Aurland's dingy boat dock area, walk one block up the paved street into the heart of town. On your right is the Spar supermarket (handy for picnic supplies) and Marianne Bakeri and Café (at the bridge). To your left is the Vangsgården Guest House and, behind it, Aurland Fjordhotel. To reach the TI, go straight ahead and bear right, then look behind the white church (800 years old and worth a peek). The bus stop, with buses to Flåm, is in front of the TI. For attractions near Aurland, see "Sights and Activities in and near Flåm," earlier.

Tourist Information: The TI stocks English-language brochures about hikes and day trips from the area, and sells local maps (daily 9:00-16:00, closed in off-season; behind the church— look for green-and-white *i* sign; mobile +47 91 79 41 64, https:// en.sognefjord.no).

Sleeping in Aurland

$$$$ Aurland Fjordhotel is big, modern, and centrally located. While it has a business-hotel vibe, most of its 30 rooms come with gorgeous fjord-view balconies (+47 57 63 35 05, www.aurland-fjordhotel.com, post@aurland-fjordhotel.com, Steinar Kjerstein).

$$$ Vangsgården Guest House, closest to the boat landing, is a complex of old buildings dominating the old center of Aurland and run from one reception desk (Wi-Fi in main building, +47 57 63 35 80, www.vangsgaarden.no, booking@vangsgaarden.no, open all year, Astrid). The main building is a simple, old guesthouse offering basic rooms and a fine old-timey living room. Their old-fashioned **Aabelheim Pension** is Aurland's best *koselig* (cozy)-like-a-farmhouse place (same prices). And lining the waterfront are their six adorable wood **$$$$** cabins with balconies, kitchen, bathroom, and two bedrooms (sleeps 2-6 people, sheets and breakfast extra, book 2 months in advance). The owners also run the recommended Duehuset Pub and rent bikes.

NEAR AURLAND

$$ Skahjem Gard is an active farm run by Aurland's former deputy mayor, Nils Tore. He's converted his old sheep barn into seven spic-and-span family apartments with private bathrooms and kitchenettes, each sleeping up to four people (sheets and towels included, two miles up the valley—road #50, follow *Hol* signs, mobile +47 95 17 25 67, nskahjem@online.no). It's a 25-minute walk from town, but Nils will pick up and drop off travelers at the ferry. This is best for families and foursomes with cars.

¢ Winjum Huts, about a half-mile from Aurland's dock, rents 14 basic cabins on a peaceful perch overlooking the majestic fjord. The washhouse/kitchen is where you'll find the toilets and showers. Follow the road uphill past the Aurland Fjordhotel; the huts are after the first hairpin curve (apartment available, sheets extra, showers extra, no food available—just beer, mobile +47 41 47 47 51).

Eating in Aurland

$$$ Marianne Bakeri and Café is a basic little bakery/café serving the best-value food in town. It's a block from the main square, at the bridge over the river. Sit inside or on its riverside terrace (sandwiches, pizza, and quiche; daily 10:00-17:00, mobile +47 90 51 29 78).

$$$ Duehuset Pub ("The Dove's House"), run by Vangsgården Guest House, serves up decent food in the center of town (daily 15:00-23:00, only open Fri-Sun for dinner in off-season).

The **$$$$ Aurland Fjordhotel** is your only alternative for splurges (dinner buffet, daily 19:00-22:00, shorter hours off-season, bar open later, +47 57 63 35 05, www.aurland-fjordhotel.com).

For cheap eats on dockside benches, gather a picnic at the **Spar** supermarket (Mon-Fri 9:00-20:00, Sat until 18:00, closed Sun).

Undredal

This almost impossibly remote community is home to about 80 people and 400 goats. A huge percentage of the town's former population (300 people) emigrated to the US between 1850 and 1925. Undredal was accessible only by boat until 1988, when the road from Flåm opened. There's not

much in the town, which is famous for its tiny stave church and its goat cheese, but I'll never forget the picnic I had on the ferry wharf. While appealing, Undredal is quiet (some say better from the boat) and difficult to reach—you'll have to be patient to connect to other towns. For more information on the town, see www. explore-undredal.no.

Getting There: The 15-minute drive from Flåm is mostly through a tunnel. By sea, you'll sail past Undredal on the Flåm-Gudvangen boat (you can request a stop). To get the ferry to pick you up in Undredal, turn on the blinking light (though some express boats will not stop).

Visiting Undredal: Undredal has Norway's smallest still-used **stave church,** seating 40 people for services every fourth Sunday. The original church was built in 1147 (look for the four original stave pillars inside). It was later expanded, pews added, and the interior painted in the 16th century in a way that resembles the traditional Norwegian *rosemaling* style (which came later). You can get in only with a 30-minute tour (70 NOK, June-mid-Aug daily 10:00-17:00, less in shoulder season, closed Oct-April, mobile +47 95 29 76 68).

Undredal's farms exist to produce **cheese.** The beloved local cheese comes in two versions: brown and white. The brown version is unaged and slightly sweet, while the white cheese has been aged and is mild and a bit salty. For samples, visit the Undredalsbui grocery store at the harbor (Mon-Fri 9:00-16:30, Sat until 15:00, Sun 12:00-16:00, shorter hours and closed Sun off-season).

Sleeping in Undredal: $ **Undredal Overnatting** rents four modern, woody apartments in two fjordside cottages. The reception is at the café on the harbor, while the accommodations are at the top of town (sheets included, breakfast extra, +47 57 63 30 80, www.visitundredal.no, visit@undredal.no).

MORE ON THE SOGNEFJORD

Balestrand • Lustrafjord • Scenic Drives

Norway's world of fjords is decorated with medieval stave churches, fishing boats, cascading waterfalls, dramatic glaciers, and brightly painted shiplap villages. Travelers in a hurry zip through the fjords on the Norway in a Nutshell route (see previous chapter). Their heads spin from all the scenery, and most wish they had more time on the Sognefjord. If you can linger in fjord country, this chapter is for you.

Snuggle into the fjordside village of Balestrand, which has a variety of walking and biking options and a fun local arts scene. Balestrand is also a handy jumping-off spot for adventures great and small, including a day trip up the Fjærlandsfjord to gaze at a receding tongue of the Jostedal Glacier, or across the Sognefjord to the truly medieval-feeling Hopperstad Stave Church. Farther east is the Lustrafjord, a tranquil branch of the Sognefjord offering drivers an appealing concentration of visit-worthy sights. On the Lustrafjord, you'll enjoy enchanting hamlets with pristine fjord views (such as Solvorn), historic churches (including Norway's oldest stave church at Urnes and the humble Dale Church in the village of Luster), an opportunity to touch and even hike on a glacier (the Nigard), and more stunning fjord views.

This region is important to the people of Norway. After four centuries under Danish rule, the soul of the country was nearly lost. With partial independence and its own constitution in the early 1800s, the country experienced a resurgence of national pride. Urban Norwegians headed for the fjord country here in the west. Norway's first Romantic painters and writers were drawn to Balestrand, inspired by the unusual light and dramatic views of mountains plunging into the fjords. The Sognefjord, with its many

Sognefjord Overview

500 KM
250 MI

SWE.
FIN.
NOR.
DEN.

To Florø

To Utvik &
Stryn

Breimsvatnet

E-39

Mykebust
Glacier

Skei

Bøya
Glacier

TUNNEL

Jølstravatnet

Grova
Glacier

NORWEGIAN
GLACIER
MUSEUM

Førdefjorden

Førde

Haukedalsvatnet

Fjærland
(Mundal)

Viksdalvatnet

Lorem ipsum

To Lavik
& Bergen
(by car and boat)

Dragsvik

Hella

*Fjærlands-
fjord*

Balestrand

Vangsnes

To Bergen
(by boat)

Sognefjord

55

Vik

HOPPERSTAD
STAVE CHURCH

N

10 Kilometers

10 Miles

Gudvangen

Tvinde-
fossen
Waterfall

Vinje

BUS

STALHEIM
(HOTEL & VIEW)

E-16

To
Bergen

Voss

OSLO-BERGEN

branches, is featured in more Romantic paintings than any other fjord.

PLANNING YOUR TIME

If you can spare a day or two off the Norway in a Nutshell route, spend it here. Balestrand is the best home base, especially if you're relying on public transportation (it's well connected by express boat both to the Nutshell scene and to Bergen). If you have a car, consider staying in the heart of the Lustrafjord region in sweet little Solvorn (easy ferry connection to the Urnes Stave Church and a short drive to the Nigard Glacier). As fjord home bases go, Balestrand and Solvorn are both better—but less convenient—than Flåm or Aurland on the Nutshell route.

With one night in this area, you'll blitz the sights on the way between destinations; with two nights, you can slow your pace (and your pulse) to enjoy the fjord scenery and plenty of day-trip possibilities.

Balestrand

The pleasant fjord town of Balestrand (pop. 1,300) has a long history of hosting tourists, thanks to its landmark Kviknes Hotel. But it also feels real and lived-in, making Balestrand a nice mix of cuteness and convenience. The town is near, but not *too* near, the Nutshell bustle across the fjord—and yet it's an easy express-boat trip away if you'd like to dive into the Nuttiness. In short, consider Balestrand a worthwhile detour from the typical fjord visit—allowing you to dig deeper into the Sognefjord, just like the glaciers did during the last ice age.

With two nights, you can relax and consider some day trips: Cruise up the nearby Fjærlandsfjord for a peek at a distant tongue of the ever-less-mighty Jostedal Glacier, or head across the Sognefjord to the beautiful Hopperstad Stave Church in Vik. Balestrand also has outdoor activities for everyone, from dreamy fjordside

strolls and strenuous mountain hikes to wildly scenic bike rides. For dinner, splurge on the memorable smorgasbord-style *koldt bord* dinner in the Kviknes Hotel dining room, then sip coffee from its balcony as you watch the sun set (or not) over the fjord.

PLANNING YOUR TIME

Balestrand's key advantage is its easy express-boat connection to Bergen, offering an alternative route to the fjord from the typical Nutshell train-bus combo. Consider zipping here on the Bergen boat, then continuing on via the Nutshell route.

One night is enough to get a taste of Balestrand. But spending two nights buys you some time for day trips. Note that the first flurry of day trips departs early, around 8:00 (includes the boat to Vik/Hopperstad Stave Church or the full-day Fjærlandsfjord glacier excursion), and the next batch departs around noon (the half-day Fjærlandsfjord glacier excursion and the last boat to Flåm). If you wait until after 12:00 to make your choice, you'll miss the boat...literally.

Balestrand pretty much shuts down from mid-September through mid-May—when most of the activities, sights, hotels, and restaurants listed here are likely closed.

Orientation to Balestrand

Most travelers arrive in Balestrand on the express boat from Bergen or Flåm. The tidy harbor area has a TI, two grocery stores, a couple of galleries, a town history museum, and a small aquarium devoted to marine life found in the fjord. The historic wooden Kviknes Hotel and its ugly modern annex dominate Balestrand's waterfront.

Even during tourist season, Balestrand is quiet. How quiet? The police station closes on weekends. And it's tiny—from the harbor to the Balestrand Hotel is a five-minute stroll, and you can walk from the aquarium to Kviknes Hotel in less time than that.

Balestrand became accessible to the wider world in 1858 when an activist minister (from the church you see across the fjord from town) brought in the first steamer service. That put Balestrand on the Grand Tour map of the Romantic Age. Even the German Kaiser chose to summer here. Today, people from around the world come here to feel the grandeur of the fjord country and connect with the essence of Norway.

TOURIST INFORMATION

At the TI, located between two supermarkets at the harbor, pick up the free, helpful *Outdoor Activities in Balestrand* brochure. The TI has numerous brochures about the Sognefjord area, including

MORE SOGNEFJORD

Balestrand

To Fjærland &
Norwegian Glacier Museum

Esefjord

AQUARIUM

To Dragsvik
& Car Ferry
to Hella &
Vangsnes

55

Express boat
to Nutshell area
(Aurland
& Flåm)

BOAT
DOCK

GOLDEN HOUSE

KVIKNES
HOTEL

Express boat
to Vik
(Hopperstad
Stave Church)
& Bergen

Sognefjord

TUNNEL

To
Kallestad

ST.
OLAF'S

OLD ROAD (KING BELE'S WAY)

N

200 Meters
200 Yards

VIKING
BURIAL
MOUNDS

To Villas

Accommodations
1 Kviknes Hotel & Restaurant
2 Balestrand Hotel
3 Thuegården Apartments
4 Kringsjå Balestrand Hostel

Eateries & Other
5 Gekken's
6 The Viking Ship & Co-op Supermarket
7 Joker Supermarket
8 Mü's Bakery
9 "The Kaiser's Stairs"
10 Norwegian Travel Museum (Historic Photos)
11 Golden House Gallery

many great hikes, with detailed information on the more challenging routes. It rents e-bikes (from 350 NOK) and sells tickets for the Norled ferry and various fjord, kayak, and fishing tours (daily 10:00-16:00 in summer, closed weekends in spring and fall and all of Oct-April; mobile +47 94 87 75 01—answered all year, https://en.sognefjord.no).

Local Guide: Various guides lead 1.5-hour tours around the village (www.balestrandadventure.no), or you can try **Bjørg Bjøberg,** who runs an art gallery along with her husband Arthur Adamson at the Golden House (Det Gylne Hus). She knows the town well and is happy to show visitors around (1,000-1,500 NOK/2 hours per group—gather several people and share the cost, mobile +47 91 56 28 42, bjoergfb@online.no).

Car Rental: The **Balholm Car Rental** agency usually will deliver a car to your Balestrand hotel, and pick it up, too (daily

8:00-20:00, +47 41 24 82 53, www.leigebil.no, booking@leigebil.
no). The **Kviknes Hotel** can likely arrange a one-day car rental for
you (+47 57 69 42 00).

Sights in Balestrand

Balestrand Harborfront Stroll

The tiny harbor stretches from the aquarium to the big, old Kviknes
Hotel. Stroll its length, starting at the aquarium (described later)
and little marina. Across the street, at the recommended Viking
Ship shack, a German woman named Carola sells German sau-
sages with an evangelical zeal. A couple of doors down, the Spin-
delvev ("Spider's Web") shop sells handicrafts made by people with
physical and mental disabilities. A local home for the disabled was
closed in the 1980s, but many of its former residents stayed in Balestrand because the government gave them pensions and houses in
town.

Then, in the unsightly modern strip mall, you'll find the TI,
Joker supermarket, and a community bulletin board with the
schedule for the summer cinema (the little theater, 800 yards away,
runs films nightly). On the corner is the Golden House art gallery.
Behind it— built into solid rock—is the boxy home of the Norwegian Travel Museum (Norsk Reiselivsmuseum), featuring photos
showing this part of Norway over the past 150 years, interactive
exhibits, and souvenirs. And just beyond that is the dock where the
big Bergen-Sognefjord express catamaran ties up.

Across the street is a cute white house (at #8), which used
to stand at the harborfront until the big Joker supermarket and
Kviknes Hotel, with its modern annex, partnered to ruin the town
center. This little house was considered historic enough to be air-
lifted 100 yards to this new spot. It's flanked by two other historic
buildings, which house a gallery and an artisans' workshop.

Farther along, find the rust-red building that was the waiting
room for the 19th-century steamer that first brought tourism to
town. Walk a few steps farther and stop at the tall stone monument erected to celebrate the North Bergen Steamship Company.
Its boats first connected Balestrand to the rest of the world in 1858.
In front of the monument, some nondescript concrete steps lead
into the water. These are "The Kaiser's Stairs," built for the German emperor, Kaiser Wilhelm II, who made his first summer visit
(complete with navy convoy) in 1899 and kept returning until the
outbreak of World War I.

Behind the monument stands one of the largest old wooden
buildings in Norway, Kviknes Hotel. It was built in the 1870s and
faces the rare little island in the fjord, which helped give the town
its name: "Balestrand" means the strand or promenade in front of

an island. (The island is now connected to the hotel's front yard and is part of a playground for its guests.) Hike up the black driveway that leads from the monument to the hotel's modern lobby. Go inside and find (to your left) the plush old lounge, a virtual painting gallery. All the pieces are by artists from this area, celebrating the natural wonder of the fjord country—part of the trend that helped 19th-century Norway reconnect with its heritage. (While you're here, consider making a reservation and choosing a table for a smorgasbord dinner tonight.) Leave the hotel lobby (from the door opposite to the one you entered), and head up to St. Olaf's Church. To continue this stroll, take King Bele's Way up the fjord.

Golden House (Det Gylne Hus)

This golden-colored house facing the ferry landing was built as a general store in 1928. Today it houses an art installation and a quirky museum created by local watercolorist and historian Bjørg Bjøberg, and her husband, Arthur Adamson. On the ground floor you'll find Bjørg's gallery, with her watercolors celebrating the beauty of Norway, and Arthur's paintings, celebrating the beauty of women. Upstairs is a room focusing on their local nature pilgrimage program, along with an exhibit of historical knickknacks contributed by locals wanting to preserve treasures from their families' past.

Cost and Hours: Free entry to the ground floor, 25 NOK for the second floor and the glass dome; optional private one-hour tour-50 NOK; May-Aug daily 10:00-22:00, shorter hours late April and Sept, closed in winter; mobile +47 91 56 28 42, www.detgylnehus.no.

St. Olaf's Church

This distinctive wooden church was built in 1897. Construction was started by Margaret Sophia Kvikne, the wife of Knut Kvikne

(of the Kviknes Hotel family; her portrait is in the rear of the nave), but she died in 1894, before the church was finished. This devout Englishwoman wanted a church in Balestrand where English services were held...and to this day, bells ring to announce services by British clergy. Saint Olaf, who brought Christianity to Norway in the 11th century, was the country's patron saint in Catholic times. The church was built in a "Neo-stave" style, with lots of light from its windows and an altar painting inspired by the famous *Risen Christ* statue in Copenhagen's Cathedral of Our Lady. Here, Christ is flanked by fields of daisies (called

"priests' collars" in Norwegian) and peace lilies. From the door of the church, enjoy a good view of the island in the fjord.

Cost and Hours: Free, open daily, services in English every Sun from late May through August.

Strolling King Bele's Way up the Fjord

For a delightful walk (or bike ride), head west out of town up the "old road"—once the main road from the harbor—for about a mile. It follows the fjord's edge, passing numerous "villas" from the late 1800s. At the time, this Swiss style was popular with some locals, who hoped to introduce a dose of Romanticism into Norwegian architecture. Look for the dragons' heads (copied from Viking-age stave churches) decorating the gables. Along the walk, you'll pass a swimming area, a campground, and two burial mounds from the Viking age, marked by a ponderous statue of the Viking King Bele. Check out the wooden shelters for the mailboxes; some give the elevation (*m.o.h.* stands for "meters over *havet*"—the sea)—not too high, are they? The walk is described in the *Outdoor Activities in Balestrand* brochure (free at the TI or your hotel).

Sognefjord Aquarium (Sognefjord Akvarium)

The tiny aquarium gives you a good look at marine life in the Sognefjord. For descriptions, borrow the English booklet at the front desk. While not thrilling, the well-explained place is a decent rainy-day option. The last room is filled with wood carvings depicting traditional everyday life in the fjordside village of Munken. The fish-filled tanks on the dock outside are also worth a look.

Cost and Hours: 70 NOK, daily 9:00-19:00, closed mid-Sept-April, +47 57 69 13 03.

Biking

You can cycle around town, or circle the scenic Esefjord (north of town, en route to the ferry landing at Dragsvik—about 6 miles each way). Or pedal west up Sognefjord along the scenic King Bele's Way (described earlier). Roads here are relatively flat. Rental bikes are usually available at the TI and through Kviknes Hotel.

Boat Tours

Balestrand Fjord Adventure specializes in Zodiac-type boat tours on the Sognefjord. Passengers wear full-body weather suits, life vests, and goggles. Join their daily round-trip cruise departing at 13:00 (800 NOK, 1.5 hours) or take the more extensive Nærøyfjord tour (1,350 NOK, 2.5 hours, 3/week, mobile +47 47 85 53 23, www.balestrandadventure.no).

NEAR BALESTRAND

These two side-trips are possible only if you've got the better part of a day in Balestrand. With a car, you can see Hopperstad Stave Church on the drive to Bergen.

▲▲Hopperstad Stave Church (Hopperstad Stavkyrkje) in Vik

The most accessible stave church in the area—and perhaps the most scenically situated in all of Norway—is located just a 20-minute

express-boat ride across the Sognefjord, in the town of Vik. Hopperstad Stave Church boasts a breathtaking exterior, with several tiers of dragon heads overlooking rolling fields between fjord cliffs. The interior is notable for its emptiness. Instead of being crammed full of later additions, the church is blissfully uncluttered, as it was when it was built in the mid-12th century. (For more on stave churches, see page 116.)

Cost and Hours: 80 NOK; daily 10:00-17:00, mid-June–mid-Aug from 9:00, closed Oct–mid-May; good 30-NOK color booklet in English, +47 57 69 52 70, www. stavechurch.com/hopperstad.

Tours: Attendants will give you a free tour at your request, provided they're not too busy. (Ask where the medieval graffiti is, and they'll grab a flashlight and show you.)

Getting There: Pedestrians can ride the express passenger boat between Balestrand and Vik (98 NOK each way). The only way to get to the church and back in one day is to take the 7:50 departure from Balestrand, then return on the 11:35 departure from Vik, arriving back in Balestrand at 11:55—just in time to join a 12:00 glacier excursion (described on the next page). Because schedules can change, be sure to double-check times at the TI or www.norled.no, under "Expressboat." The church is a 20-minute walk up the valley from Vik's harbor. From the boat landing, walk up the main street from the harbor about 200 yards (past the TI, a grocery store, and hotel). Take a right at the sign for *Hopperstad Stavkyrkje,* walk 10 minutes, and you'll see the church perched on a small hill in the distance.

Since cars can't go on the express boat, **drivers** must go around the small Esefjord to the town of Dragsvik, then catch the ferry across the Sognefjord to Vangsnes (a 20-minute drive from Vik and the church).

Visiting the Church: Originally built around 1140 and retaining most of its original wood, Hopperstad was thoroughly restored

and taken back to basics in the 1880s by renowned architect Peter Blix. Unlike the famous stave church at Urnes (described later), which has an interior that has been rejiggered by centuries of engineers and filled with altars and pews, the Hopperstad church

looks close to the way it did when it was built. You'll see only a few added features, including the beautifully painted canopy that once covered a side altar (probably dating from around 1300), and a tombstone from 1738. There are just a few colorful illustrations and some very scant medieval "graffiti" carvings and runic inscriptions.

Notice the intact chancel screen (the only one surviving in Norway), which separates the altar area from the congregation. As with the iconostasis (panel of icons) in today's Orthodox faith, this screen gave priests privacy to do the spiritual heavy lifting. Because Hopperstad's interior lacks the typical adornments, you can really grasp the fundamentally vertical nature of stave church architecture, leading your gaze to the heavens. Follow that impulse and look up to appreciate the Viking-ship rafters. Imagine the comfort this ceiling brought the church's original parishioners, whose seafaring ancestors had once sought refuge under overturned boats. For a unique angle on this graceful structure, lay your camera on the floor and shoot the ceiling.

▲Excursion to Fjærland and the Jostedal Glacier

From Balestrand, cruise up the Fjærlandsfjord to visit the Norwegian Glacier Museum in Fjærland and to see a receding tongue of the Jostedal Glacier (Jostedalbreen). Half-day (890 NOK) and full-day (925 NOK) excursions are sold by Balestrand's TI or onboard the boat. Reservations are smart (tours offered daily June-Aug only, +47 57 63 14 00, www. visitflam.com and follow links for "Fjærlandsfjord").

While the museum and the glacier's tongue are underwhelming, it's a pleasant excursion with a dreamy fjord cruise (1.5 hours each way). To take the all-day trip, catch the 8:00 ferry; for the shorter trip, hop on the 12:00 boat. Either way, you can return

on the 15:30 boat, getting you back to Balestrand at 16:45 (just in time to catch the fast boat back to Bergen). Both tours offer the same fjord ride, museum visit, and trip to the glacier. The all-day version, however, gives you a second glacier viewing point and about 2.5 hours to hang out in the town of Fjærland. (This sleepy village, famous for its secondhand book shops, is about as exciting as Walter Mondale, the former US vice president whose ancestors came from here.)

The ferry ride (no stops, no narration) is just a scenic glide with the gulls. Bring a picnic, as there's almost no food sold on-board, and some bread to toss to the gulls (they do acrobatics to catch whatever you loft into the air). You'll be met at the ferry dock (labeled *Mundal*) by a bus—and your guide, who reads a script about the glacier as you drive up the valley for about 15 minutes. You'll stop for an hour at the **Norwegian Glacier Museum** (Norsk Bremuseum). After watching an 18-minute aerial tour of the dramatic Jostedal Glacier in the theater, you'll learn how glaciers were formed, experiment with your own hunk of glacier, weigh evidence of the woolly mammoth's existence in Norway, and learn about the effect of climate change on the fjords (way overpriced at 140 NOK, included in excursion price; daily June-Aug 10:00-19:00, April-May and Sept-Oct until 16:00, closed Nov-March; +47 57 69 32 88, www.bre.museum.no). From the museum, the bus runs you up to a café near a lake, at a spot that gives you a good look at the Bøyabreen, a tongue of the Jostedal Glacier. Marvel at how far the glacier has retreated—10 years ago, the visit was more dramatic. With global warming, glacier excursions like this become more sad than majestic. I wonder how long they'll even be able to bill this as a "glacier visit."

Considering that the fjord trip is the highlight of this journey, you could save time and money by just riding the ferry up and back (8:00-11:25). At 475 NOK for the round-trip boat ride, it's much cheaper than the tour.

Note that if you're into glaciers, a nearby arm of the Jostedal, called the **Nigard Glacier,** is a more dramatic and boots-on experience (described later, under "Sights on the Lustrafjord"). It's easy for drivers to reach; see "Orientation to Balestrand," earlier, for car-rental info.

Sleeping in Balestrand

$$$$ Kviknes Hotel is the classy grande dame of Balestrand, dominating the town and packed with tour groups. The picturesque wooden hotel—and five generations of the Kvikne family—have welcomed tourists to Balestrand since the late 19th century. The hotel has two parts: a new wing, and the historic wooden sec-

tion, with 25 older, classic rooms, and no elevator. All rooms come with balconies. The elegant Old World public spaces in the old section make you want to just sit there and sip tea all afternoon (family rooms, closed Oct-April, +47 57 69 42 00, www.

kviknes.com, booking@kviknes.no). Part of the Kviknes ritual is gorging on the *koldt bord* buffet dinner—open to nonguests, and a nice way to soak in the hotel's old-time elegance without splurging on an overnight (see "Eating in Balestrand," later; cheaper if you stay at the hotel for 2 or more nights).

$$$ Balestrand Hotel, family-run by Unni-Marie Kvikne, her California-born husband Eric Palmer, and their three children, is your best fjordside home. Open mid-May through early September, this cozy, welcoming place has 30 well-appointed, comfortable, quiet rooms; a large, modern common area with lots of English paperbacks; laundry service, balconies (in some rooms), and outdoor benches for soaking in the scenery. The waterfront yard has inviting lounge chairs and a mesmerizing view. When reserving, let them know your arrival time, and they'll pick you up at the harborfront (5-minute walk from dock, past St. Olaf's Church—or free pickup, +47 57 69 11 38, www.balestrand.com, info@balestrand.com).

$ Thuegården offers five clean, bright, modern doubles with kitchenettes, conveniently located near the ferry dock and just up the street from the Co-op grocery store. Some rooms have balconies and some come with a fjord view (discount if staying more than 3 nights, no breakfast, office inside ground-floor hair salon, +47 57 69 15 95, mobile +47 97 19 92 63, www.thuegaarden.com, thuegaarden@gmail.com).

¢-$$ Kringsjå Balestrand Hostel, a camp school for sixth-graders, rents beds and rooms to budget travelers from mid-June to mid-August. Three-quarters of their 58 beds are in doubles. All the rooms have private bathrooms and most have view balconies (private and family rooms, includes sheets and towels, game room, +47 57 69 13 03, www.kringsja.no, hotel@kringsja.no).

Eating in Balestrand

Balestrand's dining options are limited, but good.

$$$$ Kviknes Hotel offers a splendid, spendy *koldt bord* buffet dinner in a massive yet stately old dining room. For a memorable fjordside smorgasbord experience, it doesn't get any better

than this. Don't rush. Consider taking a preview tour—surveying the reindeer meat, lingonberries, and fjord-caught seafood—before you dive in, so you can budget your stomach space. Get a new plate with each course and save room for dessert. Each dish is labeled in English (575 NOK/person, May-Sept daily

18:30-21:00, closed Oct-April). They also offer a four-course, locally sourced dinner for 695 NOK. After dinner, head into the rich lounge to pick up your cup of coffee or tea (included), which you'll sip sitting on classy old-fashioned furniture and basking in fjord views.

$$ Gekken's is an informal summer restaurant serving good-value meat, fish, and vegetarian dishes, along with burgers, fish-and-chips, and other fried fare. Sit in the simply decorated interior, or out on the shaded little terrace. Geir Arne "Gekken" Bale can trace his family's roots back 400 years in Balestrand. He has filled his walls with fascinating historic photos and paintings, making his dining hall an art gallery of sorts (May-Aug daily 12:00-22:00, closed Sept-April, above and behind the TI from the harbor, +47 57 69 14 14).

$ The Viking Ship, the hot-dog stand facing the harbor, is proudly run by Carola. A bratwurst missionary from Germany, she claims it took her years to get Norwegians to accept the tastier bratwurst over their beloved *pølser* weenies. Eat at her picnic tables or across the street on the harbor park (fine sausages, fish-and-chips, May-Sept daily 11:00-20:00, closed Oct-April).

Picnic: The delightful waterfront park next to the aquarium has benches and million-dollar fjord views. The Co-op and Joker **supermarkets** at the harbor have basic grocery supplies, including bread, meats, cheeses, and drinks; the Co-op is bigger and has a wider selection (both open generally Mon-Fri 8:00-20:00, shorter hours on Sat, closed Sun). **$ Mü's Bakery** offers a healthy assortment of sandwiches and fresh-baked goodies (Mon-Sat 9:30-18:00, Sun until 15:00, closed mid-Sept-early May, just inside the aquarium entrance).

Balestrand Connections

Because Balestrand is separated from the Lustrafjord by the long Fjærlandsfjord, most Balestrand connections involve a boat trip.

Express Boat Between Bergen and the Sognefjord

The made-for-tourists express boat makes it a snap to connect Bergen with Balestrand and other Sognefjord towns (for foot passengers only—no cars). In summer, the boat links Bergen, Vik, Balestrand, Aurland, and Flåm. You can also use this boat to connect towns on the Sognefjord, such as zipping from quiet Balestrand to busy Flåm, in the heart of the Nutshell action (reservations are smart—call +47 51 86 87 00 or visit www. norled.no and select "Expressboat"; discounts for students and seniors, tickets also sold on boat and at TI). The following times were good as of press time—confirm locally.

Between Bergen and the Sognefjord: The boat trip between Bergen and Balestrand takes four hours (760 NOK, departs Bergen May-Sept daily at 8:00 and 16:30, Oct-April Sun-Fri at 16:30, Sat at 14:15; departs Balestrand May-Sept Mon-Sat at 7:50 and 16:50, some Sun at 11:30 and 16:50, Oct-April Mon-Sat at 7:50, Sun at 16:25). In summer, the 8:00 boat from Bergen continues to Flåm.

Between Flåm and Balestrand: Going by boat between Flåm and Balestrand with the Norled ferry takes about 1.5 hours (300 NOK, departs Flåm May-Sept daily at 15:30, stops at Aurland, arrives in Balestrand at 16:50; departs Balestrand daily at 11:55 arriving Flåm at 13:25; no express boats between Flåm and Balestrand Oct-April). Another option is The Fjords express-ferry, which also stops at Leikanger, Undredal, and Aurland (300 NOK, only runs June-mid-Aug, takes 2 hours, departs Flåm Mon-Fri at 6:00, departs Balestrand at 8:30, no boats Sat-Sun, +47 57 63 14 00, www.visitflam.com). In peak season book ahead for any of the Flåm-Balestrand ferries.

From Oslo to Balestrand via the Nutshell: This variation on the standard Norway in a Nutshell route is called "Sognefjord in a Nutshell" (Oslo-Myrdal-Flåm-Balestrand-Bergen). From Oslo, you can take an early train to Flåm (no later than the 8:25 train as part of the Norway in a Nutshell route), then catch the 15:30 express boat to Balestrand and spend the night. The next day, continue on the express boat to Bergen, or return to the Nutshell route by taking the express boat to Flåm, and transferring to the next boat to Gudvangen.

BY BOAT

Express Passenger Boat: The easiest way to reach Balestrand is on the handy express boat, which connects to **Bergen, Vik** (near Hopperstad Stave Church), **Aurland,** and **Flåm** (see sidebar for schedules). Note that you can also use this boat to join the Nutshell trip in Flåm. From here, continue on the Nutshell boat down the Nærøyfjord to Gudvangen, where you'll join the crowd onward to Voss, then Bergen or Oslo. As you're making schedule and sightseeing decisions, consider that the Balestrand-Flåm boat skips the Nærøyfjord, the most dramatic arm of the Sognefjord.

Car Ferry: Balestrand's main car-ferry dock is at the village of **Dragsvik,** a six-mile, 15-minute drive around the adorable little Esefjord. From Dragsvik, a car ferry makes the short crossing east to **Hella** (a 30-minute drive from Sogndal and the Lustrafjord), then crosses the Sognefjord south to **Vangsnes** (a 20-minute drive to Hopperstad Stave Church and onward to Bergen). The ferry goes at least once per hour (2/hour in peak times, fewer boats Sun; Dragsvik-Vangsnes, 107 NOK for car and driver; Dragsvik-Hella, 74 NOK).

Note that you can also drive through Sogndal to catch the **Kaupanger-Gudvangen** or **Mannheller-Fodnes** ferries (described under "Lustrafjord Connections," near the end of this chapter).

BY BUS

A local bus links Balestrand to **Sogndal** (5/day Mon-Fri, 3/day Sat-Sun, 1.5 hours, includes ride on Dragsvik-Hella ferry, get details at TI).

The Lustrafjord

This arm of the Sognefjord is rugged country—only 2 percent of the land is fit to build on or farm. The Lustrafjord is ringed with tiny villages where farmers sell cherries and giant raspberries. A few interesting attractions lie along the Lustrafjord: the Dale Church at Luster; the impressive Nigard Glacier (a 45-minute drive up a valley); the postcard-pretty village of Solvorn; and, across the fjord, Norway's oldest stave church at Urnes. While a bit trickier to explore by public transportation, this beautiful region is easy by car, but still feels remote. There are no ATMs between Lom and Gaupne—that's how remote this region is.

SUGGESTED ROUTE FOR DRIVERS

The Lustrafjord can be seen either coming from the north (over the Sognefjell pass from the Jotunheimen region—see next chapter) or from the south (from Balestrand or the Norway in a Nutshell route—see previous chapter). Note that public buses between Lom and Sogndal follow this same route (see "Lustrafjord Connections," later).

Here's what you'll see if you're driving from the north (if you're coming from the south, read this section backward): Descending from Sognefjell, you'll hit the fjord at the village of Skjolden (decent TI in big community center, mobile +47 99 23 15 00). Follow highway 55 along the west bank of the fjord. In the village of Luster, consider visiting the beautifully decorated Dale Church. Farther along, near the hamlet of Nes, you'll have views across the fjord of the towering Feigumfoss waterfall. Drops and dribbles come from miles around for this 650-foot tumble. Soon highway 55 veers along an inlet to the town of Gaupne, where you can choose to detour about an hour to the Nigard Glacier (up Route 604). After Gaupne, the road enters a tunnel and cuts inland, emerging at a long, fjord-like lake at the town of Hafslo. Just beyond is the turn-off for Solvorn, a town with the ferry across to Urnes and its stave church. Highway 55 continues to Sogndal, where you can choose to turn off for the Kaupanger and Mannheller ferries across the Sognefjord, or continue on highway 55 to Hella and the boat across to either Dragsvik (near Balestrand) or Vangsnes (across the Sognefjord, near Vik and Hopperstad Stave Church).

Route Timings: If you're approaching from Lom in the Gudbrandsdal Valley, figure about 1.5 hours over Sognefjell to the start of the Lustrafjord at Skjolden, then another 30 minutes to Gaupne (with the optional glacier detour: 2 hours to see it, 4 hours to hike on it). From Gaupne, figure 20 minutes to Solvorn or 30 minutes to Sogndal. Solvorn to Sogndal is about 25 minutes. Sogndal to Hella, and its boat to Balestrand, takes about one hour. These estimated times are conservative, but they don't include photo stops.

Sights on the Lustrafjord

These attractions are listed as you'll reach them driving from north to south along the fjordside highway 55. If you're sleeping in this area, you could visit all four sights in a single day (but it'd be a busy, somewhat rushed day). If you're just passing through, Dale Church and Solvorn are easy, but the other two involve major detours—choose one or skip them both.

▲Dale Church (Dale Kyrkje) in Luster

The namesake village of Luster, on the west bank of the Lustrafjord, boasts a unique 13th-century Gothic church. In a land of wooden

stave churches, this stone church, with its richly decorated interior, is worth a quick stop as you pass through town.

Cost and Hours: Free entry but donation requested, daily 10:00-20:00 but often closed for services and off-season,

good posted English info inside, just off the main road—look for red steeple, WC in graveyard, fresh goodies at bakery across the street.

Visiting the Church: The soapstone core of the church dates from about 1250, but the wooden bell tower and entry porch were

likely built around 1600. As you enter, on the left you'll see a tall, elevated platform with seating, surrounded by a wooden grill. Nicknamed a "birdcage" for the feathery fashions worn by the ladies of the time, this high-profile pew—three steps higher than the pulpit—was built in the late 17th century by a wealthy parishioner. The beautifully painted pulpit, decorated with faded images of the four evangelists, dates from the 13th century. In the chancel (altar area), restorers have uncovered frescoes from three different time periods: the 14th, 16th, and 17th centuries.

Most of the ones you see here were likely created around the year 1500. The crucifix high over the pews, carved around 1200, predates the church, as does the old bench (with lots of runic carvings)—making them more than eight centuries old.

▲▲Jostedal's Nigard Glacier

The Nigard Glacier (Nigardsbreen) is the most accessible branch of mainland Europe's largest glacier (the Jostedalsbreen, 185 square miles). Hiking to or on the Nigard offers Norway's best easy opportunity for a hands-on glacier experience. It's a 45-minute detour from the Lustrafjord up Jostedal Valley. Visiting a glacier is a quintessential Norwegian experience, bringing you face-to-face

with the majesty of nature. If you can spare the time, it's worth the detour (even if you don't do a guided hike). But if glaciers don't give you tingles and you're feeling pressed, skip it.

Getting There: It's straightforward for **drivers.** When the main highway 55 along the Lustrafjord reaches Gaupne, turn onto highway 604, which you'll follow for 25 miles up the Jostedal Valley to the Breheimsenteret Glacier Information Center. Access to the glacier itself is down the toll road past the information center.

From mid-June through August, a **Glacier Bus** connects the Nigard Glacier to various home-base towns around the region (leaves Sogndal at 8:35 and 13:45, arrives at the glacier around 10:00 and 15:30, morning bus passes through Solvorn en route; departs glacier at 12:25 and 16:55, arrives back in Sogndal around 14:20 and 18:35; buses or boats from other towns, including Flåm and Aurland, may coordinate to meet this bus in Sogndal—ask at TI; combo-tickets include various glacier visits and hikes; for complete timetable, see www.visitnorway.no).

Visiting the Glacier: The architecturally striking Breheimsenteret Glacier Information Center services both Breheimen and Jostedalsbreen national parks. Drop by to confirm your glacier plans; you can also book excursions here. The center features a relaxing 15-minute film with highlights of the region, along with interactive glacier-related exhibits that explain these giant, slow-moving rivers of ice. The center also has a restaurant and gift shop (information center-free, exhibits and film-85 NOK; daily mid-June-mid-Aug 9:00-18:00, May-mid-June and mid-Aug-Sept 10:00-17:00, closed Oct-April; +47 57 68 32 50, www.jostedal.com.

The best quick visit is to walk to, but not on, the glacier. (If you want to walk *on* it, see "Hikes on the Glacier," next.) From the information center, an 80-NOK toll road continues two miles to a lake facing the actual tongue of the glacier. About 75 years ago, the glacier reached all the way to today's parking lot. (It's named for the ninth farm—*ni gard*—where it finally stopped, after crushing

eight farms higher up the valley.) From the lot, you can hike all the way to the edge of today's glacier (about 45 minutes each way); or, to save about 20 minutes of walking, take a special boat to a spot that's a 20-minute hike from the glacier (40 NOK one-way, 60 NOK round-trip, 10-minute boat trip, 4/hour, mid-June-mid-Sept daily 10:00-18:00).

The walk is uneven but well-marked—follow the red *T*'s and take your time. You'll hike on stone polished smooth by the glacier, and scramble over and around boulders big and small that were deposited by it. The path takes you right up to the face of the Nigardsbreen. Respect the glacier. It's a powerful river of ice, and fatal accidents do happen. If you want to walk on the glacier, see below.

Hikes on the Glacier: Don't attempt to walk on the glacier by yourself. The Breheimsenteret Glacier Information Center has

information on local companies that offer guided, family-friendly walks that include 1-2 hours on the ice. Prices and minimum age varies by the company (470-950 NOK, from 520 NOK for kids, minimum age 4-8; I'd rate the walks PG-13 myself, book in advance, www.jostedal.com). One hour roped up with your group gives you the essential experience. You'll find yourself marveling at how well your crampons work on the 5,000-year-old-ice. Even if it's hot, wear long pants, a jacket, and your sturdiest shoes. (Think ahead. It's awkward to empty your bladder after you're roped up.)

Longer, more challenging, and much more expensive hikes get you higher views, more exercise, and real crampons. If you're adventurous, ask about even longer hikes and glacier kayaking. While it's legal to go on the glacier on your own, it's dangerous and crazy to do so without crampons.

▲▲Solvorn

On the west bank of the Lustrafjord, 10 miles northeast of Sogndal,

idyllic Solvorn is a sleepy little Victorian town with colorful wooden sheds lining its waterfront. My favorite town on the Lustrafjord is tidy and quaint, well away from the bustle of the Nutshell action. Its tiny ferry crosses the fjord regularly to Urnes and its famous stave

church. While not worth going far out of your way for, Solvorn is a mellow and surprisingly appealing place to kill some time waiting for the ferry...or just munching a picnic while looking across the fjord. A pensive stroll or photo shoot through the village's back lanes is a joy (look for plaques that explain historic buildings in English). Best of all, Solvorn also has a pair of excellent accommodations: a splurge (Walaker Hotel) and a budget place (Eplet Bed & Apple), described later under "Sleeping on the Lustrafjord."

Getting There: Solvorn is a steep five-minute **drive** down a switchback road from the main highway 55. The main road into town leads right to the Urnes ferry (see next listing) and dead-ends into a handy parking lot (free, 2-hour posted—but unmonitored—limit). It's a 30-minute drive or bus trip into Sogndal, where you can transfer to other **buses** (2-4 buses/day between Solvorn and Sogndal, including the Glacier Bus to the Nigard Glacier—described earlier).

▲▲Urnes Stave Church

The hamlet of Urnes (sometimes spelled "Ornes") has Norway's oldest surviving stave church, dating from 1129. While not easy to reach (it's across the Lustrafjord from other attractions), it's worth the scenic ferry ride. The exterior is smaller and simpler than most stave churches, but its interior—modified in fits and starts over the centuries—is uniquely eclectic. For more on stave churches, see page 116. If you want to pack along a bike (rentable in Solvorn), see "Bring a Bike?" at the end of this listing.

Cost and Hours: 100 NOK, includes 20-minute English tour (generally departs at :40 past the hour to coincide with ferry arrival); May-Sept daily 10:30-17:45, closed off-season, +47 57 68 39 56, www.stavechurch.com.

Getting There: Urnes is perched on the east bank of the Lustrafjord (across the fjord from highway 55 and Solvorn). Ferries generally depart Solvorn at the top of the hour and Urnes at 30 minutes past the hour (45 NOK one-way passenger fare, 121 NOK one-way for car and driver, no round-trip discount, 15-minute ride, mobile +47 91 72 17 19, www.lustrabaatane.no). You can either drive or walk onto the boat—but, since you can't drive all the way up to the church, you might as well leave your car in Solvorn. Once across, it's about a five-minute uphill walk to the main road and parking lot (where drivers must leave their cars; parking lot at the

church only for disabled visitors). From here, it's a steep 15-minute walk up a switchback road to the church (follow signs for *Urnes*).

Planning Your Time: Don't dawdle on your way up to the church, as the tour is scheduled to depart at :40 past most hours, about 25 minutes after the ferry arrives (giving most visitors just enough time to make it up the hill to the church; last tour at 16:40). The first boat of the day departs Solvorn at 10:00 and the last boat at 16:50; the last boat back to Solvorn departs Urnes at 18:00. Confirm these times locally, especially the "last boat" times, and keep an eye on your watch to avoid getting stranded in Urnes.

Eating: A little café/restaurant is at the farm called Urnes Gard, across from the church (same hours as church, homemade apple cakes, +47 57 68 39 44).

Visiting the Church: Most visitors to the church take the included 20-minute tour (scheduled to begin soon after the ferry arrives—described earlier). Here are some highlights:

Buy your ticket in the white house across from the church. Visit the little museum here after you see the church, so you don't miss the tour.

Many changes were made to the exterior to modernize the church after the Reformation (the colonnaded gallery was replaced,

the bell tower was added, and modern square windows were cut into the walls). Go around the left side of the church, toward the cemetery. This is the third church on this spot, but the carved doorway embedded in the wall here was inherited from the second church. Notice the two mysterious beasts—a warm-blooded predator (standing) and a cold-blooded dragon—weaving and twisting around each other, one entwining the other. Yet, as they bite each other on the neck, it's impossible to tell which one is "winning"... perhaps symbolizing the everlasting struggle of human existence. The door you see in

the middle, however, has a very different message: the harmony of symmetrical figure-eights, an appropriately calming theme for those entering the church.

Now go around to the real entry door (with a wrought-iron lock and handle probably dating from the first church) and head inside. While it feels ancient and creaky, a lot of what you see in here is actually "new" compared to the 12th-century core of the church. The exquisitely carved, voluptuous, column-topping capitals are remarkably well-preserved originals. The interior was initially stark (no pews) and dark—lit not by windows (which were added much later), but by candles laid on the floor in the shape of a cross. Look-

ing straight ahead, you see a cross with Mary on the left (where the women stood) and John the Baptist on the right (with the men). When they finally added seating, they kept things segregated: Notice the pews carved with hearts for women, crowns for men.

When a 17th-century wealthy family wanted to build a special pew for themselves, they simply sawed off some of the pineconetopped columns to make way for it. When the church began to lean, it was reinforced with the clumsy, off-center X-shaped supports. Churchgoers learned their lesson, and never cut anything again.

The ceiling, added in the late 17th century, prevents visitors from enjoying the Viking-ship roof beams. But all of these additions have stories to tell. Experts can read various cultural influences into the church decorations, including Irish (some of the carvings) and Romanesque (the rounded arches).

Bring a Bike? To give your Lustrafjord excursion an added dimension, take a bike on the ferry to Urnes (free passage, rentable for 300 NOK/day with helmets from Eplet Bed & Apple hostel in Solvorn, where you can park your car for free). From the stave church, bike the super-scenic fjordside road nine miles—with almost no traffic—to the big Feigumfossen waterfall, and back.

Sleeping on the Lustrafjord

These accommodations are along the Lustrafjord, listed from north to south.

IN NES

$$ Nes Gard Farmhouse B&B rents 15 homey rooms, offering lots of comfort in a grand 19th-century farmhouse (includes breakfast, three-course dinner extra, discount for staying multiple days, rooms in main building more traditional, family apartment, bike rental, mobile +47 95 23 26 94, www.nesgard.no, post@nesgard. no, Månum family—Mari and Asbjørn).

¢ **Viki Fjord Camping** has great fjordside huts—many directly on the water, with views and balconies—located directly across from the Feigumfossen waterfall (no breakfast, sheets extra, +47 57 68 64 20, mobile +47 99 53 97 30, www.vikicamping.no, post@ vikicamping.no, Berit and Svein).

IN SOLVORN

For more on this delightful little fjordside town—my favorite home base on the Lustrafjord—see the description earlier in this chapter. While it lacks the handy boat connections of Flåm, Aurland, or Balestrand, that's part of Solvorn's charm.

$$$$ Walaker Hotel, a former inn and coach station, has

been run by the Walaker family since 1690 (that's a lot of pressure on ninth-generation owner Ole Henrik). The hotel, set right on the Lustrafjord (with a garden perfect for relaxing and, if necessary, even convalescing), is open May through September. In the main house, the halls and living rooms are filled with tradition. Notice the patriotic hymns on the piano. The 22 rooms are divided into two types: nicely appointed standard rooms in the modern annex; or recently renovated "historic" rooms with all the modern conveniences in two different old buildings: rooms with Old World elegance in the main house, and brightly painted rooms with countryside charm in the Tingstova house next door (sea kayak rentals, +47 57 68 20 80, www.walaker.com, hotel@walaker.com). They serve excellent four-course dinners (625 NOK plus drinks, nightly at 19:30, savor your dessert with fjordside setting on the balcony). Their impressive gallery of Norwegian art is in a restored, historic farmhouse out back (free for guests; Ole Henrik leads one-hour tours of the collection, peppered with some family history, nightly after dinner).

¢ **Eplet Bed & Apple** is my kind of hostel: innovative and friendly. It's creatively run by Trond and Agnethe, whose entrepreneurial spirit and positive attitude attract enjoyable guests. With welcoming public spaces and 22 beds in seven rooms (all with views, some with decks), this place is worth considering even if you don't normally sleep at hostels (open mid-April-Sept only, private rooms, no breakfast, no elevator, pay laundry, kitchen, +47 41 64 94 69, www.eplet.net, post@eplet.net). It's about 300 yards uphill from the boat dock—look for the white house with a giant red apple painted on it. It's surrounded by a raspberry-and-apple farm (they make and sell tasty juices from both). The hostel provides free loaner bikes for guests and rents them to nonguests for 300 NOK/day (helmets available).

Eating in Solvorn: The **$$$ Linahagen Kafé,** next door to Walaker Hotel, serves good meals (June-Aug Mon-Fri 12:00-18:00, Sat until 16:00, Sun 13:00-18:00, closed Sept-May, run by Tordis and her family).

IN SOGNDAL

Sogndal is the only sizeable town in this region. While it lacks the charm of Solvorn and Balestrand, it's big enough to have a busy shopping street and a helpful **TI** (daily 9:30-23:00, inside the MIX minimart at Parkvegen 5, mobile +47 41 78 13 00).

¢ **Sogndal Youth Hostel** rents good, cheap beds (private

rooms, June-mid-Aug only, closed 10:00-17:00, near the bridge at Helgheimsvegen 9, +47 57 62 75 75, www.hihostels.no/sogndal, sogndal@hihostels.no).

Lustrafjord Connections

Sogndal is the transit hub for the Lustrafjord region.

FROM SOGNDAL BY BUS

Buses go to **Lom** over the Sognefjell pass (2/day late June-Aug only, road closed off-season, 3.5 hours, likely 1/day off-season, goes around the pass, 5 hours, change in Skei), **Solvorn** (3/day, fewer Sat-Sun, 30 minutes), **Balestrand** (5/day Mon-Fri, 3/day Sat-Sun, 2 hours, includes ride on Hella-Dragsvik ferry), **Nigard Glacier** (Glacier Bus runs 2/day mid-June-Aug only, see listing earlier for times). Most buses run less (or not at all) on weekends—check the latest at https://entur.no.

BY BOAT

Car ferry reservations are generally not necessary except for the boat to Gudvangen, and on many short rides, aren't even possible (confirm schedules at https://entur.no). From near Sogndal, various boats fan out to towns around the Sognefjord. Most leave from two towns at the southern end of the Lustrafjord: **Kaupanger** (a 15-minute drive from Sogndal) and **Mannheller** (a 5-minute drive beyond Kaupanger, 20 minutes from Sogndal).

From Kaupanger: While Kaupanger is little more than a ferry landing, the small stave-type church at the edge of town merits a look. Boats go from Kaupanger all the way down the gorgeous Nærøyfjord to **Gudvangen,** which is on the Norway in a Nutshell route (where you catch the bus to Voss). Taking this leisurely boat allows you to see the best part of the Nutshell fjord scenery (the Nærøyfjord), but misses the other half of that cruise (Aurlandsfjord). From June through August, boats leave Kaupanger daily at 9:00 and 15:00 (July-mid-Aug also at 12:00 and 18:00) for the nearly 3-hour trip; check in 15 minutes before departure (car and driver-830 NOK, adult passenger-395 NOK; reserve at least one day in advance—or longer in July-Aug; +47 57 63 14 00, www.visitflam.com—follow links to "Fjord Cruise Sognefjord"). Prices are high because this route is mainly taken by tourists, not locals. Verify schedules and prices online. Boats also connect Kaupanger to **Lærdal,** but the crossing from Mannheller to Fodnes is easier (described next).

From Mannheller: Ferries frequently make the speedy 15-minute crossing to **Fodnes** (91 NOK for a car and driver, 3/hour, no reservations possible). From Fodnes, drive through the

five-mile-long tunnel to Lærdal and the main E-16 highway (near Borgund Stave Church, the long tunnel to Aurland, and the scenic overland "Snow Road" to the Stegastein fjord viewpoint—all described in the previous chapter).

To Balestrand: To reach Balestrand from the Lustrafjord, you'll take a short ferry trip (Hella-Dragsvik). For information on the car ferries to and from Balestrand, see "Balestrand Connections," earlier.

Scenic Drives from the Sognefjord

If you'll be doing a lot of driving, buy a good local map. The 1:335,000-scale *Sør-Norge nord* map by Cappelens Kart is excellent (available at local TIs and bookstores). If you are following our recommended three-week itinerary, use these directions to connect the Lustrafjord and Bergen.

▲▲From the Lustrafjord to Aurland

The drive to the pleasant fjordside town of Aurland (see previous chapter) takes you either through the world's longest car tunnel, or over an incredible mountain pass. If you aren't going as far as Lom and Jotunheimen, consider taking the pass, as the scenery here rivals the famous Sognefjell pass drive.

From Sogndal, drive 20 minutes to the Mannheller-Fodnes ferry (described earlier, under "Lustrafjord Connections"), float across the Sognefjord, then drive from Fodnes to Lærdal. From Lærdal, you have two options to Aurland: The speedy route is on E-16 through the 15-mile-long **tunnel** from Lærdal, or the Aurlandsvegen **"Snow Road"** over the pass.

The tunnel is free, and impressively nonchalant—it's signed as if it were just another of Norway's countless tunnels. But driving it is a bizarre experience: A few miles in, as you find yourself trying not to be hypnotized by the monotony, it suddenly dawns on you what it means to be driving under a mountain for 15 miles. To keep people awake, three rest chambers, each illuminated by a differently colored light, break up the drive visually. Stop and get out—if no cars are coming, test the acoustics from the center.

The second, immeasurably more scenic route is a breathtaking one-hour, 30-mile drive that winds over a pass into Aurland, cresting at over 4,000 feet and offering classic aerial fjord views (it's worth the messy pants). From the Mannheller-Fodnes ferry, take the first road to the right (to Erdal), then leave E-68 at Erdal (just west of Lærdal) for the Aurlandsvegen. This road, while well-maintained, is open only in summer, and narrow and dangerous during snowstorms (which can hit with a moment's notice, even in warm weather). Even in good weather, parts of the road can be a white-knuckle adventure, especially when meeting oncoming vehicles on the tiny, exposed hairpin turns. You'll enjoy vast and terrifying views of lakes, snowfields, and remote mountain huts and farmsteads on what feels like the top of Norway. As you begin the 12-hairpin zigzag descent to Aurland, you'll reach the sideways 7-shaped **Stegastein viewpoint**—well worth a stop. The "Snow Road" and viewpoint are both described on page 115.

▲From the Lustrafjord to Bergen, via Nærøyfjord and Gudvangen

Car ferries take tourists between Kaupanger and the Nutshell town of Gudvangen through an arm and elbow of the Sognefjord, including the staggering Nærøyfjord (for details on the ferry, see "Lustrafjord Connections," earlier). From Gudvangen, it's a 90-mile drive to Bergen via Voss (figure about one hour to Voss, then about an hour and a half into Bergen). This follows essentially the same route as the Norway in a Nutshell (Gudvangen-Voss bus, Voss-Bergen train) route. For additional commentary on the journey, see page 108.

Get off the ferry in Gudvangen and drive up the Nærøy valley past a river. You'll see the two giant falls and then go uphill through a tunnel. After the tunnel, look for a sign marked *Stalheim* and turn right. Stop for a break at the touristy Stalheim Hotel to enjoy the fabulous view down the valley. Then follow signs marked *Stalheimskleiva*. This incredible road doggedly worms its way downhill back into the depths of the valley. My brakes started overheating in a few minutes. Take it easy. As you wind down, you can view the falls from several turnouts.

The road rejoins E-16. You retrace your route through the tunnel and then continue into a mellower beauty, past lakes and farms, toward Voss. Just before you reach Voss itself, watch the right side of the road for Tvindefossen, a terraced waterfall with a handy campground/WC/kiosk picnic area that's worth a stop. Highway E-16 takes you through Voss and into Bergen. If you plan to visit Edvard Grieg's Home and the nearby Fantoft Stave Church, now is the ideal time, since you'll be driving near them—and they're

a headache to reach from downtown. Both are worth a detour if you're not rushed (see the Bergen chapter).

▲▲From Balestrand to Bergen, via Vik

If you're based in Balestrand and driving to Bergen, you have two options: Take the Dragsvik-Hella ferry, drive an hour to Kaupanger (via Sogndal), and drive the route just described; or, take the following slower, twistier, more remote, and more scenic route, with a stop at the beautiful Hopperstad Stave Church. This route is slightly longer, with more time on mountain roads and less time on the boat. Take the Hella-Vangsnes ferry, then figure 15 minutes from Vangsnes to Vik, then about 1.5 hours to Voss, then another 1.5 hours into Bergen.

From Vangsnes, head into Vik on the main highway 13. In Vik, follow signs from the main road to Hopperstad Stave Church (described earlier in this chapter). Then backtrack to highway 13 and follow it south, to Voss. You'll soon begin a series of switchbacks that wind you up and out of the valley. The best views are from the Storesvingen Fjellstove restaurant (on the left). Soon after, you'll crest the ridge, go through a tunnel, and find yourself on top of the world, in a desolate and harshly scenic landscape of scrubby mountaintops, snowbanks, lakes, and no trees, scattered with vacation cabins. After cruising atop the plateau for a while, the road twists its way down (next to a waterfall) into a very steep valley, which it meanders through the rest of the way to Voss. This is an hour-long, middle-of-nowhere journey, with few road signs—you might feel lost, but keep driving toward Voss. When highway 13 dead-ends into E-16, turn right (toward Voss and Bergen) and re-enter civilization. From here, the route follows the same roads as in the Lustrafjord-Bergen drive described earlier (including the Tvindefossen waterfall).

GUDBRANDSDAL VALLEY & JOTUNHEIMEN MOUNTAINS

Lillehammer • Lom • Drive and Hikes

Norway in a Nutshell is a great day trip (see earlier chapter), but with more time and a car, consider a scenic meander from Oslo to Bergen. You'll arc up the Gudbrandsdal Valley and over the Jotunheimen Mountains, then travel along the Lustrafjord.

After an introductory stop in Lillehammer, with its fine folk museum, you might spend the night in a log and sod farmstead-turned-hotel, tucked in a quiet valley under Norway's highest peaks. Next, Norway's highest pass takes you on an exhilarating roller-coaster ride through the heart of the myth-inspiring Jotunheimen, bristling with Norway's biggest mountains. Then the road hairpins down into Sognefjord country (covered in the previous chapter).

PLANNING YOUR TIME

While you could spend five or six days here, with two days you can cover a good slice of the region. By car, I'd spend them like this:

Day 1: Leave Oslo early, and spend midday at Lillehammer's Maihaugen open-air folk museum for a tour and picnic. Drive up the Gudbrandsdal Valley, stopping at the stave church in Lom. Stay overnight in the Jotunheimen countryside.

Day 2: Drive the Sognefjell road over the mountains, then down along the Lustrafjord, stopping to visit the

Gudbrandsdal Valley & Jotunheimen Mountains

- ① Røisheim Hotel
- ② Elvesæter Hotel
- ③ Bøverdalen Youth Hostel
- ④ Strind Gard
- ⑤ Besseggen Trailhead
- ⑥ Spiterstulen Lodge & Trailhead
- ⑦ Juvasshytta Lodge & Trailhead
- ⑧ Leirvassbu Lodge & Trailhead

Dale Church and the Nigard Glacier (see previous chapter). End your day with an overnight in your choice of fjord towns, such as Solvorn, Balestrand, or Aurland (all described in previous chapters).

This plan can be condensed into one day if you skip the Nigard Glacier side trip.

The Gudbrandsdal Valley

The Gudbrandsdal Valley is the tradition-steeped country of Peer Gynt, the Norwegian Huck Finn. This romantic valley of time-worn hills, log cabins, and velvet farms has connected northern and southern Norway since ancient times. While not as striking as other parts of the Norwegian countryside, Gudbrandsdal offers

a suitable first taste of the natural wonders that crescendo farther north and west (in Jotunheimen and the Sognefjord). Throughout this region, the government subsidizes small farms to keep the countryside populated and healthy.

Lillehammer

The de facto capital of the Gudbrandsdal Valley, Lillehammer is a pleasant winter and summer resort town of 27,000. It's best known for its brush with Olympic greatness as the host of the 1994 Winter Olympics.

Orientation to Lillehammer

Today Lillehammer is largely a jumping-off point for Gudbrands-dal Valley adventures, and it's the logical place to break up the long drive between Oslo and the Jotunheimen region. If you do have time to spare here, spend it at the excellent Maihaugen open-air folk museum. The town itself has happy, old woody pedestrian zones (Gagata and Storgata) to stroll.

Tourist Information: Lillehammer's TI is inside the train station (Mon-Fri 8:00-18:00, Sat-Sun 10:00-16:00; shorter hours and closed Sun off-season; Jernbanetorget 2, +47 61 28 98 00, www.lillehammer.com).

Sights in Lillehammer

Lillehammer's two most worthwhile sights, Maihaugen and the Olympics Museum, are up the hill behind the center of town. From the train station, it's a fairly steep 15-minute walk to either sight, and the route is not well signed. To avoid this walk, consider catching the bus from in front of the train station (bus #002, #004, or #005 to Olympics Museum, 2/hour; bus #007 to Maihaugen, 1/ hour; 37 NOK one-way for either bus). At the top, it's a 10-minute, mostly level walk between the two sights (follow the busy main road that connects them).

▲▲Maihaugen Open-Air Folk Museum (Maihaugen Friluftsmuseet)

This idyllic park, full of old farmhouses and pickled slices of folk culture, provides a good introduction to what you'll see as you drive

through the Gudbrandsdal Valley. Anders Sandvig, a local dentist, started the collection in 1887 (he originally displayed artifacts in his waiting room). You'll divide your time between the fine indoor museum at the entrance and the sprawling exterior exhibits.

Upon arrival, ask about special events, crafts, or musical performances. A monitor shows what's going on in the park. Summer is busy with crafts in action and people re-enacting life in the past, à la Colonial Williamsburg. There are no tours, so it's up to you to initiate conversations with the "residents." Off-season it's pretty dead, with no live crafts and most buildings locked up.

Cost and Hours: 175 NOK in summer, 135 NOK off-season; discount when combined with Olympics Museum; daily 10:00-17:00; Sept-May Tue-Sun 11:00-16:00, closed Mon; paid parking, scant English descriptions—consider purchasing the English guidebook; +47 61 28 89 00, www.maihaugen.no.

Visiting the Museum: The outdoor section, with 200 buildings from the Gudbrandsdal region, is divided into three areas: the Rural Collection, with old sod-roof log houses and a stave church; the Town Collection, with reconstructed bits of old-time Lillehammer; and the Residential Area, with 20th-century houses that look like most homes in today's Norway. The time trip can be jarring: In the 1980s house, a bubble-gum-chewing girl enthuses about her new "wireless" TV remote and plays ABBA tunes from a cassette-tape player.

The museum's excellent "We Won the Land" exhibit (at the entry) sweeps you through Norwegian history from the Ice Age to the Space Age. The Gudbrandsdal art section shows village life at its best. And you can walk through Dr. Sandvig's old dental office and the original shops of various crafts- and tradespeople.

Though the museum welcomes picnickers and has a simple cafeteria, Lillehammer's town center (a 15-minute walk below the museum) has lots of fun eateries and is better for lunch.

Norwegian Olympics Museum (Norges Olympiske Museum)

This cute museum is housed in the huge Olympic ice-hockey arena, Håkon Hall. With brief English explanations, an emphasis on Norwegians and Swedes, and an endearingly gung-ho Olympic spirit, it's worth a visit on a rainy day or for sports fans. The ground-floor exhibit traces the ancient history of the Olympics, then devotes one wall panel to each of the summer and winter Olympiads

of the modern era (with special treatment for the 1952 Oslo games). Upstairs, walk the entire concourse, circling the arena seating while reviewing the highlights (and lowlights) of the 1994 games (remember Tonya Harding?). While you're up there, check out the gallery of great Norwegian athletes and the giant egg used in the Lillehammer opening ceremony.

Cost and Hours: 135 NOK, discount when combined with Maihaugen; daily 10:00-17:00; Sept-May Tue-Sun 11:00-16:00, closed Mon; +47 61 28 89 00, https://eng.ol.museum.no.

Nearby: On the hillside above Håkon Hall (a 30-minute hike or quick drive) are two ski jumps that host more Olympics sights, including a ski lift, the ski jump tower, and a bobsled ride (www.olympiaparken.no). In the summer, ski jumpers practice on the jumps, which are sprayed with water.

Sleeping and Eating in the Gudbrandsdal Valley

I prefer sleeping in the more scenic and Norwegian-feeling Jotunheimen area (described later). But if you're sleeping here, Lillehammer and the surrounding valley offer several good options. My choices for Lillehammer are near the train station; the accommodations in Kvam provide a convenient stopping point in the valley.

IN LILLEHAMMER

Sleeping: True to its name, **$$ Mølla Hotell** is situated in an old mill along the little stream running through Lillehammer. The 58 rooms blend Old World charm with modern touches. It's more cutesy-cozy and less businesslike than other Lillehammer hotels in this price range (elevator, a block below Gågata at Elvegata 12, +47 61 05 70 80, www.mollahotell.no, post@mollahotell.no).

$$ First Hotel Breiseth is a business-class hotel with 89 rooms in a handy location directly across from the train station (free parking, Jernbanegaten 1, +47 61 24 77 77, www.firsthotels.no/breiseth, breiseth@firsthotels.no).

¢ Vandrerhjem Stasjonen, Lillehammer's youth hostel, is upstairs inside the train station. With 100 beds in 33 institutional but new-feeling rooms—including 21 almost hotel-like doubles—it's a winner (elevator, Jernbanetorget 2, +47 61 26 00 24, www.stasjonen.no, lillehammer@hihostels.no).

Eating: Good restaurants are scattered around the city center, but for the widest selection, head to where the main pedestrian drag (Gågata) crosses the little stream running downhill through town. Poke a block or two up and down **Elvegata,** which stretches along the river and hosts a wide range of tempting eateries—from pubs (both rowdy and upscale) to pizza and cheap sandwich stands.

IN KVAM

Gudbrandsdal is a popular vacation valley for Norwegians, and you'll find loads of reasonable small hotels and campgrounds with huts for those who aren't quite campers (*hytter* means "cottages" or "cabins," *rom* is "private room," and *ledig* means "vacancy"). These huts normally cost about 400-600 NOK, depending on size and amenities, and can hold from four to six people. Although they are simple, you'll have a kitchenette and access to a good WC and shower. When available, sheets rent for around 60 NOK per person. Here are a couple of listings in the town of Kvam, located midway between Lillehammer and Lom.

$$ Vertshuset Sinclair has a quirky Scottish-Norwegian ambience. The 15 fine rooms are in old-fashioned motel wings. The motel was named after a Scotsman who led a band of adventurers into this valley, attempting to set up their own Scottish kingdom. They failed. All were kilt (family deals, +47 61 29 54 50, www.vertshuset-sinclair.no, post@vertshuset-sinclair.no). The motel's **$$ cafeteria,** in the main building, is handy for a quick and filling bite on the road between Lillehammer and Lom (long hours daily).

¢ Kirketeigen Ungdomssenter ("Church Youth Center"), behind the town church, welcomes travelers year-round. They have camping spots, small cabins without water, cabins with kitchen and bath, plus simple four-bed rooms in the main building (sheets and blankets extra, +47 61 21 60 90, www.kirketeigen.com, post@kirketeigen.no).

Jotunheimen Mountains

Norway's Jotunheimen ("Giants' Home") Mountains feature the country's highest peaks and some of its best hikes and drives. This national park stretches from the fjords to the glaciers. You can play roller-coaster with mountain passes, take rugged hikes, wind up scenic toll roads, get up close to a giant stave church...and sleep in a time-passed rural valley. The gateway to the mountains is the unassuming town of Lom.

Lom

Pleasant Lom—the main town between Lillehammer and Sogndal—feels like a modern ski resort village. It's home to one of Norway's most impressive stave churches. While Lom has little else to offer, the church causes the closest thing to a tour-bus traffic jam this neck of the Norwegian woods will ever see.

Orientation to Lom

Park by the stave church—you'll see its dark spire just over the bridge. The church shares a parking lot with a gift shop/church museum and some public WCs. Across the street, the sod-roofed building houses the Norwegian Mountain Museum, and over the river is the TI and Co-op Mega grocery store. If you're heading over the mountains, Lom's bank (at the Kommune building) has the last ATM before Gaupne.

Tourist Information: Lom's TI, a good source of information for hikes and drives in the Jotunheimen Mountains, is near the roundabout (Mon-Sat 9:00-21:00, Sun 10:00-18:00, +47 61 21 29 90, www.visitjotunheimen.no, info@visitjotunheimen.no).

Sights in Lom

▲▲Lom Stave Church (Lom Stavkyrkje)

Despite extensive renovations, Lom's church (from 1158) remains a striking example of a Nordic stave church. For more on these distinctive medieval church-es, see page 116.

Cost and Hours: Church—90 NOK, daily 9:00-19:00 (until 17:00 last half of Aug), mid-May-mid-June and Sept 10:00-16:00, closed in winter and for funerals; museum—10 NOK, same summer hours as church, shorter hours off-season, closed Sun in winter; +47 40 43 84 86, www.lomstavechurch.no.

Tours: Try to tag along with a guided tour of the church—or, if it's not too busy, a docent can give you a quick private tour (included in ticket). Even outside of opening times—including winter—small groups can arrange a tour (60 NOK/person, 600-NOK minimum, call +47 97 07 53 97 in summer or +48 16 55 27 00 in winter).

Visiting the Church: Buy your ticket and go inside to take in the humble **interior** (still used by locals for services—notice the posted hymnal numbers). Men sat on the right, women on the left, and prisoners sat with the sheriff in the caged area in the rear. Standing in the middle of the nave, look overhead to see the earliest surviving parts of the church, such as the circle of X-shaped St. Andrew crosses and the Romanesque arches above them. High above the door (impossible to see without a flashlight—ask a docent to show you) is an old painting of a dragon- or lion-like

creature—likely an old Viking symbol, possibly drawn here to smooth the forced conversion local pagans made to Christianity. When King Olav II (later to become St. Olav) swept through this valley in 1021, he gave locals an option: convert or be burned out of house and home.

On the white town flag, notice the spoon—a symbol of Lom. Because of its position nestled in the mountains, Lom gets less rainfall than other towns, so large spoons were traditionally used to spread water over the fields. The apse (behind the altar) was added in 1240, when trendy new Gothic cathedrals made an apse a must-have accessory for churches across Europe. Lepers came to the grilled window in the apse for a blessing. When the Reformation hit in 1536, the old paintings were whitewashed over. The church has changed over the years: Transepts, pews, and windows were added in the 17th century. And the circa-1720 paintings were done by a local priest's son.

Drop into the **gift shop/church museum** in the big black building in the parking lot. Its one-room exhibit celebrates 1,000 years of the stave church—interesting if you follow the loaner English descriptions. Inside you'll find a pair of beautiful model churches, headstones and other artifacts, and the only surviving stave-church dragon-head "steeple." In the display case near the early 1900s organ, find the little pencil-size stick carved with runes, dating from around 1350. It's actually a love letter from a would-be suitor. The woman rejected him, but she saved them both from embarrassment by hiding the stick under the church floorboards beneath a pew...where it was found in 1973. (Docents inside the church like to show off a replica of this stick.)

Before or after your church visit, explore the tidy, thought-provoking **graveyard** surrounding the church. Also, check out the precarious-looking little footbridge over the waterfall (the best view is from the modern road bridge into town).

Norwegian Mountain Museum (Norsk Fjellmuseum)

This worthwhile museum traces the history of the people who have lived off the land in the Jotunheimen Mountains from the Stone Age to today (and also serves as a national park office). It is one of the better museums in fjord country, with well-presented displays and plenty of actual artifacts. The exhibit, "Spellbound" (Bergtatt), explores prehistoric human and animal migrations in the surrounding mountains based on recent archaeological finds, including a 1,300-year-old ski and a 3,400-year-old shoe made of reindeer hide.

Cost and Hours: 120 NOK; daily 9:00-16:00, July-mid-Aug until 19:00, generally closed off-season; in the sod-roofed building

across the road from the Lom Stave Church parking lot, +47 61 21 16 00, http://fjell.museum.no.

Sleeping near Lom

Lom itself has a handful of hotels, but the most appealing way to overnight in this area is at a rural rest stop in the countryside. All of these are on highway 55 south of Lom, toward Sognefjord—first is Strind Gard, then Bøverdalen, Røisheim, and finally Elvesæter (all within 20 minutes of Lom).

$$$$ Røisheim, in a marvelously remote mountain setting, is an extremely expensive storybook hotel composed of a cluster of

centuries-old, sod-roofed log farmhouses. Its posh and generous living rooms are filled with antiques. Each of the 20 rooms (in 14 buildings) is rustic but elegant, with fun "barrel bathtubs" and four-poster or canopy beds. Some rooms are in old, wooden farm buildings—*stabburs*—with low ceilings and heavy beams. The deluxe rooms are larger, with king beds and fireplaces. Call ahead so they'll be prepared for your arrival (open May-Sept; packed lunch, and an over-the-top four-course traditional dinner served at 19:30; 10 miles south of Lom on highway 55, +47 61 21 20 31, www.roisheim.no, booking@roisheim.no).

$$ Elvesæter Hotel has its own share of Old World romance, but is bigger, cheaper, and more modest. Delightful public spaces bunny-hop through its traditional shell, while its 200 beds sprawl through nine buildings. The Elvesæter family has done a great job of retaining the historic character of their medieval farm, even though the place is big enough to handle large tour groups. The renovated "superior" rooms are new-feeling, but have sterile modern furniture; the older, cheaper "standard" rooms are well-worn but more characteristic (open May-Sept, family rooms, good three-course dinners, swimming pool, farther up highway 55, just past Bøverdal, +47 61 21 12 10, www.topofnorway.no, elveseter@topofnorway.no). Even if you're not staying here, stop by to wander through the public spaces and pick up a flier explaining the towering Sagasøyla (Saga Column) that stands on the grounds. It was started in 1926 to celebrate the Norwegian constitution, and was to stand in front of Oslo's parliament building—but the project stalled after World War II (thanks to the artist's affinity for things

German and membership in Norway's fascist party). It was eventually finished and erected here in 1992.

¢ **Bøverdalen Youth Hostel** offers cheap but comfortable beds and a far more rugged clientele—real hikers rather than car hikers. While a bit institutional, it's well priced and well run (open late May-Sept, sheets extra, breakfast extra, hot meals, self-serve café, +47 61 21 20 64, www.hihostels.no, boverdalen@hihostels.no, Anna Berit). It's in the center of the little community of Bøverdal (store, campground, and toll road up to Galdhøpiggen area).

¢ **Strind Gard** is your very rustic option if you can't spring for Røisheim or Elvesæter, but still want the countryside-farm experience. This 150-year-old farmhouse, situated by a soothing waterfall, rents two rooms and one apartment, plus four sod-roofed log huts. The catch: Many of the buildings have no running water, so you'll use the shared facilities at the main building. While not everyone's cup of tea, this place will appeal to romantics who always wanted to sleep in a humble log cabin in the Norwegian mountains—it's downright idyllic for those who like to rough it (sheets and towels extra, no breakfast, low ceilings, farm smells, valley views, 2 miles south of Lom on highway 55, +47 61 21 12 37, www.strind-gard.no, post@strind-gard.no, Anne Jorunn and Trond Dalsegg).

Drives and Hikes in the Jotunheimen Mountains

Highway 55, which runs between Lom and the Sognefjord to the south, is the sightseeing spine of this region. From this main (and already scenic) drag, other roads spin upward into the mountains—offering even better views and exciting drives and hikes. Many of these get you up close to Norway's highest mountain, Galdhøpiggen (8,100 feet). I've listed these attractions from north to south, as you'll reach them driving from Lom to the Sognefjord; except for the first, they all branch off from highway 55. Another great high-mountain experience nearby—the hike to the Nigard Glacier near Lustrafjord—is covered in the previous chapter.

Remember that the Norwegian Mountain Museum in Lom acts as a national park office, offering excellent maps and advice for drivers and hikers—a stop here is obligatory if you're planning a jaunt into the mountains.

Besseggen Trail

This trail offers an incredible opportunity to walk between two lakes separated by a narrow ridge and a 1,000-foot cliff. It's one of Norway's most beloved hikes, which can make it crowded in the summer. To get to the trailhead, drivers detour down highway 51 after Otta south to Maurvangen. Turn right to Gjendesheim to park your car. From Gjendesheim, catch the boat to Memurubu, where the path starts at the boat dock. Hike along the ridge—with a blue lake (Bessvatnet) on one side and a green lake (Gjende) on the other—and keep your balance. The nine-mile trail loops back to Gjendesheim; plan on a seven- to eight-hour hike. Because the boat runs sporadically, time your visit to catch one (150 NOK for 20-minute ride, 3 morning departures daily, check schedules at www.gjende.no, mobile +47 91 30 67 44). This is a thrilling but potentially hazardous hike, and it's a major detour: Gjendesheim is about 1.5 hours and 50 miles from Lom.

Spiterstulen Drive and Hikes

From Røisheim, an 11-mile toll road (80 NOK) takes you from highway 55 to the Spiterstulen mountain hotel/lodge (3,600 feet) in about 30 minutes. This is the best destination for serious all-day hikes to Norway's two mightiest mountains, Glittertinden and Galdhøpiggen (a 5-hour hike up and a 3-hour hike down, doable without a guide). Or consider a guided, two-hour glacier walk (+47 61 21 94 00, www.spiterstulen.no).

Juvasshytta Drive and Glacier Hike

From Bøverdal, a private toll road (85 NOK) takes you in about 40 minutes to Juvasshytta lodge, the highest (6,040 feet) and closest you can get to Galdhøpiggen by car. From the lodge, guided, six-hour hikes go across the glacier to the summit and back (350 NOK, June-late Sept daily at 10:00, July also daily at 11:30, check in 30 minutes before, strict age limit—no kids under age 7, 4 miles each way, easy ascent but can be dangerous without a guide, hiking boots required—possible to rent from nearby ski resort). You can sleep in the updated **$$** lodge (includes breakfast, dinner optional, open June-Sept, +47 61 21 15 50, www.juvasshytta.no).

Leirvassbu Drive and Hikes

South of Elvesæter (from Bøverkinnhalsen), a scenic 11-mile toll road (50 NOK) takes you in about 30 minutes to the Leirvassbu mountain lodge at 4,600 feet, with great views and easy walks. A more serious six-mile round-trip hike goes to the lone peak, Kyrkja ("The Church", 6,600 feet), whose spire looms like a sanded-down Matterhorn on the horizon (allow 5 hours).

▲▲Sognefjell Drive to the Sognefjord

Norway's highest pass (at 4,600 feet, the highest road in northern Europe) is a thrilling drive through a cancan line of mountains,

from Jotunheimen's Bøverdal Valley to the Lustrafjord (an arm of the Sognefjord). Centuries ago, the farmers of Gudbrands-dal took their horse caravans over this difficult mountain pass on treks to Bergen. Today, the road (highway 55) is still nar-row, windy, and wild (and usu-ally closed mid-Oct-May).

As you begin to ascend just beyond Elvesæter, notice the view-point on the left for the Leirdalen Valley—capped at the end with the Kyrkja peak (described earlier). Next you'll twist up into a lake-filled valley, then through a mild canyon with grand waterfalls. Before long, as you corkscrew up more switchbacks, you're above the tree line, enjoying a "top of the world" feeling. The best views (to the south) are of the cut-glass range called Hurrungane ("Noisy Children"). The 10 hairpin turns between Turtagrø and Fortun are exciting. Be sure to stop, get out, look around, and enjoy the lavish views. Treat each turn as if it were your last.

Just before you descend to the fjord, the terrain changes, and you reach a pullout on the right, next to a hilltop viewpoint—offering your first glimpse of the fjord. The Lustrafjord village of Skjolden is just around the bend (and down several more switch-backs). Entering Skjolden, continue following highway 55, which now traces the west bank of the Lustrafjord. For more on the sights from here on out, turn to page 140.

Gudbrandsdal and Jotunheimen Connections

BY TRAIN AND BUS

Cars are better, but if you're without wheels, here are your options: Trains run from **Oslo to Lillehammer** (almost hourly, 2.25 hours, just 1.75 hours from Oslo airport) and from **Lillehammer to Otta** (5/day, 1.5 hours). Buses meet some trains (confirm schedule at the train station in Oslo) for travelers heading from **Otta to Lom** (1-2/day, 1 hour) and onward from **Lom to Sogndal** (1-2/day late June-Aug only, road closed off-season, 3.5 hours).

ROUTE TIPS FOR DRIVERS

Use low gears and lots of patience both up (to keep the engine cool) and down (to save your brakes). Uphill traffic gets the right-of-

way, but drivers, up or down, dive for the nearest fat part of the road whenever they meet. Ask backseat drivers not to scream until you've actually been hit or have left the road.

It's 2.5 hours from Oslo to Lillehammer and 3 hours after that to Lom.

From Oslo to Lillehammer: Wind out of Oslo following signs for *E-6* (not to *Drammen*, but for *Stockholm* and then to *Trondheim*). In a few minutes, you're in the wide-open pastoral countryside of eastern Norway. Norway's Constitution Hall—Eidsvoll Manor—is a five-minute detour off E-6, several miles south of Eidsvoll in Eidsvoll Verk (described on page 71; follow the signs to *Eidsvoll Bygningen*). Then E-6 takes you along Norway's largest lake (Mjøsa), through the town of Hamar, and past more lake scenery into Lillehammer. Signs direct you uphill from downtown Lillehammer to the Maihaugen open-air folk museum.

From Lillehammer to Jotunheimen: From Lillehammer, signs to *E-6/Trondheim* take you north, up the bucolic valley of Gudbrandsdal (en route to Otta and Lom), with fine but unremarkable scenery. Along the way, a pair of toll-road side-trips (Gynt Veien and Peer Gynt Seterveien) loop off the E-6 road. While they sound romantic, they're basically windy, curvy dirt roads over high, desolate heath and scrub-brush plateaus with fine mountain views. They're scenic, but pale in comparison with the Sognefjell road between Lom and the Lustrafjord (described earlier). At Otta, exit for Lom. Halfway to Lom, on the left, look for the long suspension bridge spanning the milky-blue river—a good opportunity to stretch your legs, and a scenic spot to enjoy a picnic.

BERGEN

Bergen is permanently salted with robust cobbles and a rich sea-trading heritage. Norway's capital in the 13th century, Bergen gained wealth and importance thanks to its membership in the heavyweight medieval trading club of merchant cities called the Hanseatic League. Bergen still wears her rich maritime heritage proudly—nowhere more scenically than at the picture-perfect Bryggen district, where colorful wooden warehouses line the harbor.

Protected from the open sea by a lone sheltering island, Bergen is a place of refuge from heavy winds for the giant working boats that serve the North Sea oil rigs. (Much of Norway's current affluence is funded by the oil it drills just offshore.) Bergen is also one of the most popular cruise-ship ports in northern Europe, hosting over 300 ships a year and up to five ships a day in peak season. Each morning is rush hour, as cruisers hike past the imposing Bergenhus fortress and into town.

Bergen gets an average of 80 inches of rain annually (compared to 30 inches in Oslo). A good year has 60 days of sunshine. The natives aren't apologetic about their famously lousy weather. In fact, they seem to wear it as a badge of pride. "Well, that's Bergen," they'll say matter-of-factly as they wring out their raincoats. When I complained about an all-day downpour, one resident cheerfully informed me, "There's no such thing as bad weather—just inappropriate clothing"...a local mantra that rhymes in Norwegian.

With about 280,000 people, Bergen has big-city traffic and high prices, but visitors sticking to the old center find it charming. Enjoy Bergen's salty market, then stroll the easy-on-foot old quarter, with cute lanes of delicate old wooden houses. From downtown

Greater Bergen

Runnhovde
To Knarvik & Brekke
E-39
Breistein
Sørfjorden
To Sognefjord
Aske-vatnet
Byfjorden
EIDSVÅG
Jordals-vatnet
E-39
E-16
To Voss, Myrdal & Oslo
562
Askøy
SANDVIKEN SJØBAD
B
GAMLE BERGEN
NORWEGIAN FISHERIES MUSEUM
Strusshamn
SKOLTEN CRUISE PORT
Bergen
▲Mt. Fløyen
TRAIN STN.
Store Lungegårds-vannet
To Voss, Myrdal & Oslo
Mt. Ulriken
ASKØY BRIDGE
LAKSEVÅG
To Fjell
LODDEFJORD
See detail maps
JEKTEVIKEN/ DOKKEN CRUISE PORT
ULRIKEN643 CABLE CAR
MONTANA HOSTEL
555
540
E-39
585
Paradis T
LANDÅS
Stora-vatnet
FYLLINGS-DALEN
582
FANTOFT STAVE CHURCH
580
Grime-vatnet
Raunafjorden
580
Hop
NESTTUN
TROLDHAUGEN
(EDVARD GRIEG'S HOME)
T
T
Nesttun
FLESLAND
582
580
E-39
1 Kilometer
1 Mile
Bergen Lufthavn
T
Apeltun-vatnet
To Stavanger & Setesdal
Flesland
580
Lagunen
556
To Fana
Kalands-vatnet

BERGEN

Bergen, a funicular zips you up a little mountain for a bird's-eye view of this sailors' town. A short foray into the countryside takes you to a variety of nearby experiences: a dramatic cable-car ride to a mountaintop perch (Ulriken643); an evocative stave church (Fantoft); and the home of Norway's most beloved composer, Edvard Grieg, at Troldhaugen.

PLANNING YOUR TIME

Bergen is worth at least one full day. It can even be enjoyed on the tail end of a day's scenic train ride from Oslo before returning on

the overnight train. But that teasing taste will make you wish you had more time.

Bergen in One Day

For a busy day, you could do this:

9:00   Stroll through the Fish Market and Bryggen shops.

10:00   Take the Bryggen Walking Tour (mid-May–mid-Sept; reserve ahead), then grab lunch. Consider returning to the Bryggens Museum using your tour ticket while you're in the area.

14:00   Visit Håkon's Hall and Rosenkrantz Tower (joining a guided tour).

15:00   Stroll through Torgallmenningen square to the KODE Art Museums to see works by famous Norwegian landscape artists and Edvard Munch.

17:00   Enjoy some free time in town, or catch the bus out to Gamle Bergen.

18:00   Ride up the Fløibanen funicular (buy ticket online to avoid the line).

More Bergen Planning Tips

Although Bergen has plenty of charms of its own, it's most famous as a springboard for fjord country. You have three options: Pick up a rental car here (fjords are a 3-hour drive away); take the express boat down the Sognefjord (about 4 hours to Balestrand, 5.5 hours to Flåm/Aurland); or do "Norway in a Nutshell" as a scenic loop from Bergen. The Nutshell option also works well as a detour midway between Bergen and Oslo (hop the train from either city to Voss or Myrdal, then take a bus or spur train into the best of the Sognefjord; scenic ferry rides depart from there). While there are a million ways to enjoy the fjords, first-timers should start with this region (covered thoroughly in the Norway in a Nutshell and More on the Sognefjord chapters).

Also note that Bergen, a geographic dead-end, is an efficient place to begin or end your Scandinavian travels. Consider flying into Bergen and out of another city, such as Helsinki (or vice versa).

Orientation to Bergen

Bergen clusters around its harbor—nearly everything listed in this chapter is within a few minutes' walk. The busy Torget (the square with the Fish Market) is at the head of the harbor. As you face the sea from here, Bergen's TI is at the left end of the Fish Market. The town's historic Hanseatic Quarter, Bryggen (BRUHY-gun), lines the harbor on the right. Express boats to the Sognefjord (Balestrand and Flåm) dock at the harbor on the left.

Charming cobbled streets surround the harbor and climb the

encircling hills. Bergen's
popular Fløibanen funicu-
lar climbs high above the
city to the top of Mount
Fløyen for the best view
of the town. Surveying
the surrounding islands
and inlets, it's clear why
this city is known as the
"Gateway to the Fjords."

TOURIST INFORMATION

The centrally located TI is upstairs in the long, skinny, modern
Torghallen market building, next to the Fish Market (daily June-
Aug 8:30-22:00, May and Sept 9:00-20:00; Oct-April 9:00-16:00;
handy budget eateries downstairs and in Fish Market; +47 55 55 20
00, www.visitbergen.com).

The TI covers Bergen and western Norway, provides tour info
and tickets, has a fjord info desk, books rooms, will exchange currency, and maintains a handy events board listing today's and to-
morrow's slate of tours, concerts, and other events. Pick up this
year's edition of the free *Bergen Guide* (also likely at your hotel),
which includes a fine map. This booklet can answer most of your
sightseeing questions.

Bergen Card: You have to work hard to make this greedy
little card pay off (280 NOK/24 hours, 360 NOK/48 hours, 430
NOK/72 hours; sold at the TI, the Deli de Luca store at the Bergen
airport, and the Montana Family & Youth Hostel). It gives you free
use of the city's tram and buses, half off the Fløibanen funicular,
and free or discounted admission to many sights. For details on
what's covered, see the TI website.

ARRIVAL IN BERGEN

By Train or Bus: Bergen's train and bus stations are on Strømgat-
en, facing a park-rimmed lake. The small, manageable train station
is open long hours for booking all your travel in Norway, including
Nutshell reservations if available—and you haven't reserved ahead
(Mon-Fri 6:45-19:15, Sat-Sun 7:30-16:00). You'll find the usual
train station amenities, pay baggage lockers (daily 6:00-23:30), and
pay WCs. To get to the bus station, follow the covered walkway
behind the Narvesen newsstand via the Storsenter shopping mall.

Taxis wait to the right (with the tracks at your back); a tram
stop is to your left, just around the corner. From the train station,
it's a 10-minute walk to the TI: Cross the street (Strømgaten) in
front of the station and take Marken, a cobbled street that eventu-

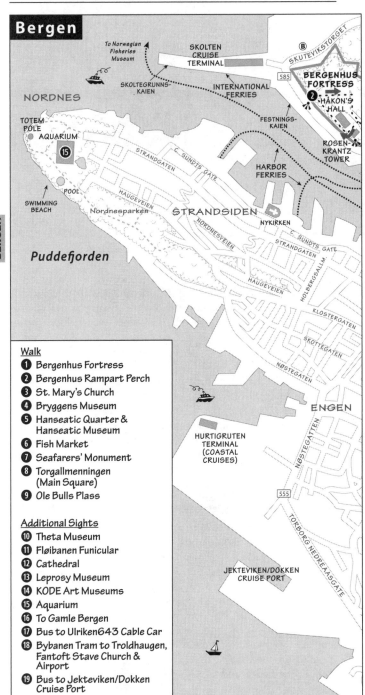

Bergen

To Norwegian Fisheries Museum

SKOLTEN CRUISE TERMINAL

SKOLTEGRUNNS-KAIEN

INTERNATIONAL FERRIES

SKUTEVIKSTORGET

Ⓑ

585

BERGENHUS FORTRESS

❷ HÅKON'S HALL

FESTNINGS-KAIEN

ROSEN-KRANTZ TOWER

NORDNES

TOTEM POLE

AQUARIUM

⑮

STRANDGATEN

C. SUNDTS GATE

HARBOR FERRIES

SWIMMING BEACH

POOL

HAUGEVEIEN

Nordnesparken

STRANDSIDEN

NORDNESVEIEN

NYKIRKEN

C. SUNDTS GATE

STRANDGATEN

HOLBERGSALLM.

HAUGEVEIEN

Puddefjorden

KLOSTERGATEN

SKOTTEGATEN

NØSTEGATEN

ENGEN

HURTIGRUTEN TERMINAL (COASTAL CRUISES)

NØSTEGATTEN

555

TORBORG NEDREAASGATE

JEKTEVIKEN/DOKKEN CRUISE PORT

Walk
❶ Bergenhus Fortress
❷ Bergenhus Rampart Perch
❸ St. Mary's Church
❹ Bryggens Museum
❺ Hanseatic Quarter & Hanseatic Museum
❻ Fish Market
❼ Seafarers' Monument
❽ Torgallmenningen (Main Square)
❾ Ole Bulls Plass

Additional Sights
❿ Theta Museum
⓫ Fløibanen Funicular
⓬ Cathedral
⓭ Leprosy Museum
⓮ KODE Art Museums
⓯ Aquarium
⓰ To Gamle Bergen
⓱ Bus to Ulriken643 Cable Car
⓲ Bybanen Tram to Troldhaugen, Fantoft Stave Church & Airport
⓳ Bus to Jekteviken/Dokken Cruise Port

BERGEN

BERGEN

ally turns into a modern retail street. Continue walking in the same direction until you reach the water.

By Plane: Bergen's sleek and modern Flesland Airport is 12 miles south of the city center (code: BGO, +47 67 03 11 00, www.avinor.no/bergen). The airport **bus** runs between the airport and downtown Bergen, stopping at the Radisson Blu Royal Hotel in Bryggen, the harborfront area near the TI (if you ask), Festplassen (in the modern part of town, near Ole Bulls Plass), and the bus station (about 120 NOK, pay driver, 6/hour at peak times, fewer in slow times, 30-minute ride). **Taxis** take up to four people and cost about 400 NOK for the 20-minute ride (depending on time of day).

The cheapest option is to take the Bybanen **tram** to the end of the line at Byparken (38 NOK, departs every 5-10 minutes, 45-minute trip, schedule at www.skyss.no). This stop—on Kaigaten, between Bergen's little lake and Ole Bulls Plass—is several blocks from most of my recommended hotels. For tram ticket details, see "Getting Around Bergen," later.

By Car: Driving is a headache in Bergen; avoid it if you can. Approaching town on E-16 (from Voss and the Sognefjord area), follow signs for *Sentrum,* which spits you out near the big, modern bus station and parking garage. Parking is difficult and costly—ask your hotelier for tips. Note that Bergen collects a congestion toll on cars entering the city (25 NOK, 51 NOK during rush hour; fee collected via transponder—your car-rental company will bill you).

By Cruise Ship: Bergen is easy for cruise passengers, regardless of which of the city's two ports your ship uses. The **Skolten** cruise terminal is on the main harborfront road, a 15-minute walk from the Fish Market and TI. On the way, you'll pass the Bergenhus fortress—the starting point for my self-guided walk. The **Jekteviken/Dokken** cruise port is farther out, south of the center. A free shuttle bus drops you off along Rasmus Meyers Allé in front of the KODE Art Museums (and near the end of my self-guided walk). For more in-depth cruising information, pick up my *Rick Steves Scandinavian & Northern European Cruise Ports* guidebook.

HELPFUL HINTS

Museum Tours: Many of Bergen's sights are barren and hard to appreciate without a guide. Fortunately, several offer wonderful and intimate guided tours. Make the most of the following sights by taking advantage of their tours: Håkon's Hall and Rosenkrantz Tower, Bryggens Museum, Hanseatic Museum (closed through 2024), Leprosy Museum, Gamle Bergen, and Edvard Grieg's Home.

Crowd Control: In high season, cruise-ship passengers mob the waterfront between 10:00 and 15:00; to avoid the crush, con-

sider visiting an outlying sight during this time, such as Gamle
Bergen or Edvard Grieg's Home.

Laundry: Drop your laundry off at **Hygienisk Vask & Rens** and
pick it up clean the next day (no self-service; Mon-Fri 8:30-
16:30, closed Sat-Sun; Halfdan Kjerulfsgate 8, +47 55 31 77
41).

GETTING AROUND BERGEN

Most in-town sights are no more than a 10-minute walk from the
TI. But buses and trams come in handy for reaching the aquarium,
Norwegian Fisheries Museum, Gamle Bergen, and farther-flung
sights such as the Fantoft Stave Church, Edvard Grieg Museum
at Troldhaugen, and the Ulriken643 cable car. For schedules and a
travel planner, see Skyss.no.

BERGEN

By Bus: City buses cost 60 NOK per ride (pay driver in cash),
or 39 NOK per ride if you buy a single-ride ticket from a machine
or at a convenience store such as Narvesen, 7-Eleven, Rimi, and
Deli de Luca. The best buses for a Bergen joyride are #6 (north
along the coast) and #11 (into the hills).

By Tram: Bergen's Bybanen light-rail line is a convenient way
to visit Edvard Grieg's home and the Fantoft Stave Church, or to
get to Flesland Airport. The tram begins next to Byparken (on Kaigaten, between Bergen's lake and Ole Bulls Plass), then heads to
the train station and continues south, ending at the airport. Buy
your 39-NOK ticket from the machine before boarding (accepts
credit card with PIN or coins). You can also buy single-ride tickets
at convenience stores—you'll get a gray *minikort* pass. Validate the
pass when you board by holding it next to the card reader (watch
how other passengers do it). Ride about 20 minutes to the Paradis
stop for **Fantoft** Stave Church (don't get off at the "Fantoft" stop,
which is farther from the church); continue to the next stop, Hop,
to hike to **Troldhaugen.**

By Ferry: The *Beffen,* a little orange ferry, chugs across the
midpoint of the harbor every half-hour, from a dock near the
Bryggens Museum to one near the Nykirken church (single ride-
65 NOK, day pass-130 NOK, buy tickets onboard or at the dock,
Mon-Fri 7:30-16:00, plus Sat May-Aug 11:00-16:00, none on Sun,
4-minute ride). Other ferries run from the Fish Market to the Norwegian Fisheries Museum and the aquarium (details in those sight
listings, later). All of these "poor man's cruises" offer good harbor
views.

By Taxi: For a local taxi, which can be pricey, call +47 55 99
70 00.

Bergen at a Glance

▲▲▲Bryggen Walking Tour Wonderful 1.5-hour tour of the historic Hanseatic district that covers 900 years of history and includes short visits to the Bryggens Museum, Hanseatic Assembly Rooms, Hanseatic Museum, a medieval wine cellar, plus a walk through Bryggen. **Hours:** Mid-May-mid-Sept daily at 10:00, 11:00, and 12:00. See below.

▲▲Bryggens Museum Featuring early bits of Bergen (1050-1500), found in an archaeological dig. **Hours:** Daily 9:00-16:00; mid-Sept-mid-May 11:00-15:00. See page 184.

▲▲Hanseatic Museum and Schøtstuene Museum highlighting Bryggen's glory days, featuring an old merchant house and a separate building housing assembly rooms—most interesting with a guided tour. **Hours:** Daily 10:00-18:00, May and Sept until 17:00, Oct-April 11:00-15:00. See page 185.

▲▲Fløibanen Funicular Zippy lift to top of Mount Fløyen for super views of Bergen, islands, and fjords, with picnic ops, an eatery, playground, and hiking trails. **Hours:** Daily 7:30-23:00. See page 188.

▲Fish Market Lively market with cheap seafood eateries and free samples. **Hours:** Daily 8:00-23:00; shorter hours Oct-April. See page 181.

▲Bergenhus Fortress: Håkon's Hall and Rosenkrantz Tower Fortress with a 13th-century medieval banquet hall, a climbable tower offering a history exhibit and views, and a worthwhile guided tour. **Hours:** daily 10:00-16:00; mid-Sept-mid-May daily 12:00-15:00. See page 183.

Tours in Bergen

▲▲▲Bryggen Walking Tour

This tour of the historic Hanseatic district is one of Bergen's best activities. Local guides take visitors on a 1.5-hour walk in English through 900 years of Bergen history via the old Hanseatic town. You'll spend 20 to 30 minutes at each of the following: Bryggens Museum, medieval Hanseatic Assembly Rooms

▲**St. Mary's Church** Bergen's oldest church, dating to the 12th century. **Hours:** Mon-Fri 10:00-16:00, closed mid-Sept-May. See page 189.

▲**KODE Art Museums** Collection spread among four neighboring lakeside buildings: KODE 4 (international and Norwegian artists), KODE 3 (Norwegian artists, including Munch), KODE 2 (contemporary art), and KODE 1 (decorative arts). **Hours:** Daily 10:00-17:00 (KODE 2 Thu until 20:00), closed Mon mid-Sept-mid-May. See page 190.

▲**Aquarium** Well-presented sea life, with a walk-through "shark tunnel" and feeding times at the top of most hours in summer. **Hours:** Daily 9:00-18:00, Sept-April from 10:00. See page 191.

▲**Gamle Bergen (Old Bergen)** Quaint gathering of 50 homes and shops dating from 18th-20th century, with guided tours of museum interiors at the top of the hour. **Hours:** Daily 10:00-16:00, closed Sept-mid-May. See page 191.

Near Bergen
▲▲**Edvard Grieg Museum, Troldhaugen** Home of Norway's greatest composer, with artifacts, tours, and concerts. **Hours:** Daily 9:00-18:00, Oct-April 10:00-16:00. See page 194.

▲**Ulriken643 Cable Car** A quick ride up to the summit of Ulriken, Bergen's tallest mountain, with nonstop views, a restaurant, and hiking trails. **Hours:** Daily 9:00-21:00, off-season until 17:00. See page 193.

BERGEN

(Schøtstuene), the Bryggen quarter, a medieval wine cellar, and Hanseatic Museum (when it reopens—closed until 2024). Tours leave from the Bryggens Museum (next to the Radisson Blu Royal Hotel). The tour price includes entry tickets to these sights, making it an especially good value (250 NOK; daily at 10:00, 11:00, and 12:00; no tours mid-Sept-mid-May, +47 55 30 80 30, www.bymuseet.no). While the museum visits are a bit rushed, your tour ticket allows you to re-enter the museums for the rest of the day. The tours are popular and can sell out, especially in July; to be safe, buy tickets in advance online or from the reception desk at the Bryggens Museum.

Local Guide

Sue Lindelid is a British expat who has spent more than 25 years showing visitors around Bergen (1,250 NOK/2-hour tour, 1,650 NOK/3-hour tour; mobile +47 90 78 59 52, suelin@hotmail.no).

▲Bus Tours

The TI sells tickets for various bus tours, including a 3.5-hour Grieg Lunch Concert tour that goes to Edvard Grieg's Home at Troldhaugen—a handy way to reach that distant sight (290 NOK, see the listing under "Sights Near Bergen," later). Buses are comfy, with big views and a fine recorded commentary. There are also several full-day tour options from Bergen, including bus/boat tours to nearby Hardanger and Sogne fjords. The TI is packed with brochures describing all the excursions.

Hop-On, Hop-Off Buses

Sightseeing Bergen links most of Bergen's major sights and also stops at the Skolten cruise port, but doesn't go to the Fantoft Stave Church, Troldhaugen, or Ulriken643 cable car. If your sightseeing plans don't extend beyond the walkable core of Bergen, skip this (300 NOK/24 hours, May-mid-Sept 9:00-16:00, every 30 minutes, also stops in front of Fish Market, mobile +47 97 78 18 88, www.sightseeingbergen.no).

Inflatable Boat Tour

After a scenic cruise along the Bergen harborfront, you'll zip out into the open fjord past islands and rocky skerries aboard a fast and breezy **Fjord Tours** rigid inflatable boat (RIB). Before heading out you'll don a survival suit and goggles for the thrilling high-speed part of the journey. Tours last 50 minutes and depart from near the Radisson Blue Royal Hotel (in Bryggen), at Bradbenken 2. Get tickets at the TI (595 NOK, daily at 13:10, www.fjordtours.com).

Bergen Walk

For a quick self-guided orientation stroll through Bergen, follow this walk from the city's fortress, through its old wooden Hanseatic Quarter and Fish Market, to the modern center of town. This walk is also a handy sightseeing spine, passing most of Bergen's best museums; ideally, you'll get sidetracked and take advantage of their excellent tours along the way. I've pointed out the museums you'll pass en route—all are described in greater detail later, under "Sights in Bergen." To trace the route of this walk, see the "Bergen" map, earlier.

• *Begin where Bergen did, at its historic fortress. To get there from the harborfront road, 50 yards before the stone tower with the water on your*

left, veer up the ramp behind the low stone wall on the right, through a gate, and into the fortress complex. Stand before the stony skyscraper.

❶ Bergenhus Fortress

In the 13th century, Bergen became the Kingdom of Norway's first real capital. (Before then, kings would circulate, staying on royal farms.) This fortress complex—built in the 1240s and worth ▲— was a garrison, containing a tower for the king's residence (Rosenkrantz Tower) and a large hall for his banquets (Håkon's Hall).

This south end of the fortress complex is marked by **Rosenkrantz Tower,** the keep of the 13th-century castle. It was expanded in the 16th century by the Danish-Norwegian king, who wanted to exercise a little control over the German merchants who dominated his town. He was tired of the Germans making all the money without paying taxes. This tower—with its cannon trained not on external threats but toward Bryggen—while expensive, paid for itself many times over as Germans got the message and paid their taxes.

• *Find the gate 20 yards to the right of the tower, marked 1728. Head through this gate and into the courtyard of the Bergenhus Fortress. In front of you stands Håkon's Hall with its stepped gable. Tours for both the hall and the tower leave from the building to the right of Håkon's Hall.*

Pop into the museum lobby to enjoy a free exhibit about the massive 1944 explosion of the German ammunition ship in the harbor. For the best view of Håkon's Hall, walk through the gate to the left of the building and onto the grassy ramparts between the hall and the harbor.

Håkon's Hall is the largest secular medieval building in Norway. When the pope sent a cardinal to perform Håkon's coronation there was no suitable building in Norway for such a VIP. King Håkon fixed that by having this impressive banqueting hall built in the mid-1200s. When Norway's capital moved to Oslo in 1299, the hall was abandoned and eventually used for grain storage. For a century it had no roof. In the 19th century, it was appreciated and restored. It's essentially a giant, grand reception hall used today just as it was eight centuries ago: for banquets.

• *Continue walking along the rampart (climbing some steps and going about 100 yards past Håkon's Hall) to the far end of Bergenhus Fortress, where you'll find a statue of a king and a fine harbor view.*

❷ Bergenhus Rampart Perch and Statue of King Håkon VII

The cannon on the ramparts here illustrates how the fort protected this strategic harbor. The port is busy with both cruise ships and supply ships for the nearby North Sea oil rigs. Long before this modern commerce, this is where the cod fishermen of the north met the traders of Europe. Travelers in the 12th century described

how there were so many trading vessels here "you could cross the harbor without getting your feet wet." Beyond the ships is an island protecting Bergen from the open sea.

Look left and right at the dangerous edge with no railing. If someone were to fall and get hurt here and then try to sue, the Norwegian judge's verdict would be: stupidity—case dismissed. Around you in the distance are Bergen's "seven mountains." One day each summer, locals race to climb each of these in rapid succession, accomplishing the feat in less than 12 hours.

The statue is of the beloved King Håkon VII (1872-1957), grandfather of today's king. While exiled in London during World

War II, King Håkon kept up Norwegian spirits through radio broadcasts. The first king of modern Norway (after the country won its independence from Sweden in 1905), he was a Danish prince married to Queen Victoria's granddaughter—a savvy monarch who knew how to play the royalty game.

A few steps behind the statue (just right of tree-lined lane) is the site of Bergen's first cathedral, built in 1070. A hedge grows where its walls once stood. The statue of Mary marks the place of the altar, its pedestal etched with a list of 13th-century kings of Norway crowned and buried here.

These castle grounds (notice the natural amphitheater on the left) host cultural events and music festivals; Elton John, Paul McCartney, and Norwegian DJ Kygo have all packed this outdoor venue.

Continuing around Håkon's Hall, follow the linden tree-lined lane. On the left looms a massive concrete structure disguised by ivy. It was a German bunker built during the Nazi occupation—easier now to ignore than dismantle.

Twenty yards ahead on the right is a rare set of free public toilets. Notice they come with blue lights to discourage heroin junkies from using these WCs as a place to shoot up. The blue lights make it hard to see veins.

• *You've now returned to the tower and circled the castle grounds. Before leaving, consider taking a guided tour of the hall and tower. Otherwise, head back down the ramp, out to the main road, and continue with the harbor on your right. (After a block, history buffs could follow* Bergenhus *signs, up the street to the left, to the free and fascinating* **Fortress Museum**—*with its collection of Norwegian military history and Nazi occupation exhibits.) Proceed one more block along the harbor until you reach an open, parklike space on your left. Walk 100 yards (just past a handy Rema 1000 supermarket) to the top of this park to reach...*

❸ St. Mary's Church (Mariakirken)

Dating from the 12th century, this is Bergen's oldest preserved building. This stately church of the Hanseatic merchants has a

dour stone interior, but it's enlivened by a colorful, highly decorated pulpit.

In the park below the church, find the statue of Snorri Sturlason. In the 1200s, this Icelandic scribe and scholar wrote down the Viking sagas. Thanks to him, we have a better understanding of this Nordic era. A few steps to the right, look through the window of the big modern building at an archaeological site showing the oldest remains of Bergen—stubs of the 12th-century trading town's streets tumbling to the harbor before land reclamation pushed the harbor farther out.

• *The window is just a sneak peek at the excellent* ❹ *Bryggens Museum, which provides helpful historical context for the Hanseatic Quarter we're about to visit. The museum's outstanding* **Bryggen Walking Tour** *is your best bet for seeing this area (see "Tours in Bergen," earlier). Continue down to the busy harborfront. On the left is the most photographed sight in town, the Bryggen quarter. To get your bearings, first read the "Bryggen's History" sidebar; if it's nice out, cross the street to the wharf and look back for a fine overview of this area. (Or, in the rain, huddle under an awning.)*

❺ Bergen's Hanseatic Quarter (Bryggen)

Bergen's fragile wooden old town is its iconic front door. The long "tenements" (rows of warehouses) hide atmospheric lanes that creak and groan with history.

While we think of Bergen as "Norwegian," Bryggen was German— the territory of *Deutsch*-speaking merchants and traders. (The most popular surname in Bergen is the German name Hanson—"son of Hans.") From the front of Bryggen, look back at the Rosenkrantz Tower. The little red holes at its top mark where cannons once pointed at the German quarter, installed by Norwegian royalty who wanted a slice of all that taxable trade revenue. Their threat was countered by German grain—without which the Norwegians would've starved.

Bryggen's History

Pretty as Bryggen is today, it has a rough-and-tumble history. A horrific plague decimated the population and economy of Norway in 1350, killing about half of its people. A decade later, German merchants arrived and established a Hanseatic trading post.

For the next four centuries, from 1370 to 1754, the port of Bergen was essentially German territory, with German merchants controlling the city's trade. In 1550, Bergen was a Germanic city of 1,000 workaholic merchants—surrounded and supported by some 5,000 Norwegians.

This wasn't a military occupation, but a mutually beneficial economic partnership. The Norwegian fishermen of the far north shipped their dried cod to Bergen, where the Hanseatic merchants marketed it to Europe. Norwegian cod, an easy-to-preserve protein, provided much of Europe with food, and cod oil lit European lamps until about 1850.

In its earlier heyday, Bergen was one of the largest wooden cities in Europe (the original town dates from 1070). But those jammed-in wooden buildings, heated with lots of hearth fires, spelled disaster for Bergen. Over the centuries, the city suffered countless fires, with major blazes every 20 or so years. Each time the warehouses burned, the merchants would toss the refuse into the bay and rebuild. Gradually, the land crept out, and so did the buildings. Looking at the Hanseatic Quarter from the harborfront, you can see how the buildings have settled as the fire debris decomposed.

Notice that the first six houses are perfectly straight; they were built in the 1980s to block the view of a modern hotel behind. The more ramshackle stretch of 11 houses beyond date from the early 1700s. Each front hides a long line of five to ten businesses.

• *To wander into the heart of this woody medieval quarter, head down Bredsgården, the lane a couple of doors before the shop sign featuring the anatomically correct unicorn. We'll make a loop to the right: down this lane nearly all the way, under a passage into a square (with a well, a vibrant outdoor restaurant, and a big wooden cod), and then back to the harbor down a parallel lane. Read the information below, then explore, stopping at the big wooden cod.*

Bit by bit, Bryggen is being restored using medieval techniques and materials. As you explore, you may stumble upon a rebuilding project in action.

After the last big fire in 1702, the city rebuilt using more stone and brick, and suffered fewer fires thereafter. But one small wooden quarter—Bryggen—was built after the fire, in the early 1700s. To prevent future blazes, the Germans forbade all fires and candles for light or warmth except in isolated and carefully guarded communal houses behind each tenement. It was in these communal houses that apprentices studied, people dried out their soggy clothes, hot food was cooked, and the men drank and partied. When there was a big banquet, one man always stayed sober—a kind of designated fire watchman.

Flash forward to the 20th century. One of the biggest explosions of World War II occurred in Bergen's harbor on April 20, 1944. An ammunition ship loaded with 120 tons of dynamite blew up just in front of the fortress. The blast leveled entire neighborhoods on either side of the harbor (notice the ugly 1950s construction opposite the fortress) and did serious damage to Håkon's Hall and Rosenkrantz Tower. How big was the blast? There's a hut called "the anchor cabin" a couple of miles away in the mountains. That's where the ship's anchor landed. The blast is considered to have been accidental, despite the fact that April 20 happened to be Hitler's 55th birthday and the ship blew up about 100 yards away from the Nazi commander's headquarters (in the fortress).

After World War II, Bryggen was slated for destruction. Most of the locals wanted it gone—it reminded them of the Germans who had occupied Norway for the miserable war years. Then excavators discovered rune stones indicating that the area predated the Germans. This boosted Bryggen's approval rating, and the quarter was saved. Today this picturesque and historic zone is the undisputed tourist highlight of Bergen.

BERGEN

Strolling through Bryggen, you feel swallowed up by history. Long rows of planky buildings (medieval-style double tenements) lean haphazardly across narrow alleys. The last Hanseatic merchant moved out centuries ago, but this is still a place of (touristy) commerce. You'll find artists' galleries, T-shirt boutiques, leather workshops, atmospheric restaurants, fishing tackle shops, sweaters, sweaters, sweaters...and trolls.

Look up at the winch-and-pulley systems on the buildings. These connected ground-floor workrooms with

top-floor storerooms. Notice that the overhanging storerooms up-stairs were supported by timbers with an elbow created by a tree trunk and its root—considered the strongest way to make a right angle in construction back then. Turning right at the top of the lane, you enter a lively cobbled square. On the far side is that big wooden fish.

The wooden cod (next to a well) is a reminder that the eco-nomic foundation of Bergen—the biggest city in Scandinavia until 1650 and the biggest city in Norway until 1830—was this fish. The stone building behind the carved cod was one of the fireproof cookhouses serving a line of buildings that stretched to the harbor. Today it's the Hetland Gallery, filled with the entertaining work of a popular local artist famous for fun caricatures of the city. Facing the same square is the Bryggen visitors center, worth peeking into.

• *Enjoy the center and the shops. Then return downhill to the harbor-front, turn left, and continue the walk.*

Half of Bryggen (the brick-and-stone stretch to your left be-tween the old wooden facades and the head of the bay) was torn down around 1900. Today the stately buildings that replaced it—far less atmospheric than Bryggen's original wooden core—are filled with tacky trinket shops and touristy splurge restaurants. They do make a nice architectural cancan of pointy gables, each with its date of construction indicated near the top.

Head to the lone wooden red house at the end of the row, which houses the **Hanseatic Museum** (closed until 2024 for reno-vation). The man who owned this building recognized the value of the city's heritage and kept its 18th-century interior intact. Once considered a nutcase, today he's celebrated as a visionary, as his de-cision has left visitors with a fine example of an old merchant house.

• *The Fish Market is just across the street. But first, we'll circle a few blocks inland and around to the right.*

The red-brick building (with frilly white trim, stepped gable, and a Starbucks) is the old **meat market**. It was built in 1877, after the importance of hygiene was recognized and the meat was moved inside from today's Fish Market. At the intersection just beyond, look left (uphill past the meat market) to see the **Fløibanen sta-tion.** Ahead, on the right, is an unusually classy McDonald's in a 1710 building that was originally a bakery. A few steps uphill on Kong Oscars Gate, the tiny red shack flying the Norwegian flags is the popular, recommended 3-Kroneren hot-dog stand.

Turn right to wander the length of **Hollendergaten,** a cute, narrow lane of 200-year-old buildings. Its name comes from a time when the king organized foreign communities of traders into vari-ous neighborhoods; this was where the Dutch lived. The curving street marks the former harborfront—these buildings were origi-nally right on the water.

Hooking left, you reach the end of Hollendergaten, then turn right onto Nedre Korskirkeallmenningen. You'll pass the grand, red stone **Børsen** building, once the stock exchange and now a hotel with a few trendy restaurants. Step inside to enjoy its 1920s Art Deco-style murals celebrating Bergen's fishing heritage.

• *Turn right to go back toward the harborfront, then cross the street (Torget) and immerse yourself in Bergen's beloved Fish Market.*

❻ Fish Market (Fisketorget)

A fish market has thrived here since the 1500s, when fishermen rowed in with their catch and haggled with hungry residents.

While it's now a food circus of eateries selling fishy treats to tourists—no local would come here to actually buy fish—this famous market is still worth ▲, offering lots of smelly photo fun and free morsels to taste (daily 8:00-23:00, but vendors may close earlier if they're not busy, shorter hours Oct-April). Watch your wallet: If you're going to get pickpocketed in Bergen, it'll likely be here.

Many stands sell premade smoked-salmon *(laks)* sandwiches, fish soup, and other snacks ideal for a light lunch (confirm prices before ordering). To try Norwegian jerky, pick up a bag of dried cod snacks *(tørrfisk)*. The red meat is minke (pronounced mink-ee) whale, caught off the coast of northern Norway. Norwegians, notorious for their whaling, defend it as a traditional livelihood for many of their people. They point out that they only harvest the minke whale, which is not on an endangered list. In recent years, Norway has assigned itself a quota of nearly 1,000 minke whales a year, with the actual catch coming to a bit over half of that.

• *When done exploring, with your back to the market, hike a block to the right (note the pointy church spire in the distance and the big blocky stone monument dead ahead) into the modern part of town and a huge wide square. Pause at the intersection just before crossing into the square, about 20 yards before the blocky monument. Look left to see Mount Ulriken with its TV tower. A cable car called Ulriken643 takes you to its 2,110-foot summit (shuttle buses to the cable car station leave from this corner; for summit details, see page 193.) Now, walk up to that big square monument and meet some Vikings.*

❼ Seafarers' Monument

Nicknamed "the cube of goat cheese" for its shape, this 1950 monument celebrates Bergen's contact with the sea and remembers those

who worked on it and died in it. Study the faces: All social classes are represented. The statues relate to the scenes depicted in the reliefs above. Each side represents a century (start with the Vikings and work clockwise): 10th century—Vikings, with a totem pole in the panel above recalling the pre-Columbian Norwegian "discovery" of America; 18th century—equipping Europe's ships; 19th century—whaling; 20th century—shipping and war. For the 21st century, see the real people—a cross-section of today's Norway—sitting at the statue's base. Major department stores (Galleriet, Xhibition, and Telegrafen) are all nearby.

• The monument marks the start of Bergen's main square…

❽ Torgallmenningen

Allmenningen means "for all the people." Torg means "square." While this is the city's main gathering place, it was actually created as a firebreak. The residents of this wood-built city knew fires were inevitable. The street plan was designed with breaks, or open spaces like this square, to help contain the destruction. In 1916, it succeeded in stopping a fire, which is why it has a more modern feel today.

Walk the length of the square to a low angled slab of blue stone at the far end. This is a monument to King Olav V, who died in 1991, and a popular meeting point: Locals like to say, "Meet you at the Blue Stone."

• You're at the center of a parklike swath known as…

❾ Ole Bulls Plass

This drag leads from the National Theater (above on right) to a little lake (below on left).

Detour a few steps up for a better look at the **National Theater,** built in Art Nouveau style in 1909. Founded by violinist Ole Bull in 1850, this was the first theater to host plays in the Norwegian language. After 450 years of Danish and Swedish rule, 19th-century Norway enjoyed a cultural awakening, and Bergen became an artistic power. Ole Bull collaborated with the playwright Henrik Ibsen. Ibsen commissioned Edvard Grieg

to compose the music for his play *Peer Gynt.* These three lions of Norwegian culture all lived and worked right here in Bergen.

Head downhill on the square to a delightful fountain featuring a **statue of Ole Bull** in the shadow of trees. Ole Bull was an 1800s version of Elvis. A pop idol and heartthrob in his day, Ole Bull's bath water was bottled and sold by hotels, and women fainted when they heard him play violin. Living up to his name, he fathered over 40 children. Speaking of children, I love to hang out here watching families frolic in the pond, oblivious to the waterfall troll (see the statue with the harp below Ole Bull). According to legend, the troll bestows musical talent on anyone—like old Ole—who gives him a gift (he likes meat).

From here, the park spills farther downhill to a cast-iron pavilion given to the city by Germans in 1889, and on to the little man-made lake (Lille Lungegårdsvannet), which is circled by an enjoyable path.

• *If you're up for a lakeside stroll, now's your chance. Alongside the lake (to the right as you face it from here) is a row of buildings housing the enjoyable* **KODE Art Museums.** *And to the left of the lake are some fine residential streets (including the picturesque, cobbled Marken); within a few minutes' walk is the* **Leprosy Museum** *and the* **cathedral.**

Sights in Bergen

Several museums listed here—including the Bryggens Museum, Håkon's Hall, Rosenkrantz Tower, Leprosy Museum, and Gamle Bergen—are part of the Bergen City Museum (Bymuseet) organization. If you buy a ticket to any of them, you'll pay half-price at any of the others simply by showing your ticket. In summer, note that many of these sights are included in the recommended Byrggen Walking Tour (see "Tours in Bergen," earlier).

▲Bergenhus Fortress: Håkon's Hall and Rosenkrantz Tower

The tower and hall, sitting boldly out of place on the harbor just beyond Bryggen, are reminders of Bergen's importance as the first permanent capital of Norway. Both sights feel vacant and don't really speak for themselves; a guided tour, which provides a serious introduction to Bergen's history, is essential for grasping their significance.

Cost and Hours: Hall and tower-150 NOK for both, 100 NOK for one; open daily 10:00-16:00, mid-Sept-mid-May 12:00-15:00; free WC; +47 55 30 80 30, www.bymuseet.no.

Tours: 30 NOK extra for worthwhile guided tour that includes both buildings (mid-June-mid-Aug tours leave daily at 10:00 and 14:00 from the building to the right of Håkon's Hall).

Visiting the Hall and Tower: Dating from the 13th century, **Håkon's Hall** was built as a banqueting hall, and that's essentially what it still is today. It was restored in the early 20th century but was heavily damaged in World War II when a munitions ship exploded in the harbor, leaving nothing but the walls standing. In the 1950s it was restored with a grand wooden ceiling and roof modeled after the medieval roof on a church in northern Norway. Beneath the hall is a whitewashed cellar likely used for storage.

Rosenkrantz Tower, the keep of a 13th-century castle, is today a stack of barren rooms connected by tight spiral staircases, with a good history exhibit on the top two floors and a commanding view from its rooftop. In the 16th century, the ruling Danish-Norwegian king enlarged the tower and trained its cannon on the German-merchant district, Bryggen, to remind the merchants of the importance of paying their taxes.

Fortress Museum (Bergenhus Festningmuseum)

This humble museum (which functioned as a prison during the Nazi occupation), set back a couple of blocks from the fortress, will interest historians with its thoughtful exhibits about military history, especially Bergen's WWII experience (look for the Norwegian Nazi flag). You'll learn about the resistance movement in Bergen (including its underground newspapers), the role of women in the Norwegian military, and Norwegian troops who have served with UN forces in overseas conflicts.

Cost and Hours: Free, daily 11:00-17:00, ask to borrow a translation of the descriptions, just behind Thon Hotel Orion at Koengen, +47 55 54 63 87.

▲▲Bryggens Museum

Built over the 12th-century rubble of medieval Bergen, this modern museum displays artifacts from the ruins and explains the 1950s archaeological dig that uncovered the earliest bits of the city (1050-1500). A trove of artifacts, including ceramics, rune inscriptions, and a 1000-year-old tunic, shed light on the everyday lives of the medieval people who inhabited Bergen and western Norway.

Cost and Hours: 100 NOK; in summer, entry included with Bryggen Walking Tour (see "Tours in Bergen," earlier); open daily 9:00-16:00, mid-Sept-mid-May 11:00-15:00; inexpensive cafeteria; in big, modern building just beyond the end of Bryggen and the Radisson Blu Royal Hotel, +47 55 30 80 30, www.bymuseet.no.

Tours: It's best to visit as part of the Bryggen Walking Tour. From mid-September through mid-May, when there is no tour, consider buying the good museum guidebook to supplement the brief English explanations.

Visiting the Museum: The manageable, well-presented permanent exhibit occupies the ground floor. First up are the foundations from original wooden tenements dating back to the 12th century (displayed right where they were excavated) and a giant chunk of the hull of a 100-foot-long, 13th-century ship that was found here. Next, an exhibit (roughly shaped like the long, wooden double-tenements outside) shows off artifacts and explains lifestyles from medieval Bryggen. Behind that is a display of items you might have bought at the medieval market. You'll finish with exhibits about the church in Bergen, the town's role as a royal capital, and its status as a cultural capital.

▲▲Hanseatic Museum and Schøtstuene
(Det Hanseatiske Museum og Schøtstuene)

The **Hanseatic Museum**—closed until at least 2024 for an extensive renovation—offers the best look inside the trademark wooden houses of Bergen. The creaky old rooms—with hundred-year-old cod hanging from the ceiling—offer a time-tunnel experience back to Bryggen's glory days. It's located in an atmospheric old merchant house furnished with dried fish, antique ropes, an old oxtail (used for wringing spilled cod-liver oil back into the bucket), sagging steps, and cupboard beds from the early 1700s—one sporting what some claim is a medieval pinup girl.

During the museum's closure, you can still visit the nearby Hanseatic Assembly Rooms at **Schøtstuene,** where Hanseatic merchants would cook and gather to feast, hold court, conduct ceremonies, be schooled, and get warm. The rooms are in a building near St. Mary's Church (follow Øvregaten behind Bryggen—Schøtstuene is on your left). Fires were allowed in this building only because it was separate from the other (highly flammable) Bryggen offices. A glass floor reveals medieval ruins of

BERGEN

The Hanseatic League, Blessed by Cod

Middlemen in trade, the clever German merchants of the Hanseatic League, or Hanse, ruled the waves of northern Europe for 500 years (c. 1250-1750). These sea traders first banded together in a merchant guild to defend themselves against pirates. As they spread out from Germany, they established trading posts in foreign lands, cut deals with local leaders for trading rights, built boats and wharves, and organized armies to protect ships and ports.

By the 15th century, these merchants had organized more than a hundred cities into the Hanseatic League, a free-trade zone that stretched from London to Russia. The league ran a profitable triangle of trade: Fish from Scandinavia was exchanged for grain from the eastern Baltic and for luxury goods from England and Flanders. Everyone benefited, and the German merchants—the middlemen—reaped the profits.

At its peak in the 15th century, the Hanseatic League was the dominant force—economic, military, and political—in northern Europe. This was a chaotic age when much of Europe was fragmented into petty kingdoms and dukedoms. Revenue-hungry kings and robber-baron lords levied extortionist tolls. Pirates plagued shipments. It was the Hanseatic League that brought the stability that allowed trade to flourish.

Bergen that predate the Hanseatic era. Until the Hanseatic Museum reopens, Schøtstuene is displaying some of the Hanseatic collection and runs a short film about the ongoing restoration project.

Cost: 130 NOK (includes Hanseatic Museum when it reopens), 50 percent discount with your Norwegian Fisheries Museum ticket (or save your Schøtstuene ticket for discount at Norwegian Fisheries Museum); in summer, entry included with Bryggen Walking Tour.

Hours: Daily 10:00-18:00, May and Sept until 17:00, Oct-April 11:00-15:00; Øvregaten 50, +47 53 00 61 10, www.museumvest.no.

Tours: Included with your ticket is a 40-minute guided tour of Schøtstuene (check online to confirm tour schedule, generally Tue-Fri at 12:00 and 14:00). If you won't make this tour, your best alternative is joining the Bryggen Walking Tour, which includes a 25-minute tour inside Schøtstuene.

Bergen's place in this Baltic economy was all about cod—a form of protein that could be dried, preserved, and shipped anywhere. Blessed with a good harbor conveniently located between the rich fishing spots of northern Norway and the markets of Europe, Bergen shipped dried cod and fish oil southward and imported grain, cloth, beer, wine, and ceramics.

Bryggen, along with London, Bruges, and Novgorod, was one of four principal Hanseatic trading posts known as "kontors." It was the last kontor opened (c. 1360), the least profitable, and the final one to close. Bryggen had warehouses, offices, and living quarters. Ships docked here were unloaded by counterpoise cranes. At its peak, as many as a thousand merchants, journeymen, and apprentices lived and worked here.

Bryggen was a self-contained German enclave within the city. The merchants came from Germany, worked a few years here, and retired back in the home country. They spoke German, wore German clothes, and attended their own churches. By law, they were forbidden to intermarry or fraternize with the Bergeners, except on business.

The Hanseatic League peaked around 1500, then slowly declined. Rising nation-states were jealous of the German merchants' power and wealth. The Reformation tore apart old alliances. Dutch and English traders broke the Hanseatic monopoly. Cities withdrew from the league and kontors closed. In 1754, Bergen's kontor was taken over by the Norwegians. When it closed its doors on December 31, 1899, a sea-trading era was over, but the city of Bergen had become rich...by the grace of cod.

Norwegian Fisheries Museum (Norges Fiskerimuseum)

Just up the coast from Bryggen is the Norwegian Fisheries Museum, located in a well-preserved wharfside warehouse with exhibits about life along and on the sea. Antique boats are displayed in the harbor just outside.

Cost and Hours: 100 NOK, 50 percent discount if you show your Schøtstuene ticket (or save your Fisheries ticket for discount at Schøtstuene); June-Aug daily 10:00-18:00, May and Sept until 17:00, Oct-April 11:00-15:00; Sandviksboder 23, +47 55 69 96 01, www.museumvest.no.

Getting There: From the Schøtstuene Assembly Rooms, it's a 15- to 20-minute walk along curving Nye Sandviksveien. From Schøtstuene, follow Øvregaten—which becomes Nye Sandviksveien—north for about 10 minutes. The street soon splits with Ladegårdsgaten—but keep straight, then turn left onto Johan Mohrs Gate. After Johan Mohrs Gate joins Sjøgaten, the museum is two minutes ahead, on the left.

You can also catch bus #3, #4, or #6 from the Bryggen stop (in front of the Radisson Blu Royal Hotel) and ride 5 minutes to the museum (stop: Sandvikstorget). Or, if it is running, cruise 20 minutes aboard the *Beffen* ferry (65 NOK one-way, 130 NOK day pass, June-Aug hourly 11:00-16:00, departs from the Bryggen side of the Fish Market).

Theta Museum

This small museum highlights Norway's resistance movement. You'll peek into the hidden world of a 10-person cell of courageous students, whose group—called Theta—housed other fighters and communicated with London during the Nazi occupation in World War II. It's located in Theta's former headquarters—a small upstairs room in a wooden Bryggen building.

Cost and Hours: 50 NOK, June-Aug Tue, Sat, and Sun 14:00-16:00, closed Mon, Wed-Fri, and Sept-May, Enhjørningsgården.

▲▲Fløibanen Funicular

Bergen's popular funicular climbs 1,000 feet in seven minutes to the top of Mount Fløyen for the best view of the town, surrounding islands, and fjords all the way to the west coast. The top is the perfect picnic spot for enjoying the sunset. The **$$ Fløien Folkerestaurant,** the white building at the top of the funicular, offers affordable self-service food all day in season. Behind the station, you'll find a playground and a fun giant troll

photo op. The top is also the starting point for many peaceful hikes.

You'll buy your funicular ticket at the base of the Fløibanen (notice the photos in the entry hall of the construction of the funicular and its 1918 grand opening).

Cost and Hours: 130 NOK round-trip, 65 NOK one-way, cheaper online and off-season; daily 7:30-23:00, departures 4/hour—on the quarter-hour most of the day, runs continuously if busy; +47 55 33 68 00, www.floyen.no.

Advance Tickets: While you can buy tickets on-site, there can be huge lines if cruise ships are in town. Online tickets are cheaper and let you skip the ticket-buying line at the funicular.

Hiking Down: If you plan to hike down from the top, buy a

one-way ticket and ask for the Fløyen hiking map. From the top, walk behind the station and follow the signs to the city center. The top half of the 30-minute hike is a gravelly path through a forest with fine views. The bottom is a paved lane passing charming old wooden homes. It's a steep descent. To save your knees, you could ride the lift most of the way down and get off at the Promsgate stop to wander through the delightful cobbled and shiplap lanes (note that only the :00 and :30 departures stop at Promsgate—and this option requires a round-trip ticket).

▲St. Mary's Church (Mariakirken)

The oldest parish church and preserved building in Bergen dates to between 1130 and 1170 and is said to be one of the best-decorated medieval churches in Norway. For many years, St. Mary's Church was known as the "German Church," as it was used by German merchants of the Hanseatic League from 1408 to 1766. The last service in German was held in 1906. The stony interior is accented with a golden altarpiece, a Baroque pulpit of Dutch origin partly made from exotic materials (such as turtle skin), and artworks from various time periods.

Cost and Hours: 50 NOK, Mon-Fri 10:00-16:00, closed mid-Sept-May, 25-minute English guided tour (25 NOK) runs June-Aug Mon-Fri at 15:30, http://bergendomkirke.no, +47 55 59 71 75.

Bergen Cathedral (Bergen Domkirke)

Bergen's main church, dedicated to St. Olav (the patron saint of Norway), dates from 1301. Drop in to enjoy its stoic, plain interior with stuccoed stone walls and a giant wooden pulpit. Sit in a hard, straight-backed pew and just try to doze off. Like so many old Norwegian structures, its roof makes you feel like you're huddled under an overturned Viking ship. The church is oddly lopsided, with just one side aisle. Before leaving, look up to see the gorgeous wood-carved organ over the main entrance. In the entryway, you'll see portraits of each bishop dating all the way back to the Reformation.

Cost and Hours: Free, Mon-Fri 10:00-16:00, Sun 9:30-13:00, closed Sat, shorter hours mid-Aug-mid-June.

Leprosy Museum (Lepramuseet)

Leprosy is also known as "Hansen's Disease," because in the 1870s a Bergen man named Armauer Hansen did groundbreaking work in understanding the ailment. This unique museum is in St. Jørgens Hospital, a leprosarium that dates to about 1700. Until the 19th century, as much as 3 percent of Norway's population had leprosy. This hospital—once called "a graveyard for the living" (its last patient died in 1946)—has a meager exhibit in a thought-provoking dorm for the dying. It's most worthwhile if you read the translation of the exhibit (borrow a copy at the entry) or take the free tour

(at the top of each hour). As you leave, if you're interested, ask if you can see the medicinal herb garden out back.

Cost and Hours: 100 NOK, daily 10:30-15:30, closed Sept-mid-May, between train station and Bryggen at Kong Oscars Gate 59, +47 55 30 80 37, www.bymuseet.no.

▲KODE Art Museums (KODE Kunstmuseer)

If you need to get out of the rain, check out this collection, filling four neighboring buildings facing the lake along Rasmus Meyers Allé. The KODE 3 branch specializes in Norwegian artists and has an especially good Munch exhibit. Many visitors focus on the KODE 4 building (which may be closed during your visit—check locally), on the far left, for its eclectic cross-section of international and Norwegian artists. The KODE 2 building has installations of contemporary art and a big bookstore on the first floor, while the KODE 1 building has decorative arts and silver crafts from Bergen.

Cost and Hours: 160 NOK, daily 10:00-17:00 (KODE 2 Thu until 20:00), closed Mon mid-Sept-mid-May, Rasmus Meyers Allé 3, +47 53 00 97 04, www.kodebergen.no.

Visiting KODE 3 and 4: KODE 3 presents one of the finest collections of work by Edvard Munch, including such masterpieces

as *Jealousy, Melancholy, Woman in Three Stages,* and *Evening on Karl Johan.* Also on hand is a representative collection from Norway's golden age of painting (1880-1905), including highlights from the careers of Romantic landscape painters Hans Gude and J. C. Dahl. And don't miss the iconic troll and folktale drawings and watercolors by Theodor Kittelsen.

When it's open, **KODE 4** features an easily digestible collection (from outside, enter through door 4). The ground floor includes an extensive display of works by Nikolai Astrup (1880-1928), who depicts Norway's fjords with bright colors and Expressionistic flair. One flight up, "Bergen and the World, 1400-1900" creates a visual history of Norway and Bergen with portraits, landscapes, genre scenes, and religious works. Look for paintings by J. C. Dahl and his students, who captured the majesty of Norway's natural

wonders (don't miss Adelsteen Normann's impressive, photorealistic view of Romsdalsfjord). "Norwegian Art 1840-1900" includes works by Christian Krohg, as well as some portraits by Harriet Backer and realistic scenes of everyday life by Frits Thaulow.

Up on the third floor, things get modern. The Tower Hall (Tårnsalen) features Norwegian modernism and a large exhibit of Bergen's avant-garde art (1966-1985). The International Modernism section has four stars: Pablo Picasso (sketches, etchings, collages, and a few Cubist paintings), Paul Klee (Swiss color-theory painter), and the dynamic Norwegian duo of Edvard Munch and Ludvig Karisten. Rounding it out are a smattering of Surrealist, Abstract Expressionist, and Op Art pieces.

▲Bergen Aquarium (Akvariet i Bergen)

Small but fun, this aquarium claims to be the second most-visited sight in Bergen. It's wonderfully laid out and explained in English. Check out the view from inside the "shark tunnel" in the tropical shark exhibit.

Cost and Hours: Adults-295 NOK, kids-195 NOK; daily 9:00-18:00, Sept-April from 10:00, feeding times at the top of most hours in summer; cheery cafeteria with light sandwiches, Nordnesbakken 4, +47 55 55 71 71, www.akvariet.no.

Getting There: It's at the tip of the peninsula on the south end of the harbor—about a 20-minute walk or short ride on bus #11 from the city center. Or hop on the handy little harbor ferry that sails from the Fish Market to near the aquarium (65 NOK one-way, 130 NOK for day pass, less for kids, runs Mon-Fri 7:30-16:00, show ferry ticket for discount on aquarium entry, 2/hour, 10-minute ride, June-Aug 10:00-17:30, off-season until 16:00).

Nearby: The lovely park behind the aquarium has views of the sea and a popular swimming beach (described later, under "Activities in Bergen"). The totem pole erected here was a gift from Seattle, Bergen's sister city in the US.

▲Gamle Bergen Museum (Old Bergen Museum)

This Disney-cute open-air gathering of 50-some 18th- through 20th-century homes and shops was founded in 1946 to save them from destruction as Bergen modernized. Each wooden building was moved from elsewhere in Bergen and reconstructed here. Together, they create a virtual town that offers a cobbled look at the old life. It's free to wander through the town and park to enjoy

the facades of the historic buildings, but to enter the 20 or so museum buildings, you'll have to join a tour (departing on the hour 10:00-16:00).

Cost and Hours: 120 NOK, daily 10:00-16:00, closed Sept-mid-May, +47 55 39 43 04, www.bymuseet.no.

Getting There: Take any bus heading west from Bryggen (such as #4, #5, or #6, direction: Lønborglien) to Gamle Bergen (stop: Gamle Bergen). The stop is just after the tunnel. When you get off, backtrack a few steps (toward the tunnel) before peeling left downhill. Follow the sidewalk as it curves under the highway—you should see a small sign for *Gamle Bergen*. At the fork under the highway, cross the road and turn left, then head right down the hill. When you reach the apartment building on your right, take a hairpin turn left down the small road (signs should direct you). You'll see the museum's white arch ahead of you. Any bus heading back into town takes you to the center (buses come by every few minutes).

BERGEN

ACTIVITIES IN BERGEN
▲Strolling
Bergen is a great town for wandering. Enjoy a little Norwegian paseo. On a balmy Norwegian summer evening, I'd stroll from the castle, along the harborfront, up the main square to Ole Bulls Plass, and around the lake.

For a slightly more strenuous yet rewarding walk, head up the zig-zagging road behind the Fløibanen funicular station to a viewpoint in front of a white building with a lookout tower. The building was once a fire station (which explains the tower). The lake next to it used to be a reservoir. Firefighters built the white houses beyond the lake on land given to them so that they could live close to the station. After enjoying the city views, you can either return to town the way you came, or follow Øvre Blekeveien down past the lake and white houses; then take any road to the left off Blekeveien back down to the harbor.

Shopping
Most shops are open Monday through Friday 9:00-17:00, Thursday until 19:00, and Saturday 9:00-15:00, and are closed Sunday. Many touristy shops along the harborfront strip are open daily—even during holidays—until 20:00 or 21:00. You'll see the same products offered at different prices, so shopping around can be a good idea.

Ting (Things) offers a fun alternative to troll shopping, with contemporary housewares and quirky gifts (daily 9:00-22:30, at Bryggen 13, a block past the Hanseatic Museum, +47 55 21 54 80).

Nilssen på Bryggen, next to the Hanseatic Museum, is one of the oldest shops in Bergen. You'll find Norwegian yarn for knitting

and modern-style Sandnes wool sweaters, along with souvenirs and hand-embroidered Christmas items (Mon-Sat 10:00-18:00, closed Sun, Bryggen 3, +47 55 31 67 90).

Husfliden is popular for its handmade goodies and reliably Norwegian sweaters (fine variety and quality but expensive, just off Torget at Vågsallmenninge 3, +47 55 54 47 40).

The Galleriet Mall, a shopping center on Torgallmenningen, holds six floors of shops, cafés, and restaurants. You'll find a pharmacy, clothing, sporting goods, bookstores, mobile-phone shops, and a basement grocery store (Mon-Fri 9:00-21:00, Sat until 18:00, closed Sun).

Swimming

On a hot sunny day you'll find a great local scene at Bergen's public swimming areas. One is at the aquarium, and another is in Gamle Bergen. **Nordnes Sjøbad,** near the aquarium, offers swimmers an outdoor heated pool and a protected area of the sea (80 NOK, kids-35 NOK, mid-May-Aug Mon-Fri 7:00-19:00, Sat 9:00-14:00, Sun 10:00-14:00, Sat-Sun until 19:00

in good weather, closed off-season, Nordnesparken 30, +47 53 03 91 90). **Sandviken Sjøbad,** at Gamle Bergen, is free and open all summer. It comes with changing rooms, a roped-off bit of the bay (no pool), a high dive, and lots of sunbathing space. And by 2023, a new waterfront park called **True Blue** will offer a beach, pool, and sauna, as well as play areas and gardens, in a modern, mile-long recreational space just south of the city center, along the shore of Store Lungegårdsvannet lake (get info at TI).

SIGHTS NEAR BERGEN
▲Ulriken643 Cable Car

It's amazingly easy and quick to zip up six minutes to the 643-meter-high (that's 2,110 feet) summit of Ulriken, the tallest mountain near Bergen. The cable car has undergone a face lift and should reopen—with updated, more spacious gondolas—by the time you visit. Stepping out of the

cable car, you enter a different world, with views stretching to the ocean. A chart clearly shows the many well-marked and easy hikes that fan out over the vast, rocky, grassy plateau above the tree line (circular walks of various lengths, a 40-minute hike down, and a 4-hour hike to the top of the Fløibanen funicular). For less exercise, you can simply sunbathe, unpack a picnic, or enjoy the Ulriken restaurant.

Cost and Hours: 125 NOK one-way, 195 NOK round-trip; about 8/hour, daily 9:00-21:00, off-season until 17:00; +47 53 64 36 43, www.ulriken643.no.

Getting There: It's about three miles southeast of Bergen. From the Fish Market, you can take a blue double-decker shuttle bus that includes the cost of the cable-car ride (285 NOK, ticket valid 24 hours, April-Sept daily 9:00-18:00, 2/hour, departs from the corner of Torgallmenningen and Strandgaten, buy ticket as you board or at TI). Alternatively, public buses #2 and #3 run from Småstrandgaten in the city center and stop 200 yards from the lift station.

▲▲Edvard Grieg Museum, Troldhaugen

Norway's greatest composer spent his last 22 summers (1885-1907) at his country home, soaking up inspirational fjord beauty and
composing many of his greatest works. Grieg fused simple Norwegian folk tunes with the bombast of Europe's Romantic style. In a dreamy Victorian setting, Grieg's Troldhaugen ("Hill of the Trolls") is pleasant for anyone and essential for diehard fans. You can visit his house on your own, but it's more
enjoyable if you take the included 20-minute tour. The house and adjacent museum are full of memories and artifacts, including the composer's Steinway. The walls are festooned with photos of the musical and literary superstars of his generation. When the hugely popular Grieg died in 1907, 40,000 mourners attended his funeral. His little studio hut near the water makes you want to sit down and modulate.

Cost and Hours: 130 NOK, includes guided tour in English, daily 9:00-18:00, Oct-April 10:00-16:00, café, +47 55 92 29 92, https://griegmuseum.no.

Grieg Lunch Concert: Troldhaugen offers a great guided tour/concert package that includes a shuttle bus from the Bergen TI to the doorstep of Grieg's home on the fjord (departs 11:00), an hour-long tour of the home, a half-hour concert (Grieg's greatest

piano hits, at 13:00), and the ride back into town (you're back in the center by 14:30). Your guide will narrate the ride out of town as well as take you around Grieg's house (290 NOK, daily May-mid-Oct). Lunch isn't included, but there is a café, or you could bring a picnic. You can skip the return bus ride and spend more time in Troldhaugen. While the tour rarely sells out, it's wise to drop by the TI earlier that day to reserve your spot.

Evening Concerts: Ask at the TI about piano performances in the concert hall at Grieg's home—a gorgeous venue with the fjord stretching out behind the grand piano (390 NOK, concerts roughly mid-June-Sept Sun at 18:00, free round-trip shuttle bus leaves TI at 16:30, show your concert ticket).

Getting to Troldhaugen: It's six miles south of Bergen. The Bybanen tram drops you a long 20-minute walk away from Troldhaugen. Catch the tram in the city center at its terminus near Byparken (between the lake and Ole Bulls Plass), ride it for about 25 minutes (stop: Hop). Walk in the direction of Bergen (about 25 yards), cross at the crosswalk, and follow signs to Troldhaugen. Part of the way is on a pedestrian/bike path; you're halfway there when the path crosses over a busy highway. If you want to make the 13:00 lunchtime concert, leave Bergen at 12:00.

To avoid the long walk from the tram stop, consider the Grieg Lunch Concert package (described earlier). If you're driving into Bergen from the east (such as from the Sognefjord), you'll drive right by Troldhaugen on your way into town.

Fantoft Stave Church (Fantoft Stavkirke)

Situated in a quiet forest next to a mysterious stone cross, this replica of a huge, preserved-in-tar 12th-century stave church is bigger, though no better, than others covered in this book. But it's worth a look if you're in the neighborhood, even after-hours, for its atmospheric setting. The original wooden church burned down in 1992. It was rebuilt and reopened in 1997, but it will never be the same (for more on stave churches, see page 116).

Cost and Hours: 65 NOK, daily

10:30-18:00, interior closed mid-Sept-mid-May, no English information, +47 55 28 07 10.

Getting There: It's three miles south of Bergen on E-39 in Paradis. Take the Bybanen tram (from Byparken, between the lake and Ole Bulls Plass) or bus #83 (from Torget, by the Fish Market) to the Paradis stop (not the "Fantoft" stop). From Paradis, walk uphill to the parking lot on the left, and find the steep footpath to the church.

BERGEN NIGHTSPOTS

At such a high latitude, Bergen stays light until 23:00 in the summer. On warm evenings, people are out enjoying the soft light and the mellow scene.

For a selection of cool nightspots, visit the **Pingvinen** and **Café Opera** (both described in "Eating in Bergen," later) and explore the neighboring streets.

For something a little funkier, **Skostredet** ("Shoe Street," recalling the days when cobblers set up shop here) is emerging as the hip, bohemian-chic area. You'll sort through cafés, pubs, and retro shops. There's an American-style Rock and Roll '59er Diner. And **Folk og Røvere** ("People and Robbers") is an unpretentious bar with cheap beer (nightly until late, Skostredet 12).

For candlelit elegance, enjoy a drink at the historic **Dyvekes Wine Cellar.** Named for the mistress of King Christian II of Denmark (her portrait is on the signboard hanging above the door), the atmosphere of the ground-floor bar and the cellar downstairs is hard to beat (daily from 15:00, wine by the glass, beer on tap, Hollendergaten 7).

For live music, try **Madam Felle Nightclub** (on the Bryggen strip), which usually has musicians on the weekends (sometimes without a cover). And if you're really drunk at 3:00 in the morning and need a spicy hotdog, the **3-Kroneren** *pølse* stand is open.

Sleeping in Bergen

Busy with business travelers and popular with tourists, Bergen can be jammed any time of year. Even with this crush, proud and pricey hotels may be willing to make deals. Bergen also has some fine budget alternatives that can save you money.

HOTELS

$$$$ Hotel Havnekontoret, with 116 rooms and the best location in town, fills a grand old shipping headquarters dating from the 1920s. It's an especially fine value on weekends and in summer for those who eat the included dinner. While part of a chain, it has a friendly spirit. Guests are welcome to climb its historic tower

(with a magnificent view) or enjoy its free sauna and exercise room downstairs. The room price includes virtually all your food—a fine breakfast, self-service waffles in the afternoon, fruit and coffee all day, and a light dinner buffet each evening. If you take advantage of them, these edible extras are easily worth 600 NOK per day per couple, making the cost of this fancy hotel little more than a hostel (facing the harbor across the street from the Radisson Blu Royal Hotel at Slottsgaten 1, +47 55 60 11 00, www.choicehotels. no, cc.havnekontoret@choice.no).

$$$$ Hotel Park Bergen is classy, comfortable, and in a fine residential neighborhood a 15-minute uphill walk from the town center (10 minutes from the train station). It's tinseled in Old World, lived-in charm, yet comes with all of today's amenities. The 35 rooms are split between two buildings, with 22 in the classy old-fashioned hotel and 13 in the modern annex across the street. They also offer eight fully furnished apartments (Harald Hårfagres Gate 35, +47 55 54 44 00, www.hotelpark.no, booking@hotelpark.no).

$$$$ Thon Hotel Rosenkrantz, with 129 rooms and an included light dinner, is one block behind Bryggen, between the Bryggens Museum and the Fløibanen funicular station—right in the heart of Bergen's appealing old quarter. Ask for a room with a double bed even if you're traveling alone—they go for the same price as a single (elevator, Rosenkrantzgaten 7, +47 55 30 14 00, www.thonhotels.com, rosenkrantz@olavthon.no).

$$$$ Thon Hotel Orion, beyond Bryggen near Håkon's Hall, has 219 rooms with a light dinner included. But be aware that many rooms face the fortress grounds, which sometimes host summer evening concerts. If you love music ask for a room on the concert side and enjoy the show; otherwise ask for a room on the quiet side and bring earplugs—or stay somewhere else (elevator, Bradbenken 3, +47 55 30 87 00, www.thonhotels.com, orion@ olavthon.no).

$$$ P-Hotel has 114 basic rooms just up from Ole Bulls Plass. While it's not particularly charming and some rooms come with noise from the street and a ground-floor nightclub, it's in a prime location. Ask for a room facing the courtyard in the renovated wing (credit card only, box breakfast in your room, elevator, Vestre Torggate 9, +47 55 21 00 00, www.p-hotels.no, bergen@p-hotels.no).

$$$ Best Western Plus Hotel Hordaheimen is Bergen's oldest hotel, dating back to 1918. It has 88 well-priced rooms with hardwood floors and welcoming decor. The charming breakfast room is decorated with vintage Kinsarvik wood furniture, giving it a traditional feel (elevator, +47 55 33 50 00, www.hordaheimen.no, booking@hordaheimen.no).

$$ Citybox Bergen City is a unique, no-nonsense hotel concept: plain, white, clean, and practical. You'll book one of their

Bergen Hotels & Restaurants

SKOLTEN CRUISE TERMINAL

To Norwegian Fisheries Museum

SKOLTEGRUNNS-KAIEN

INTERNATIONAL FERRIES

(B)

SKUTEVIKSTORGET

585

BERGENHUS FORTRESS

HÅKON'S HALL

NORDNES

FESTNINGS-KAIEN

ROSEN-KRANTZ TOWER

TOTEM POLE

AQUARIUM

STRANDGATEN

C. SUNDTS GATE

HARBOR FERRIES

SWIMMING BEACH

POOL

HAUGEVEIEN

Nordnesparken

STRANDSIDEN

NYKIRKEN

C. SUNDTS GATE

NORDNESVEIEN

STRANDGATEN

Puddefjorden

HAUGEVEIEN

HOLBERGSALLM.

KLOSTERGATEN

SKOTTEGATEN

NØSTEGATEN

ENGEN

HURTIGRUTEN TERMINAL (COASTAL CRUISES)

NØSTEGATTEN

555

TORBORG NEDREAASGATE

JEKTEVIKEN/DOKKEN CRUISE PORT

Accommodations

1. Hotel Havnekontoret
2. Hotel Park Bergen
3. Thon Hotel Rosenkrantz
4. Thon Hotel Orion
5. P-Hotel
6. Best Western Plus Hotel Hordaheimen
7. Citybox Bergen City
8. Guest House Skiven
9. Marken Gjestehus
10. To Montana Family & Youth Hostel

Eateries & Other

11. Enhjørningen, Restaurant To Kokker, Baker Brun & Madam Felle Nightclub
12. Bryggeloftet & Stuene
13. Pygmalion Restaurant
14. Pingvinen
15. Café Opera
16. To Fløien Folkerestaurant Cafeteria
17. Peppes Pizza
18. Deli de Luca (3)
19. Zupperia
20. Fish Market
21. 3-Kroneren Hot-Dogs
22. Söstrene Hagelin Fast Fish Joint
23. Krohnhagen Café
24. Rema 1000 Supermarket
25. Bunnpris
26. Folk og Røvere Bar
27. Dyvekes Wine Cellar
28. Laundry

BERGEN

122 rooms online or by phone and receive a confirmation number. Check-in is automated—just punch in your number and get your room key card. The call-in reception is staffed 24 hours daily (family room, no breakfast, elevator, rooftop terrace, self-service laundry, just away from the bustle in a mostly residential part of town at Nygårdsgaten 31, +47 55 31 25 00, www.citybox.no, bergen@citybox.no.

$ Guest House Skiven is a humble little place beautifully situated on a steep, traffic-free cobbled lane called "the most painted street in Bergen." Alf and Elizabeth Heskja (who live upstairs) rent four bright, nonsmoking doubles. Rooms have their own sinks, but share a shower, two WCs, and a kitchen (no breakfast, 4 blocks from train station, at Skivebakken 17, mobile +47 90 05 30 30, www.skiven.no, rs@skiven.no). From the train station, go down Kong Oscars Gate, uphill on D. Krohns Gate, and up the stairs at the end of the block on the left.

DORMS AND HOSTELS

$ Marken Gjestehus is a quiet, tidy, and conveniently positioned 100-bed place between the station and the harborfront. Its rooms, while spartan, are modern and cheery. Prices can rise with demand, especially in summer (private rooms available, breakfast extra, elevator, open all year but with limited reception hours, fourth floor at Kong Oscars Gate 45, +47 55 31 44 04, www.marken-gjestehus.com, post@marken-gjestehus.com).

Away from the Center: ¢ Montana Family & Youth Hostel (IYHF), while one of Europe's best, is high-priced for a hostel and way out of town. Still, the bus connections (#12, 20 minutes from the center) and the facilities—modern rooms, classy living room, no curfew, huge free parking lot, and members' kitchen—are excellent (private rooms available; 30 Johan Blytts Vei—for location, see the "Greater Bergen" map on page 165; +47 55 20 80 70, www.montana.no, bergen.montana@hihostels.no).

Eating in Bergen

Bergen has numerous choices: restaurants with rustic, woody atmosphere, candlelight, and steep prices; trendy pubs and cafés that offer good-value meals; cafeterias, chain restaurants, and international eateries with less ambience but better value; and takeaway sandwich shops, bakeries, and cafés for a light bite.

You can always get a glass or pitcher of water at no charge, and fancy places give you free seconds on potatoes—just ask. And if you get your food to go, it's taxed at a lower rate.

SPLURGES AT BRYGGEN

You'll pay a premium to eat at these restaurants, but you'll have a memorable meal in a pleasant setting.

$$$$ Enhjørningen Restaurant ("The Unicorn") is *the* place in Bergen for fish. With thickly painted walls and no right angles, this dressy yet old-time wooden interior wins my "Bryggen Atmosphere" award. The dishes, while not hearty, are close to gourmet and beautifully presented (small plates, main dishes, multicourse meals, nightly 16:00-23:00, reservations smart, #29 on Bryggen harborfront—look for anatomically correct unicorn on the old wharf facade and dip into the alley and up the stairs, +47 55 30 69 50, www.enhjorningen.no).

$$$$ Restaurant To Kokker, down the alley from Enhjørningen (and with the same owners), serves more meat and game. The prices and quality are equivalent, but even though it's also in an elegant old wooden building, I like The Unicorn's atmosphere much better (small plates, main dishes, multicourse meals, Mon-Sat 18:00-23:00, closed Sun, +47 55 30 69 55, www.tokokker.no).

$$$ Bryggeloftet & Stuene Restaurant, in a brick building just before the wooden stretch of Bryggen, is a vast eatery serving seafood, vegetarian, and traditional meals. To dine memorably yet affordably, this is your best Bryggen bet. Upstairs feels more elegant and less touristy than the main floor—if there's a line downstairs, just head on up (lunches, dinners, Mon-Sat 11:00-23:30, Sun from 13:00, try reserving a view window upstairs—no reservations for outside seating, #11 on Bryggen harborfront, +47 55 30 20 70, www.bryggeloftet.no).

NEAR THE FISH MARKET

$$ Pygmalion Restaurant has a happy salsa vibe, with local art on the walls and a fun, healthy international menu. It's run with creativity and passion by Sissel. Her burgers are a hit, and there are always good vegetarian options, hearty salads, and pancakes (wraps, burgers, main plates, Mon-Sat 11:00-22:00, Sun 12:00-23:00, two blocks inland from the Fish Market at Nedre Korskirkealmenning 4, +47 55 31 32 60).

BERGEN

CHARACTERISTIC PLACES NEAR OLE BULLS PLASS

Bergen's "in" cafés are stylish, cozy, small, and open very late. Around the cinema on Neumannsgate, there are numerous Italian, Middle Eastern, and Chinese restaurants.

$$$ Pingvinen ("The Penguin") is a homey place in a charming neighborhood, serving traditional Norwegian home cooking to an enthusiastic local clientele. The pub has only indoor seating, with a long row of stools at the bar and five charming, living-room-cozy tables—a great setup for solo diners. After the kitchen closes, the place stays open very late as a pub. For Norwegian fare in an untouristy atmosphere, this is a good, affordable option. Their seasonal menu (reindeer in the fall, whale in the spring) is listed on the board (nightly until 22:00, Vaskerelven 14 near the National Theater, +47 55 60 46 46).

$$$ Café Opera, with a playful, slacker vibe and chessboards for the regulars, is the hip budget choice for its loyal, youthful following. With two floors of seating and tables out front across from the theater, it's a winner (light sandwiches until 16:00, daily 10:00-23:30, Engen 18, +47 55 23 03 15).

ATOP MOUNT FLØYEN

$$ Fløien Folkerestaurant Cafeteria, at the top of the funicular, offers meals indoors and out with a panoramic view. It's self-service, with cheap sandwiches and a soup buffet (daily 10:00-22:00, Sept-April Sat-Sun only 12:00-17:00, +47 55 33 69 99).

GOOD CHAIN RESTAURANTS

You'll find these chain restaurants in Bergen and throughout Norway. All are open long hours daily. In good weather, enjoy a takeout meal with sun-worshipping locals in Bergen's parks.

$$$ Peppes Pizza on Ole Bulls Plass has cold beer and good pizzas—consider the Thai Chicken, with satay-marinated chicken, pineapple, peanuts, and coriander (Mon-Wed 11:00-23:00, Thu-Sat until 24:00, Sun 12:00-23:00, seating inside or takeaway, Olav Kyrres Gate 11, +47 22 22 55 55).

$ Baker Brun makes 75-100-NOK sandwiches, including wonderful shrimp baguettes, and pastries such as *skillingsboller*— Bergen's version of cinnamon rolls—warm out of the oven. Their shop at Bryggen is a prime spot for a simple, inexpensive bite (open from 7:00, a little later Sat-Sun, seating inside or takeaway).

$ **Deli de Luca** is a cut above other takeaway joints, adding sushi, noodle dishes, and calzones to the normal lineup of sandwiches. While a bit more expensive than the others, the variety and quality are appealing (open daily 24 hours, branches in train station and near Ole Bulls Plass at Torggaten 5, branch with indoor seating on corner of Engen and Vaskerelven, +47 55 23 11 47).

$$$ **Zupperia** is a lively, popular chain that offers burgers, salads, Norwegian fare, and Asian dishes; their Thai soup is a local favorite. For a lighter (and cheaper) meal, order off the lunch menu any time of day (Sun-Wed 12:00-22:00, Thu-Sat until 23:30). It's near the National Theater at Vaskerelven 12.

BUDGET BETS NEAR THE FISH MARKET

The **Fish Market** has lots of stalls bursting with salmon sandwiches, fresh shrimp, fish-and-chips, and fish cakes. For a tasty, memorable, and inexpensive Bergen meal, assemble a seafood picnic here (ask for prices first; May-Sept daily 8:00-23:00, vendors may close early if they're not busy; Oct-Dec Mon-Sat 10:00-22:00, Sun from 11:00; Jan-April Sat only 9:00-15:00). Also be sure to peruse the places next door on the ground floor of the TI building, Torghallen.

$ **3-Kroneren,** a classic hot-dog stand, sells a wide variety of sausages (including reindeer). The well-described English menu makes it easy to order your choice of artery-clogging guilty pleasures (open daily from 11:00 until 5:00 in the morning—you'll see the little hot-dog shack a block up Kong Oscars Gate from the harbor). Each dog comes with a free little glass of fruit punch.

$ **Söstrene Hagelin Fast Fish Joint** is an easygoing eatery that's cheerier than its offerings—a pale extravaganza of Norway's white cuisine. It's all fish here: fish soup, fish burgers, fish balls, fish cakes, fish wraps, and even fish pudding (Mon-Fri 9:00-19:00, Sat 10:00-17:00, closed Sun, Strandgaten 3, +47 55 90 20 13).

$ **Krohnhagen Café,** a humble community center next to a retirement home, is run by the church and partly staffed by volunteers. While it's designed to give Bergen's poor (and the retired) an inviting place to enjoy, everyone's welcome (it's a favorite of local guides). The dining area is bright and spacious, the staff friendly, and the menu is simple yet tasty (salad and dinner buffets, soup, waffles, cheap sandwiches, Mon-Fri 11:00-16:00, closed Sat-Sun, Kong Oscars Gate 54, +47 45 22 07 95).

PICNICS AND GROCERIES

While you'll be tempted to drop into 7-Eleven-type stores, you'll pay for the convenience. Pick up your groceries for half the price at a real supermarket. The **Rema 1000 supermarket,** just across from the Bryggens Museum and St. Mary's Church, is particularly

handy (Mon-Fri 7:00-23:00, Sat 8:00-21:00, closed Sun). For groceries on a Sunday, check out **Bunnpris**—just off Ole Bulls Plass, between the National Theater and Festplassen (Mon-Sat 6:00-24:00, Sun from 8:00, Torggaten 7).

Bergen Connections

Bergen is conveniently connected to **Oslo** by plane and train (trains depart Bergen daily at 7:57, 11:57, 15:57, and 22:59—but no night train on Sat, arrive at Oslo seven scenic hours later, additional departures in summer and fall, confirm times at station, 60-NOK seat reservation with second-class rail pass required—but free with first-class rail pass, book well in advance if traveling mid-July–Aug—there may be advance purchase discounts, buy tickets at Vy website). From Bergen, you can take the Norway in a Nutshell train/bus/ferry route; for information, see the Norway in a Nutshell chapter. Train info: +47 61 05 19 10 (9 for English), Vy.no.

To get to **Stockholm** or **Copenhagen,** you'll go via Oslo (see "Oslo Connections" on page 93). Before buying a ticket for a long train trip from Bergen, look into cheap flights.

By Express Boat to Balestrand and Flåm (on Sognefjord): A handy express boat links Bergen with Balestrand (4 hours) and Flåm (5.5 hours). For details, see page 137.

By Boat to Denmark: Fjordline runs a boat from Bergen to Hirtshals, Denmark (18.5 hours; departs daily at 13:30; boat from Hirtshals departs daily at 20:00, +47 51 46 40 99, www.fjordline. com).

By Boat to the Arctic: Hurtigruten coastal cruises depart nearly daily for the seven-day trip north up the scenic west coast to Kirkenes on the Russian border.

This route was started in 1893 as a postal and cargo delivery service along the west coast of Norway. Although no longer delivering mail, their ships still fly the Norwegian postal flag by special permission and deliver people, cars, and cargo from Bergen to Kirkenes. A lifeline for remote areas, the ships call at over 30 fishing villages and cities.

For the seven-day trip to Kirkenes, allow from $1,600 and up per person based on double occupancy (includes three meals per day, taxes, and port charges). Prices vary greatly depending on the season (highest June-July), cabin, and type of ship. The fleet includes those with a bit of brass built in the 1960s, but most of the ships in service were built in the mid-1990s and later. Shorter voyages are possible (including even just a day trip to one of the villages along the route). Cabins should be booked well in advance. Ship services include a 24-hour cafeteria, a launderette on newer boats, and optional port excursions. Check online for senior and

off-season (Oct-March) specials at www.hurtigruten.com or call Hurtigruten (US +1 888 645 6370, Norway +47 77 59 71 68). For most travelers, the ride makes a great one-way trip, with a flight back south as a logical last leg (rather than returning to Bergen by boat—a 12-day round-trip).

Route Tips for Drivers: For tips on connecting Bergen to Denmark via the Setesdal Valley and the Kristiansand ferry, see the South Norway chapter.

SOUTH NORWAY

Stavanger • Setesdal Valley • Kristiansand

South Norway is pleasant and pretty. Spend a day in the harborside town of Stavanger. Delve into the oil industry at the surprisingly interesting Norwegian Petroleum Museum. Admire the Stavanger Cathedral, window-shop in the old town, cruise the harbor, or hoof it up Pulpit Rock, an eerily flat-topped rock thrusting 2,000 feet above the Lysefjord, with an eagle's-eye view deep into the fjord. A series of time-forgotten towns stretch across the Setesdal Valley, with sod-roofed cottages and locals who practice fiddles and harmonicas, rose painting, whittling, and gold- and silverwork.

PLANNING YOUR TIME

The main draw in this part of Norway is the famous Pulpit Rock hike; poking around Stavanger, a pleasant port city and the springboard for reaching Pulpit Rock, helps round out your time here. The hike takes the better part of a day, requiring at least one overnight. Several cruises also call at Stavanger.

The Setesdal Valley—covered at the end of this chapter—is for people with ample time, a car, and a desire to explore a scenic corner of Norway. Since it's not "on the way" to much of anything (except dreary Kristiansand and the ferry to Denmark), it only makes the cut for Norway completists.

Stavanger

This waterfront burg of about 125,000 is mildly charming, its streets lined with unpretentious shiplap cottages that echo its perennial ties to the sea. Stavanger feels more cosmopolitan than most small Norwegian cities, thanks in part to its oil industry—which brings multinational workers (and their money) into the city. Known as Norway's festival city, Stavanger hosts several lively events, including jazz in May (www.maijazz.no), Scandinavia's biggest food festival in July (www.gladmat.no), and chamber music in August (www.kammermusikkfestivalen.no).

For most visitors, Stavanger functions a launch pad for side-tripping to the famous, iconic Pulpit Rock. Stavanger itself has barely enough to fill a day: The Norwegian Petroleum Museum is the only big-time sight in town, Gamle Stavanger (the "old town") offers pleasant wandering on cobbled lanes, and the city's fine cathedral is worth a peek.

Orientation to Stavanger

Stavanger is most interesting around its harbor, where you'll find the Maritime Museum, lots of shops and restaurants (particularly around the market plaza and along Kirkegata, which connects the cathedral to the Petroleum Museum), the indoor fish market, and a produce market. The artificial Lake Breiavatnet—bordered by Kongsgaten on the east and Olav V's Gate on the west—separates the train and bus stations from the harbor.

TOURIST INFORMATION

The centrally located TI can help with day trips, including logistics and tickets for reaching Pulpit Rock and other scenic hikes (June-Aug daily 8:00-18:00; Sept-May Mon-Fri 9:00-16:00, Sat until 14:00, closed Sun; Strandkaien 61, +47 51 85 92 00, www.regionstavanger.com).

ARRIVAL IN STAVANGER

Cruise liners dock right at the Vågen harbor in the very center of town. Some tie up on the west side of the harbor (called Strandkaien) next to the TI, and others put in along the east side (called Skagenkaien)—but both are an easy walk to the central market plaza. Stavanger's **train and bus stations** are a five-minute walk around Lake Breiavatnet to the inner harbor and cathedral.

Stavanger's **Sola Airport** is about nine miles outside the city (code: SVG, +47 67 03 10 00, www.avinor.no). The Flybussen airport bus connects to the train and bus stations, city center, and ferry terminal (see www.flybussen.no).

HELPFUL HINTS

Money: ATMs are on buildings facing the harbor, opposite the cathedral.

Laundry: Renseriet offers expensive drop-off service and affordable self-service (Mon-Fri 8:30-16:30, Thu until 19:00, Sat 9:00-15:00, closed Sun, Kongsgata 40, +47 51 89 56 53).

Stavanger

Byfjord

To Printing Museum

Sightseeing Boats to Lysefjord & Pulpit Rock

Ferries to Tau & Lysebotn

NORWEGIAN PETROLEUM MUSEUM

STRANDKAIEN CRUISE PORT

SKAGENKAIEN CRUISE PORT

Vågen

ØVRE HOLMEGATE

SKANSEGATA

HAVNERINGEN

FISKE-PIREN

GAMLE STAVANGER

To Canning Museum

BRØNNGATA

STRANDKAIEN

NEDRE STRANDGATE

VALBERGGATA

VALBERG TOWER

KIRKEGATA

BREIGATA

CULTURAL CENTER

VERKSGATA

LARS HERTERVIGS GATE

MARITIME MUSEUM

SKAGEN

LAUGMANNSGATA

NYGATA

KLUBBGATA

HOSP.

PEDERSGATA

OLAV KYRRES GATE

LØKKEVEIEN

Rosenkilde-Torget

KONGSGATA

"Plaza"

ATM

HAKON VII'S GATE

KONGSGATA

POST

CATHEDRAL

Byparken

To Ledaal & Breidablikk

Breiavatnet (Lake)

BERGELANDSGATA

KONGSGATA

LANGGATA

NY OLAVSKLEIV

OLAV V'S GATE

BREIBAKKEN

JERNBANEVEIEN

STIFTELSESGATA

TRAIN STATION

ERICHSTRUPSGATA

BUS STATION

BIRKELANDS

SAUDAGATA

200 Meters

200 Yards

MUSÉGATEN

KANNIKGATA

To Pulpit Rock via Ryfast Tunnel

To Stavanger Museum

To Airport

Accommodations
1 Thon Hotel Maritim
2 Hotel Victoria
3 Stavanger B&B

Eateries & Other
4 XO Mat & Vinhus
5 Renaa Xpress
6 Skagen Bageri
7 Supermarket
8 Market Plaza Eateries
9 Vågen Spiseri & Fish Market
10 N. B. Sørensen's Dampskibsexpedition
11 Sjøhuset Skagen
12 Bølgen og Moi
13 Launderette
14 Sightseeing Boats to Lysefjord & Pulpit Rock
15 Ferries to Tau & Lysebotn
16 Flybussen Stops (4)
17 Bus to Fjordline Terminal (Ferries to Hirtshals, Denmark)

SOUTH NORWAY

Sights in and Near Stavanger

IN STAVANGER TOWN

▲Stavanger Cathedral (Stavanger Domkirke)

Stavanger's top church—which overlooks the town center on a small ridge—has a harmonious interior and a few intriguing details worth lingering over. Good English information throughout the church brings meaning to the place. Parts of the church may be closed to visitors for restoration through 2023 as it gears up to celebrate its 900th birthday in 2025.

Cost and Hours: 30 NOK, open daily 11:00-16:00, +47 51 84 04 00, www.stavangerdomkirke.no.

Visiting the Church: The cathedral, dedicated to St. Swithun (his relic, an arm, was popular with pilgrims), was originally built in 1125 in a Norman style, with basket-handle Romanesque arches. After a fire badly damaged the church in the 13th century, a new chancel was added in the pointy-arched Gothic style. You can't miss where the architecture changes about three-quarters of the way up the aisle. On the left, behind the baptismal font, notice the ivy-lined railing on the stone staircase; this pattern is part of the city's coat of arms. And nearby, appreciate the colorful, richly detailed "gristle Baroque"-style pulpit (from 1658). Notice that the whole thing is resting on Samson's stoic shoulders—even as he faces down a lion.

Stroll the church, perusing its several fine "epitaphs" (tomb markers), which are paintings in ornately decorated frames. Go on a scavenger hunt for two unique features; both are on the second columns from the back of the church. On the right, at the top facing away from the nave, notice the stone carvings of Norse mythological figures: Odin on the left, and a wolf-like beast on the right. Although the medieval Norwegians were Christians, they weren't ready to entirely abandon all of their pagan traditions. On the opposite column, circle around the base and look at ankle level, facing away from the altar. Here you see a grotesque sculpture that looks like a fish head with human hands. Notice that its head has been worn down. One interpretation is that early worshippers would ritualistically put their foot on top of it, as if to push the evil back to the underworld. Mysteriously, both of these features are one-offs—you won't find anything like them on any other column in the church.

▲▲Norwegian Petroleum Museum (Norsk Oljemuseum)

This entertaining, informative museum—dedicated to the discovery of oil in Norway's North Sea in 1969 and the industry built

up around it—offers an unapologetic look at the country's biggest money-maker. With half of Western Europe's oil reserves, the formerly poor agricultural nation of Norway is the Arabia of the North and a world-class player, producing 1.6 million barrels a day.

Cost and Hours: 150 NOK; daily 10:00-19:00; Sept-May Mon-Sat 10:00-16:00, Sun until 18:00; +47 51 93 93 00, www.norskolje.museum.no. The small museum shop sells various petroleum-based products. The museum's recommended Bølgen og Moi restaurant has an inviting terrace over the water.

Visiting the Museum: The exhibit describes how oil was formed, how it's found and produced, and what it's used for. You'll see models of oil rigs, actual drill bits, see-through cylinders that you can rotate to investigate different types of crude, and lots of explanations (in English) about various aspects of oil. Interactive exhibits cover everything from the history of the earth (4.5 billion years displayed on a large overhead globe, showing how our planet has changed—stay for the blast that killed the dinosaurs), to day-to-day life on an offshore platform, to petroleum products in our lives (though the peanut-butter-and-petroleum-jelly sandwich is a bit much). Kids enjoy climbing on the model drilling platform, trying out the emergency escape chute at the platform outside, and playing with many other hands-on exhibits.

Several included movies delve into specific aspects of oil: The main movie, *Oljeunge (Oil Kid)*, stars a fictional character who was born in 1969—the year Norway discovered oil—and shows how that discovery changed Norwegian society over the last 50 years. Other movies (in the cylindrical structures outside) highlight intrepid North Sea divers and the construction of an oil platform. Each film runs in English at least twice hourly.

Even the museum's architecture was designed to echo the foundations of the oil industry—bedrock (the stone building), slate and chalk deposits in the sea (slate floor of the main hall), and the rigs (cylindrical platforms). While the museum has its fair share of propaganda, it also has several good exhibits on the environmental toll of drilling and consuming oil.

SOUTH NORWAY

Gamle Stavanger

Stavanger's "old town" centers on Øvre Strandgate, on the west side of the harbor. Wander the narrow, winding, cobbled back lanes, with tidy wooden houses, oasis gardens, and flower-bedecked entranceways. Peek into a workshop or gallery to find ceramics, glass, jewelry, and more. Many shops are open roughly daily 10:00-17:00.

Museum Stavanger (M.U.S.T.)

This "museum" is actually 10 different museums scattered around town (covered by a single 95-NOK combo-ticket, most closed Mon off-season, for details see www. museumstavanger.no). The various branches include the **Stavanger Museum,** featuring the history of the city and a zoological exhibit (Muségate 16); the **Maritime Museum** (Sjøfartsmuseum), near the bottom end of Vågen harbor (Nedre Strandgate 17); the **Norwegian Canning Museum** (Norsk Hermetikkmuseum—the *brisling,* or herring, is smoked the first Sunday of every month— Øvre Strandgate 88A); **Ledaal,** a royal residence and manor house (Eiganesveien 45); and **Breidablikk,** a wooden villa from the late 1800s (Eiganesveien 40A).

DAY TRIPS TO LYSEFJORD AND PULPIT ROCK

The nearby Lysefjord is an easy day trip. Those with more time (and strong legs) can hike to the top of 2,000-foot-high Pulpit Rock. The TI sells tickets for several tour companies and is a good place to confirm details before you head out.

Lysefjord Boat Tour

A boat tour here is memorable: you'll see towering mountains, waterfalls, rustic farms, and, if you're lucky, colonies of seals.

Rødne Fjord Cruise offers three-hour round-trip excursions from Stavanger to Lysefjord (including a view of Pulpit Rock—but no stops). Conveniently, boats depart from the main Vågen harbor in the heart of town (east side of the harbor, in front of Skansegata, along Skagenkaien; 580 NOK; May-Sept daily at 10:00 and 14:00, also at 12:00 July-Aug; April and Oct daily at 11:00; Jan-Feb and Nov-Dec Wed-Sun at 11:00; +47 51 89 52 70, www.rodne. no). They also offer a combined boat tour and Pulpit Rock trip (see later).

A different company, **Norled,** runs similar trips (490 NOK, July-Sept daily at 12:15, extra departures on busy days, www. norled.no). For a slower journey up the Lysefjord, it's possible to

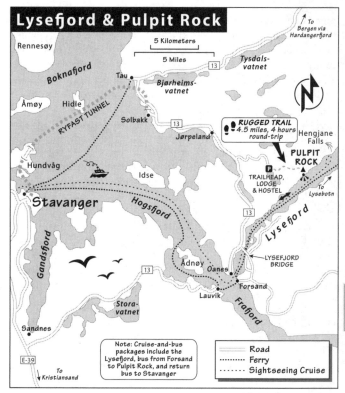

Lysefjord & Pulpit Rock

To Bergen via Hardangerfjord

Rennesøy

Boknafjord

5 Kilometers

5 Miles

13

Tau

Bjørheims-vatnet

Tysdals-vatnet

Åmøy   Hidle

RYFAST TUNNEL

Solbakk

13

Jørpeland

RUGGED TRAIL
4.5 miles, 4 hours round-trip

Hengjane Falls

PULPIT ROCK

Hundvåg

Idse

Stavanger

Hogsfjord

TRAILHEAD, LODGE & HOSTEL

To Lysebotn

13

Gandsfjord

Ådnøy

Oanes

LYSEFJORD BRIDGE

Lysefjord

Forsand

Lauvik

Fidafjord

Stora-vatnet

Sandnes

13

E-39

To Kristiansand

Note: Cruise-and-bus packages include the Lysefjord, bus from Forsand to Pulpit Rock, and return bus to Stavanger

———— Road
- - - - - - - Ferry
· · · · · · · Sightseeing Cruise

SOUTH NORWAY

ride on a car ferry that's part of the Stavanger-Lysebotn line (see the Ryfylke region timetable at www.kolumbus.no).

Pulpit Rock (Preikestolen)

Ascending to this dramatic 270-square-foot natural platform gives you a fantastic view of the fjord and surrounding mountains. Hiking up to the top of Pulpit Rock is a popular outing that will take the better part of a day; plan on 45 minutes travel time each way, about four hours of hiking (two hours up, two hours down), and time to linger at the top for photos. The rock has its own website with helpful advice (https://preikestolen365.com).

Getting There

By Car: From Stavanger, it's about a 45-minute drive via the nine-mile Ryfast Tunnel, which burrows under the sea at Stavanger and emerges near Solbakk on the other side (140-NOK toll). From there turn onto highway 13 and follow signs to *Preikestolen*. In summer you'll pay 250 NOK to park at the trailhead.

   By Bus Tour: The trailhead is easily reached in summer with a bus tour. Trips generally go daily from hotels in Stavanger (daily

June-Aug; weekends-only March-May and Sept-Oct; none Nov-Feb). Confirm schedules with the TI or the individual companies: **Go Fjords** (329 NOK, departs Stavanger at 9:15, return bus from trailhead departs at 15:30, +47 48 06 03 33, https://gofjords.com) and **Pulpit Rock Tours** (325 NOK, departs Stavanger at 9:10 or 13:10, last return bus from trailhead at 18:00, +47 51 59 90 60, www.pulpitrock.no).

By Cruise-and-Bus Combo: This option begins with a scenic Lysefjord cruise (2.5 hours) and drops you at Forsand, where you'll catch a bus to the Pulpit Rock trailhead. From there you can do the four-hour round-trip hike; afterwards, you'll catch a bus back to Stavanger. This handy trip is operated by **Rødne Fjord Cruise** (930 NOK, May-Sept daily at 10:00, also July-Aug at 12:00, see contact info earlier).

With a Guided Hike: Outdoorlife Norway offers guided tours for individuals or small groups. They'll pick you up at your hotel and even provide hiking poles. Check out their Preikestolen Off the Beaten Track Hike (1,590 NOK, May-Sept) or Preikestolen Sunrise Hike (1,390 NOK, April-Oct, +47 51 88 03 88, mobile +47 97 65 87 04, www.outdoorlifenorway.com).

Hiking to Pulpit Rock

At just over 4.5 miles round-trip, with an elevation gain of about 1,100 feet, this hike takes four hours total—longer if the trail is very crowded. The hike is fairly strenuous and includes scrambling over sometimes tricky, rocky terrain. Bring snacks and plenty of water, pack extra clothes as the weather is changeable, and wear sturdy hiking shoes or boots. Start early or you'll be sharing the trail with dogs on long leashes, toddlers navigating boulders, and the unprepared Bermuda-shorts crowd in flip-flops.

The trail starts by the big sign at the entrance to the main parking lot. From there the path climbs steadily through forest at first and eventually into open, rocky terrain. Along the way, you can thank Nepali Sherpas—who were hired to improve sections of the route—for their fine stonework on the trail.

The farther and higher you go, the rockier and more spectacular the scenery becomes. Whenever the trail disappears onto bare rock, look for the red T's painted on stones or posts marking the route. As you near Pulpit Rock, the path tiptoes along the cliff's edge with airy views out to the Lysefjord that can only be topped by those from the rock itself.

Before you head back, scramble up the mountainside behind the rock for that iconic, tourist-brochure scene of the people-speckled Pulpit Rock soaring out over the fjord 2,000 feet below.

Sleeping at the Pulpit Rock Trailhead

The Pulpit Rock trail is usually very crowded during the middle of the day, even in bad weather. I prefer to spend the night at the trailhead, and get an early start on the trail the next morning. If you don't have a car, you can get here from Stavanger by using one of the tour options listed above.

$$$$ Preikestolen Fjellstue is a modern building with 27 bright, simple, functional rooms and a pricey restaurant with a lovely lake view (includes breakfast, free parking). Below the Fjellstue and closer to the lake, the rustic, grass-roofed **$ Preikestolhytta** hostel has rooms that sleep 2-4 and bathrooms down the hall (includes breakfast). Both are run by the Norwegian

Trekking Association (+47 51 74 20 74, www.preikestolenfjellstue. no).

Sleeping in Stavanger

$$$ Thon Hotel Maritim, with 140 rooms, is two blocks from the train station near the artificial Lake Breiavatnet. It can be a good deal for a big business-class hotel (elevator, Kongsgaten 32, +47 51 85 05 00, www.thonhotels.no/maritim, maritim@olavthon.no).

$$$ Hotel Victoria has 107 business-class rooms over a stately, high-ceilinged lobby facing the Skagenkaien embankment right on the harbor (elevator, Skansegata 1, +47 51 86 70 00, www.hotel-victoria.no, post@hotel-victoria.no).

$ Stavanger B&B is Stavanger's best budget option. This large red house among a sea of white houses has tidy, tiny rooms. The lodgings are basic, verging on institutional—not cozy or doily—but they're affordable and friendly. The shared toilet is down the hall; 14 rooms have their own showers, while eight share showers down the hall. Waffles, coffee, and friendly chatter are served up every evening at 21:00 (10-minute uphill walk behind train station in residential neighborhood, Vikedalsgate 1A, +47 45 41 31 60, www.stavangerbedandbreakfast.no, post@sbb.no). If you let them know in advance, they may be able to pick you up or drop you off at the boat dock or train station.

Eating in Stavanger

CASUAL DINING

$$$ XO Mat & Vinhus, in an elegant setting, serves up big portions of traditional Norwegian food and pricier contemporary fare (Mon-Wed 14:30-23:30, Thu 11:00-23:00, Fri-Sat 11:30 until late, closed Sun, a block behind main drag along harbor at Skagen 10 ved Prostebakken, mobile +47 91 00 03 07).

$$ Renaa Xpress, popular with the locals, is inside Stavanger's library and cultural center. It's a cozy café where bakers make their own bread and pastries. In addition to a variety of sandwiches, salads, and soups, they also offer sourdough pizza after 13:00 (Mon-Thu 10:00-22:00, Fri-Sat until 24:00, Sun 12:00-22:00, Sølvberggata 2, mobile +47 94 00 93 48).

$ Skagen Bageri, in a lovely, leaning wooden building dating to the 1700s, serves baked goods and traditional open-face sandwiches at reasonable prices in a cozy, rustic-elegant setting (Mon-Fri 8:00-15:00, Sat until 16:00, closed Sun; in the blue-and-white building a block off the harborfront at Skagen 18; +47 51 89 51 71).

Meny is a large supermarket with a good selection and a fine deli for super picnic shopping (Mon-Fri 7:00-20:00, Sat 9:00-18:00, closed Sun, in Straen Senteret shopping mall, Lars Hertervigs Gate 6, +47 51 50 50 10).

Market Plaza Eateries: The busy square between the cathedral and the harbor is packed with reliable Norwegian chain restaurants. If you're a fan of **Deli de Luca, Dolly Dimple's,** or **Dickens Pub,** you'll find them within a few steps of here.

DINING ALONG THE HARBOR WITH A VIEW

The harborside street of Skansegata is lined with lively restaurants and pubs, and most serve food.

$$$$ Vågen Spiseri, in the same building as the fish market, serves tasty seafood dishes based on the catch of the day (affordable lunch specials, Mon-Wed 11:00-21:00, Thu-Sat until 24:00, closed Sun, Strandkaien 37, +47 51 52 73 50, www.fisketorget-stavanger. no).

$$$$ N. B. Sørensen's Dampskibsexpedition consists of a lively pub on the first floor (pasta, fish, meat, and vegetarian dishes; Mon-Wed 16:00-24:00, Sat 11:00-late, Sun 13:00-23:00) and a fine-dining restaurant on the second floor, with tablecloths, view tables overlooking the harbor, and a pricey menu (Mon-Sat 18:00-23:00, closed Sun, Skagenkaien 26, +47 51 84 38 20, www. herlige-stavanger.no). The restaurant is named after an 1800s company that shipped from this building, among other things, Norwegians heading to the US. Passengers and cargo waited on the first

floor, and the manager's office was upstairs. The place is filled with emigrant-era memorabilia.

$$$$ Sjøhuset Skagen, with a woodsy interior, invites diners to its historic building for lunch or dinner. The building, from the late 1700s, once housed a trading company. Today, you can choose from local seafood specialties with an ethnic flair, as well as plenty of meat options (Mon-Sat 11:30-24:00, Sun from 13:00, Skagenkaien 16, +47 51 89 51 80, www.skagenrestaurant.no).

$$$$ Bølgen og Moi, the restaurant at the Petroleum Museum, has great views over the harbor (good lunch specials, lunch daily 11:00-16:00; dinner Tue-Sat 18:00-20:00—reservations recommended; Kjeringholmen 748, +47 51 93 93 51, www.bolgenogmoi.no).

Stavanger Connections

From Stavanger by Train to: Kristiansand (5/day, 3 hours), **Oslo** (5/day, 8 hours, overnight possible).

By Bus to Bergen: Kystbussen operates buses between Stavanger and Bergen (hourly, 5.5 hours, +47 52 70 35 26, http://kystbussen.no).

By Boat to Denmark: Fjordline ferries sail overnight from Stavanger to Hirtshals, Denmark (12 hours, www.fjordline.com).

The Setesdal Valley

Welcome to the remote, and therefore very traditional, Setesdal Valley. Probably Norway's most authentic cranny, the valley is a

mellow montage of sod-roofed water mills, ancient churches, derelict farmhouses, yellowed recipes, lovely lakes, and gentle scenery. The Setesdal Valley isn't on the way to anything (except the ferry crossing from Kristiansand to Hirtshals, in Denmark).

But that's sort of the point. Come here only if you have ample time, and really want to commune with time-passed, rural Norway.

The valley is famous for its filigree jewelry, made to adorn traditional costumes and echoing the rhythmical designs of the Viking era and Middle Ages. Each town has a weekly rotating series

of hikes and activities for the regular, stay-put-for-a-week visitor. The upper valley is dead in the summer but enjoys a bustling winter.

The Setesdal Valley joined the modern age with the construction of the valley highway in the 1950s. All along the valley you'll see the unique two-story storage sheds called *stabburs* (the top floor was used for storing clothes; the bottom, food) and many sod roofs. Even the bus stops have rooftops the local goats love to munch.

In the high country, just over the Sessvatn summit (3,000 feet), you'll see herds of goats and summer farms. If you see an *ekte geitost* sign, that means genuine, homemade goat cheese is for sale. (It's sold cheaper and in more manageable sizes in grocery stores.) To some, it looks like a decade's accumulation of earwax. I think it's delicious. Remember, *ekte* means all-goat—really strong. The more popular and easier-to-eat version is made from a blend of cow and goat milk.

Without a car, the Setesdal Valley is not worth the trouble—there are no trains in the valley, and bus schedules are as sparse as the population. The sights are best for joyriding. If you're in Bergen with a car, and want to get to Denmark, this route is more interesting than repeating Oslo.

For more information on the Setesdal Valley, see www.visitsorlandet.com/setesdal.

Sights in the Setesdal Valley

I've described these roadside sights from north to south, most logically connected on a 10-hour drive from Bergen to Kristiansand. To trace this route, see the "South Norway" map at the beginning of this chapter.

From Bergen, drive about 2.5 hours, giving yourself plenty of time to catch the 9:00 Kvanndal-Utne ferry (www.norled.no). To reach **Kvanndal,** take the E-16 highway toward Voss and Oslo (signs for *Nestune, Landås, Nattland*); then, after a long tunnel, leave the Voss road and take highway 7 heading for Norheimsund, and then Kvanndal. This road, treacherous for the famed beauty of the Hardangerfjord it hugs as well as for its skinniness, is faster and safer if you beat the traffic.

The Kvanndal ferry drops you in **Utne,** where a lovely road takes you south along the Hardangerfjord. At the fjord's end, just past the huge zinc and copper industrial plant, you'll hit the industrial town of **Odda** (TI on market square at Torget 2, +47 48 07 07 77, www.visitodda.com). Odda brags that Kaiser Wilhelm came here a lot, but he's dead and I'd drive right through. If you want to visit the tongue of a glacier, drive to Buer and hike an hour to Buerbreen.

From Odda, drive into the land of boulders. The many mighty

waterfalls that line the road seem to have hurled huge rocks (with rooted trees) into the rivers and fields. Stop at the giant **double waterfall** called Låtefossen (on the left, pullout on the right, drive slowly through it if you need a car wash).

Continue over Røldalsfjellet and follow E-134 into the valley below, where the old town of **Røldal** is trying to develop some tourism (drive on by—its old church isn't worth the stop). Lakes are like frosted mirrors, making desolate huts come in pairs. Farther along on the Hardangervidda plateau is **Haukeliseter**—a group of sod-roofed buildings filled with cultural clichés and tour groups, offering light food in a lakeside setting.

At the Haukeli transportation junction, turn south on highway 9 and wind up to **Sessvatn** at 3,000 feet (toward Hovden). Enter the upper Setesdal Valley. From here, you'll follow the Otra River downhill for 140 miles south to the major port town of Kristiansand. Skip the secondary routes.

A ski resort at the top of the Setesdal Valley (2,500 feet), **Hovden** is barren in the summer and painfully in need of charm. Still, it makes a good home base if you want to explore the area and has a seasonal TI (+47 37 93 93 70, www.hovden.com). Hovden has boat rental (at Hegni Center, south edge of town, +47 37 93 93 70); a water park (Hovden Badeland, +47 37 93 93 93, www.badeland. com); the free Museum of Iron Production (Jernvinnemuseum—learn about iron production from the late Iron Age with the aid of drawings, exhibits, and recorded narration in English from a "Viking," about 100 yards behind the Hegni Center); and plenty of choices for hikes and mountain biking. Good walks offer you a chance to see reindeer, moose, arctic fox, and wabbits—so they say. Berry picking is popular in late August, when small, sweet blueberries are in season. A sporadically running chairlift sometimes takes sightseers to the top of a nearby peak, with great views in clear weather; bikers can ride the trails downhill. Hunting season starts in late August for reindeer (only in higher elevations) and later in the fall for grouse and moose *(elg)*.

For an affordable place to sleep or eat in Hovden, consider the big, old ski chalet called **¢ Hovden Fjellstoge.** Check out the mural in the balcony overlooking the lobby—an artistic rendition of this area's history. Behind the mural is a frightening taxidermy collection (www.hovdenfjellstoge.no).

Leaving Hovden, you enter the most scenic stretch of the drive. Nine miles south of Hovden is a two-mile side-trip to a 400-foot-high rock-pile dam, called **Dammar Vatnedalsvatn,** with great view and an impressive rockery. Sit out of the wind a few rows down the rock pile and ponder the vastness of Norwegian wood.

Farther south, the most interesting folk museum and church in Setesdal are in the teeny town of **Bykle.** The 17th-century

SOUTH NORWAY

church has two balconies—one for men and one for women (www.setesdalsmuseet.no).

On the east side of the main road (at the *Grasbrokke* sign) is an old water mill (1630). A few minutes farther south, at the sign for *Sanden Såre Camping*, exit onto a little road to stretch your legs at another old water mill with a fragile, rotten-log sluice.

In Flateland, the **Setesdal Museum** (Rygnestadtunet) offers more of what you saw at Bykle; unless you're a glutton for culture, I wouldn't do both (www.setesdalsmuseet.no). Past Flateland at **Honnevje** is a nice picnic and WC stop, with a dock along the water for swimming...for hot-weather days or polar bears.

Valle is Setesdal's prettiest village (but don't tell Bykle). In the center, you'll find fine silver- and gold-work, homemade crafts next to the TI (+47 37 93 75 29), and occasional *lefse* cooking demonstrations. The fine suspension bridge attracts kids of any age (b-b-b-b-bounce), and anyone interested in a great view over the river to strange mountains that look like polished, petrified mudslides. European rock climbers, tired of the over-climbed Alps, often entertain spectators with their sport. Is anyone climbing? To sleep in Valle, consider the basic **Valle Motell** (www.valle-motell.no).

South of Valle, the area has a lot more logging (and is less scenic). In **Nomeland,** the Sylvartun silversmith shop, whose owner Hallvard Bjørgum is also a renowned Hardanger fiddle player, sells Setesdal silver in a 17th-century, grass-roofed log cabin next to the main road.

Farther south, the road traces first the west shore of the freshwater Åraksfjord and then the east shore of the long and scenic (and also freshwater) Byglandsfjord to **Grendi,** where the Ardal Church (1827) has a rune stone in its yard. Three hundred yards south of the church is a 900-year-old oak tree.

A huge town by Setesdal standards (3,500 people), **Evje** is famous for its gems and mines. Fancy stones fill the shops here. Rockhounds find the nearby mines fun; for a small fee, you can hunt for gems. The **Setesdal Mineral Park** is on the main road, two miles south of town (www.mineralparken.no).

From Evje, it's about an hour's drive to this region's transportation hub, **Kristiansand.**

Kristiansand

The "capital of the south," Kristiansand has 85,000 inhabitants, a pleasant Renaissance grid-plan layout (Posebyen), a famous zoo with Norway's biggest amusement park, lots of big boats going to Denmark, and a TI (Rådhusgata 18, +47 38 07 50 00, www.visitsorlandet.com). It's the closest thing to a beach resort in Norway. Markensgate is the bustling pedestrian market street—an enjoyable place for good browsing, shopping, eating, and people-

watching. Stroll along the Strand Promenaden (marina) to Christiansholm Fortress. The otherwise uninteresting harbor area has a cluster of wooden buildings called **Fiskebasaren** ("Fish Bazaar") with an indoor fish market and numerous restaurants offering a nice dinner atmosphere.

Sleeping in Kristiansand: Hotels are expensive and nondescript; consider the **$$$$ Rica Hotel Norge** (Dronningensgate 5, +47 38 17 40 00, www.hotel-norge.no) or the **$$$$ Thon Hotel Parken** (ask for quiet room, Kirkegate 15, +47 38 17 20 40, www.thonhotels.no/wergeland).

Kristiansand Connections: Trains connect to **Stavanger** (5/day, 3 hours) and **Oslo** (5/day, 4.5 hours). Kristiansand is also a hub for the **ferry to Hirtshals, Denmark,** operated by two companies: Color Line (2/day year-round, more in summer, 3.5 hours, www.colorline.com) and Fjordline (1-2/day in summer, none in winter, 2.5 hours, www.fjordline.com). Reservations are smart. You can either drive on or walk on.

SOUTH NORWAY

PRACTICALITIES

This section covers just the basics on traveling in this region (for more comprehensive information, see the latest edition of *Rick Steves Scandinavia*). You'll find free advice on specific topics at RickSteves.com/tips.

MONEY

Norway uses the Norwegian krone (NOK): 9 kroner equals about $1. To roughly convert prices in kroner to dollars, divide by nine (100 NOK = about $11). Check www.oanda.com for the latest exchange rates.

To get cash, use a debit card to withdraw kroner from an ATM; US debit cards with a Visa or MasterCard logo will work in any European ATM. Avoid "independent" ATMs, such as Travelex, Euronet, Moneybox, Your Cash, Cardpoint, and Cashzone. These have high fees, can be less secure, and may try to trick users with "dynamic currency conversion" (see later).

In Scandinavia, credit cards are widely accepted and often preferred, even for small purchases. Before departing, call your bank or credit-card company: Confirm that your card(s) will work overseas, ask about international transaction fees, and alert them that you'll be making withdrawals in Europe. Also ask for the PIN number for your credit card—you may need it for Europe's "chip-and-PIN" payment machines. Allow time for your bank to mail your PIN to you).

European cards use no-signature chip-and-PIN technology; some chip cards issued in the US instead require a signature. European card readers may generate a receipt for you to sign—or prompt you to enter your PIN. US credit cards may not work at some self-service payment machines (transit-ticket kiosks, parking kiosks,

etc.). If your card won't work, look for a cashier who can process the transaction manually—or pay in cash. (I keep a small amount of cash on hand, just in case.)

"Tap to pay" cards and smartphone payment apps work in Europe just as they do in the US and sidestep chip-and-PIN compatibility issues.

To keep your cash, cards, and valuables safe, wear a money belt.

Dynamic Currency Conversion: When withdrawing cash or paying with a credit card, you'll often be asked whether you want the transaction processed in dollars or in the local currency. Always refuse the conversion and choose the local currency. While DCC seems convenient, it comes with a poor exchange rate, and you'll wind up losing money.

STAYING CONNECTED

The simplest solution is to bring your own device—mobile phone, tablet, or laptop—and use it just as you would at home (following the money-saving tips below). For more on phoning, see RickSteves.com/phoning. For a one-hour talk covering tech issues for travelers, see RickSteves.com/mobile-travel-skills.

To Call from a US Phone: Phone numbers in this book are presented exactly as you would dial them from a US mobile phone. For international access, press and hold the 0 key until you get a + sign, then dial the country code (47 for Norway) and phone number. To dial from a US landline, replace + with 011 (US/Canada international access code).

From a European Landline: Replace + with 00 (Europe international access code), then dial the country code (47 for Norway) and phone number. If a European phone number begins in 0, you'll typically omit the 0 when dialing from country to country.

Within Norway: To place a domestic call (from a Norwegian landline or mobile), drop the +47 and dial the phone number.

Tips: If you bring your mobile phone, consider signing up for an **international plan;** most providers offer a simple bundle that includes calling, messaging, and data.

Use **Wi-Fi** whenever possible. Most hotels and many cafés offer free Wi-Fi, and you may also find it at tourist information offices (TIs), major museums, and public-transit hubs. With Wi-Fi you can use your phone or tablet to make free or low-cost calls via a calling app such as Skype, WhatsApp, FaceTime, or Google Hangouts. When you need to get online but can't find Wi-Fi, turn on your cellular network (or turn off airplane mode) just long enough for the task at hand.

Most **hotels** charge a fee for placing calls—ask for the rates before you dial. You can use a prepaid international phone card

Sleep Code

Hotels are classified based on the average price of a standard double room with breakfast in high season.

$$$$	**Splurge:**	Most rooms over 1,500 NOK
$$$	**Pricier:**	1,200-1,500 NOK
$$	**Moderate:**	900-1,200 NOK
$	**Budget:**	600-900 NOK
¢	**Hostel/Backpacker:**	Under 600 NOK
RS%	**Rick Steves discount**	

Unless otherwise noted, credit cards are accepted, and free Wi-Fi is available. Comparison-shop by checking prices at several hotels (on each hotel's own website, on a booking site, or by email). For the best deal, always book directly with the hotel. Ask for a discount if paying in cash; if the listing includes **RS%,** request a Rick Steves discount.

(usually available at newsstands, tobacco shops, and train stations) to call out from your hotel.

SLEEPING

I've categorized my recommended accommodations based on price, indicated with a dollar-sign rating (see sidebar).

Book your accommodations as soon as your itinerary is set, especially if you want to stay at one of my top listings or if you'll be traveling during busy times. You can do this by checking hotel websites and booking sites such as Hotels.com or Booking.com.

After you've zeroed in on your choice, book directly with the hotel itself. This increases the chances that the hotelier will be able to accommodate special needs or requests (such as shifting your reservation). When you book by phone or email, the owner avoids the commission paid to booking sites, giving the hotel wiggle room to offer you a discount, a nicer room, or a free breakfast (if it's not already included).

For complicated requests, send an email with the following information: number and type of rooms; number of nights; arrival date; departure date; any special requests; and applicable discounts (such as a Rick Steves discount, cash discount, or promotional rate). Use the European style for writing dates: day/month/year.

In general, hotel prices can soften if you do any of the following: offer to pay cash, stay at least three nights, or travel off-season.

Room rates are especially volatile at larger hotels that use "dynamic pricing" to set rates. Prices can skyrocket during festivals and conventions, while business hotels can have deep discounts on weekends when demand plummets. Of the many hotels I recommend, it's difficult to say which will be the best value on a given day.

To find an apartment or room in a private home, try Airbnb, FlipKey, Booking.com, and the HomeAway family of sites (Home-Away, VRBO, and VacationRentals).

EATING

I've categorized my recommended eateries based on the average price of a typical main course, indicated with a dollar-sign rating (see sidebar).

Restaurants are often expensive—you'll save money by dining out at lunch (when there's usually a special, and food is generally cheaper) and picnicking for dinner. Many restaurants offer cheap daily *(dagens)* lunch specials and buffets to entice office workers. Ethnic eateries—Indian, Turkish, Greek, Italian, and Asian—offer a good value and a break from Norwegian fare. Basements of big department stores have huge, first-class supermarkets with lots of alternatives to sandwiches for picnic dinners. Or explore your options at market stalls and takeaway delis. Grab a park bench or waterside perch, relax, and enjoy.

If your hotel offers breakfast—even if they charge for it—take advantage of this option; these generous buffets are often a better deal than buying breakfast around town. They usually feature fruit, cereal, various milks, breads and crackers, cold cuts, pickled herring, caviar paste, and boiled eggs. The brown cheese with the texture of earwax and a slightly sweet taste is *geitost* ("goat cheese"). Give this odd but enjoyable dairy product a try—it's a tasty topping on traditional heart-shaped waffles.

The *smörgåsbord* (known in Norway as the *store koldt bord*) is a revered Scandinavian culinary tradition that locals indulge in mainly during festive times, but anyone can dig into this all-you-can-eat buffet any time of year at bigger hotels and on overnight ferries. Seek it out at least once during your visit. Begin with the fish dishes, along with boiled potatoes and *knekkebrød* (crisp bread). Then move on to salads, egg dishes, and various cold cuts. Next it's meatball time! Pour on some gravy as well as a spoonful of lingonberry sauce. Still hungry? Make a point to sample the Nordic cheeses and the racks of traditional desserts, cakes, and custards.

In Norway, alcohol is sold only at state-run liquor stores called Vinmonopolet (though weak beer is also sold at supermarkets). To avoid extremely high restaurant prices for alcohol, many Norwegians—and tourists—buy their wine, beer, or spirits at a store and then drink at a public square; this is illegal although often done. Or, they'll have a drink or a glass of wine at home (or in their hotel room) before going out, then limit themselves to one or two glasses at the restaurant. One Norwegian specialty is *akevitt*, a strong, vodka-like spirit distilled from grains or potatoes and infused with dill, caraway, or other herbs and spices—that's normally drunk

Restaurant Code

Eateries in this book are categorized according to the average cost of a typical main course. Drinks, desserts, and splurge items can raise the price considerably.

$$$$ **Splurge:** Most main courses over 225 NOK
$$$ **Pricier:** 175-225 NOK
$$ **Moderate:** 125-175 NOK
$ **Budget:** Under 125 NOK

In Norway, a takeout spot is **$**; a basic sit-down café is **$$**; a casual but more upscale restaurant is **$$$**; and a swanky splurge is **$$$$**.

at room temperature. *Lakka* is a syrupy-sweet liqueur made from cloudberries, the small orange berries grown in the Arctic.

Good service is relaxed (slow to an American). When you want the bill, say, *"Regningen, takk."*

Tipping: Tipping in restaurants is not an established practice in Scandinavia. A service charge is typically included in your bill, and you aren't expected to leave an additional tip. But if you enjoy great service and want to show your appreciation, round up the bill (about 5-10 percent of the total check). If you do tip, leave cash to be sure it goes to your server. You don't need to tip if you order your food at a counter.

TRANSPORTATION

By Train and Bus: Trains cover many of my recommended Norwegian destinations. To see if a rail pass could save you money, check RickSteves.com/rail. Rail passes cover almost all trains in the region, though you'll need paid seat reservations ($5–20) for many longer rides, express trains, and special routes such as the scenic Myrdal-Flåm portion of the Norway in a Nutshell route.

The easiest way to buy most train tickets is online or at stations from self-service kiosks. If you need help, tickets are sold at counters at bigger stations, but this can come with long lines and a surcharge. The cheapest tickets are advance purchase (up to four months ahead), nonchangeable, and nonrefundable.

To research train schedules and fares, visit the Norwegian train website, Vy.no. Or check out Deutsche Bahn's excellent all-Europe timetable: www.bahn.com. If you'll be taking a popular train on a busy day and want to be assured of having a seat, a reservation can be a good investment even if it's not required. For travel on the Norway in a Nutshell route in summer, book well in advance—four to five weeks is best (see www.fjordtours.com).

If the Norwegian railway website won't process your passholder

reservation or accept your US credit card, try ordering by phone—dial +47 61 05 19 10 (press 9 for English)—or email tog@vy.no.

Don't overlook long-distance buses, which are usually slower than trains but have considerably cheaper and more predictable fares. Big bus carriers include Norway's Nor-Way (www.nor-way.no) and Vy Buss (www.vybuss.com).

By Car: It's cheaper to arrange most car rentals from the US. For tips on your insurance options, see RickSteves.com/cdw. Bring your driver's license. Local road etiquette is similar to that in the US. Ask your car-rental company for details, or check the US State Department website (www.travel.state.gov, search for your country in the "Learn about your destination" box, then click on "Travel and Transportation"). Use your headlights day and night (it's required in most of Scandinavia) and hand-held mobile phone use is forbidden. A car is an expensive headache in any big city—it's best used to explore the countryside.

By Boat: Boats are both a necessary and spectacular way to travel through Norway's fjords or along its coast (for various routes, see www.fjordtours.no, www.fjord1.no, and www.tide.no). Reserve ahead if you're planning on taking overnight boats in summer or on weekends to link Oslo and Copenhagen (www.dfds.com). It's possible to connect Bergen or Kristiansand, Norway, with Hirtshals, Denmark, by ferry (www.fjordline.com and www.colorline.com). Bergen is also a departure point for boats to the Arctic (www.hurtigruten.com).

By Plane: SAS is the region's dominant airline (www.flysas.com). Widerøe Air (www.wideroe.no) has connections throughout Norway and a few international destinations. Another option is Norwegian Airlines (hubs in Oslo and Bergen, www.norwegian.com). Well-known cheapo airlines EasyJet (www.easyjet.com) and Ryanair (www.ryanair.com) fly into Scandinavia.

HELPFUL HINTS

Travel Advisories: For updated health and safety conditions, including any Covid entry restrictions for your destination, consult the US State Department's international travel website (www.travel.state.gov).

Emergency Help: To summon the **police** dial 112, for an **ambulance** call 113, and to report a **fire** dial 110 from a mobile phone or landline (operators typically speak English). If you get sick, do as the Norwegians do and go to a pharmacist for advice. Or ask at your hotel for help—they'll know the nearest medical and emergency services.

Travel Documents: If your passport is due to expire within six months of your ticketed date of travel, you need to renew it (www.travel.state.gov). Check for current Covid entry require-

ments, such as proof of vaccination or a negative Covid-19 test result.

For **passport problems,** contact the **US Embassy** (Oslo—appointment required, dial +47 21 30 85 40, https://no.usembassy. gov) or **Canadian Embassy** (Oslo—appointment required, dial +47 22 99 53 00, www.norway.gc.ca).

Theft or Loss: Pickpockets target tourists. Keep your cash, credit cards, and passport secure in your money belt, and carry only a day's spending money in your front pocket or wallet.

To replace a passport, you'll need to go in person to an embassy (see above). Cancel and replace your credit and debit cards by calling these 24-hour US numbers with a mobile phone: Visa (dial +1-303-967-1096), MasterCard (dial +1-636-722-7111), and American Express (dial +1-336-393-1111). From a landline, you can call these US numbers collect by going through a local operator.

File a police report either on the spot or within a day or two; you'll need it to submit an insurance claim for lost or stolen rail passes or travel gear, and it can help with replacing your passport or credit and debit cards. For more information, see RickSteves.com/ help.

Time: Norway uses the 24-hour clock. It's the same through 12:00 noon, then keep going: 13:00, 14:00, and so on. Norway, like most of continental Europe, is six/nine hours ahead of the East/West Coasts of the US. The exceptions are the beginning and end of Daylight Saving Time: Europe "springs forward" the last Sunday in March (two weeks after most of North America) and "falls back" the last Sunday in October (one week before North America).

Business Hours: Shops generally open at 10:00 and close between 17:00 and 20:00 on weekdays; bigger stores and malls tend to stay open later, while smaller stores and shops in smaller towns may have shorter hours. On Sundays banks and most shops are closed, and public transportation options are generally fewer. Many museums in Scandinavia are closed on Mondays.

Holidays and Festivals: Europe celebrates many holidays, which can close sights and attract crowds (book hotel rooms ahead). For info on holidays and festivals in Norway, check VisitNorway. com. For a simple list showing major—though not all—events, see RickSteves.com/festivals.

Numbers and Stumblers: What Americans call the second floor of a building is the first floor in Europe. Europeans write dates as day/month/year, so Christmas 2021 is 25/12/21. Commas are decimal points and vice versa—a dollar and a half is 1,50, and there are 5.280 feet in a mile. Europe uses the metric system: A

PRACTICALITIES

kilogram is 2.2 pounds; a liter is about a quart; and a kilometer is six-tenths of a mile.

RESOURCES FROM RICK STEVES

This Snapshot guide, excerpted from the latest edition of *Rick Steves Scandinavia,* is one of many titles in my series of guidebooks on European travel. I also produce a public television series, *Rick Steves' Europe,* and a public radio show, *Travel with Rick Steves.* My free online video library, Rick Steves Classroom Europe, offers a searchable database of short video clips on European history, culture, and geography (Classroom.RickSteves.com). My website, RickSteves.com, offers free travel information, a forum for travelers' comments, guidebook updates, my travel blog, an online travel store, and information on European rail passes and our tours of Europe. If you're bringing a mobile device on your trip, you can download my free Rick Steves Audio Europe app that features dozens of self-guided audio tours of the top sights in Europe and travel interviews about Europe. For more information, see RickSteves.com/audioeurope. You can also follow me on Facebook, Twitter, and Instagram.

ADDITIONAL RESOURCES

Tourist Information: www.visitnorway.com
Passports and Red Tape: www.travel.state.gov
Packing List: www.ricksteves.com/packing
Travel Insurance: www.ricksteves.com/insurance
Cheap Flights: www.kayak.com or www.skyscanner.com
Airplane Carry-on Restrictions: www.tsa.gov
Updates for This Book: www.ricksteves.com/update

HOW WAS YOUR TRIP?

To share your tips, concerns, and discoveries after using this book, please fill out the survey at RickSteves.com/feedback. Thanks in advance—it helps a lot.

INDEX